THE STYLE ENGINE

FASHION   ENGINEERING   UNIT

First published in the United States of America in 1998 by The Monacelli Press, Inc. 10 East 92nd Street, New York, New York 10128.

Copyright © 1998 The Monacelli Press, Inc., and Pitti Immagine SRL

Library of Congress Catalog Card Number: 97-76232
ISBN: 1-885254-95-4

Printed and bound in Italy

The Style Engine is the title of this book and of an exhibition; together they constitute the first creations of the FASHION ENGINEERING UNIT, a multidisciplinary research group focusing on fashion culture, produced by PITTI IMMAGINE, under the guidance and supervision of Giannino Malossi; the book and the show were conceived and produced by Giannino Malossi, with Peppino Ortoleva and Antony Shugaar. The project of The Style Engine is dedicated to the late Marco Rivetti.
Florence, January 8-February 15, 1998

President of Pitti Immagine:
Mario Boselli

General Manager and Managing Director of Pitti Immagine:
Raffaello Napoleone

Director of Corporate Communications of Pitti Immagine:
Lapo Cianchi

The following persons took part in the research of the FASHION ENGINEERING UNIT:
Andrea Balestri
Sybille Bollmann
Laird O. Borrelli
Laura Bovone
Stefano Casciani
John Durrell
Nadine Frey
Franco La Cecla
Giannino Malossi
Nancy Martin
Peppino Ortoleva
Antonio Pilati
Ted Polhemus
Marco Ricchetti
Antony Shugaar
Valerie Steele
John Thackara

Director of the Book and the Exhibition:
Giannino Malossi

Special Supervising Consultant:
Peppino Ortoleva/Cliomedia Officina

International Editions:
Antony Shugaar

Book Design:
Italo Lupi with Silvia Kihlgren

Exhibition Design:
Achille Castiglioni, Alberto Cavaglià, Italo Lupi

Press Office:
Cristina Brigidini

Public Relations:
Sibilla della Gherardesca

General Organization:
Sybille Bollmann

Photo Editor:
Giannino Malossi

Research and Supervision of the Acoustics:
Francesca Chiocci

Research and Supervision of the Work of the Artists:
Emi Fontana

Research and Supervision of the Textiles Section:
Nancy Martin

Research and Supervision of the Television Section:
Michela Moro Journò

Video Production:
Ranuccio Sodi/Show Biz Srl

Translations:
Guido Lagomarsino (Italian)
Antony Shugaar (English)

Photographic Research:
Sybille Bollmann
Laird O. Borrelli
Nicoletta Leonardi
Carla Saibene

Coordinator of the Show:
Anna Pazzagli

Production Assistants:
Francesca Chiocci
Carla Saibene

Special thanks go to:
Frans Ankone
Paola Antonelli
Giorgio Armani
Pino Bardi
Bona Bonarelli
David Colby
Enzo
Barnaba Fornasetti
Willy Moser
Paolo Roversi
Paul Smith
Vivienne Westwood

Andrea Rosen Gallery, New York
Art Department, New York
Charles Cowles Gallery, New York
Fashion Institute of Technology Museum, New York
Jessica Fredericks Gallery, New York
Metro Pictures, New York
Pat Hearn Gallery, New York
Silicon Gallery, Philadelphia
303 Gallery, New York

Camera Austria, Graz
The Manipulator Magazine, Düsseldorf

Alfa Romeo Spa
Aprilia Spa
Benelli Spa
Cagiva Motor Spa
Dainese Spa
Ermenegildo Zegna Spa
Faliero Sarti Spa
Ford Motor Company
General Motors Company
Gommatex Spa
Guy Laroche
Italjet Spa
Loro Piana Spa
Malaguti Spa
Mattel Inc.
Mercedes Benz Italia Spa
Patrick Cox Inc., New York
Piaggio Italia Spa
Volkswagen Italia Spa

THE STYLE ENGINE

Spectacle, Identity, Design, and Business:
How the Fashion Industry Uses Style to Create Wealth

edited by
Giannino Malossi

designed by
Italo Lupi
with Silvia Kihlgren

PITTI
IMMAGINE

fashion
engineering
unit

THE MONACELLI PRESS

Opening pages:
John Galliano debuts for Givenchy,
1996. Photo by Ben Coster
(Camera Press/Grazia Neri)

V-back evening dress by Trigère,
published by *Harper's Bazaar*,
July 1955, reinterpreted 1994.
Photo by Lillian Bassman (Courtesy
of the Fashion Institute of Technology Museum)

Bartolomeo Bimbi (1648–1725),
Lemons and Limes (detail),
Galleria Palatina, Florence (Photo Scala)

Lanvin runway presentation.
Photo by Sebastião Salgado (Contrasto)

Bartolomeo Bimbi (1648–1725),
Cherries (detail), Galleria Palatina,
Florence (Foto Scala).

Jean Paul Gaultier,
haute couture collection,
fall-winter 1997–98.
Photo by Pierre Vauthey
(Sygma/Grazia Neri)

Sean Connery (courtesy of Archivio Infinito)

Ivanka Trump modeling for Thierry
Mugler, haute couture collection,
fall-winter 1997–98. Photo by Thierry
Orban (Sygma/Grazia Neri)

George Hurrell, (United States,
1904–92) *Jan Olivela, 1941* toned
gelatin silver print, 8x12", unframed
(Private Collection, New York)

This page:
Ocimar Versolato, ready-to-wear
collection, fall-winter 1997–98. Photo
by Thierry Orban (Sygma/Grazia Neri)

Angelika Ullhofer, 1988, outfit by Luciano Soprani. Photo by Pino Guidolotti

PITTI IMMAGINE'S ROLE IN THE CREATION
OF A CULTURE FOR THE TEXTILE AND CLOTHING INDUSTRY

Mario Boselli
President of Pitti Immagine

For some time now, Pitti Immagine, aside from organizing and operating one of the world's most important international fashion fairs—which hosts the leading companies and individuals in the sector—has been devoting a considerable share of its resources to the planning and creation of events and projects meant to encourage the growth of fashion culture, personified by the Italian textiles and apparel industry. In this activity, Pitti Immagine has developed, year after year, a hidden potential in the world of fashion that is now widely acknowledged in the swelling interest in the fashion industry, on the part of both mass media and the world of finance.

Unless it is understood in terms of its cultural and economic implications, fashion appears as a marginal and frivolous activity, underdeveloped from a technological point of view. Nowadays, to an increasing degree, fashion appears in the pages of financial and cultural publications, and this attention in turn stimulates new and weightier public interest and opinion. The world of fashion, and its overall role, demands and increasingly commands the role of a major economic resource, the product of a sophisticated and complex industry, on the cutting edge in terms of capacity to create added value, not only through the processing of raw materials but also through the development and creation of immaterial contents. An industry, in other words, that finds its resources for growth in the relationship between technology, organization, and labor (all traditional components of the industrial sphere), and the relationship between these elements and the context of mass culture in the dynamics of the media, and in the creative development of style that embodies the spirit of the time.

In order to ensure continuity and functionality to our research in this field, Pitti Immagine has created the Fashion Engineering Unit, a research division that is exploring the engineering of style and the economics of creativity. This book and the exhibition that accompanies it are the first products of this research structure, which employs a network of scholars, experts, and authors, based in numerous schools and institutes in Italy, the rest of Europe, and the United States; the mere existence of the Fashion Engineering Unit is a new and important step forward.

The Fashion Engineering Unit serves as an attractor and collector of the knowledge and cultural analysis concerning fashion that is being produced in various fields. It is meant to trigger a generally accessible interdisciplinary dialogue, spectacular and unprecedented, and to translate the product of this dialogue into books, exhibitions, and events, which will constitute a variety of tools for the orientation of communications and the capacity for planning and creativity in the fashion industry. The Italian fashion industry has attained, over the years, a position of enormous economic importance in the markets of the world. We believe that undertakings of this sort—which have major repercussions in the fields of culture and image—should be considered with the same pragmatic attitude that we apply to investments in technology and machinery. Global competition demands that all available resources be used to their best effect. The culture of fashion, and the tools to make that culture grow, are among those resources.

Christy Turlington.

Photo by Brad Branson

Enhanced by Fritz Kok

(courtesy of *The Manipulator*)

INTELLIGENT FORMS OF LIFE ON THE PLANET FASHION
Giannino Malossi

Is there intelligent life on the planet Fashion? There is evidence that seems to rule it out entirely, and certainly, from the many photographs that have been taken, there is no clear evidence to support its existence. For centuries, fashion and intelligence have seemed to be mutually exclusive categories. We all remember how blithely fashion-unconscious Einstein was, to cite just one universal and legendary example. For that matter, books written by the top models of the moment seem to have been created precisely to confirm, and to update, the age-old skepticism concerning the intellectual capacity of fashion. Is it that the environment is too arid, or is the intelligence simply too feeble to be detected? Perhaps the instruments with which we are analyzing existing data are simply not sufficiently sophisticated. How can we detect intelligent lifeforms if the instruments that we are using to do so are not, themselves, intelligent? Flaubert's *Bouvard and Pécuchet* reminds us of that paradox.

For that matter, to imagine theoretical tools for use in a cultural analysis of fashion is already, per

se, to establish a definition of fashion in intellectual terms. To order and to classify is already to frame a language that attributes significance to the subject. In short, fashion may be banal, just as advertising, the movies, pop music, and in general, the many forms of mass communications and expression are banal; in the face of banality, however, meaning is established by the use of intelligence in analysis. A theory of fashion cannot be established by declaring, a priori, that fashion is intelligent (or even, a form of art!—as it has become fashionable lately to say of fashion) but a "lowering" of one's intelligence to the level of the banal. Recently, a number of schools of thought, even in academe, even specialized, have cautiously (or interestedly) admitted that perhaps something is moving, that there is something resembling a coherent, decipherable, analyzable form. Like Mars, the planet Fashion is distant from the Earth; therefore it arouses curiosity, fantasy, and confusion on a daily basis (and in the daily papers). It is also thought that the planet Fashion influences life on Earth with the pull of its magnetic field, but little is known about its beginning, or its end. It is true enough that it is easier to change fashion than it is to change your astrological sign. In our search for intelligent lifeforms on the planet Fashion, we have assembled a research unit, contacting in various places around the Earth experts in various fields. We brought them together, and asked them to discuss the knowledge that they have amassed thus far, in the hope that their meeting would engender new and original ideas. Out of this work, exchange, and cross-pollination, we developed a working method, a field of interdisciplinary research in which we sought evidence of the forms of intelligent life on Fashion. This book is the first product of the Fashion Engineering Unit—for that is the name that we have chosen for this (intellectual) undertaking.

Other projects will follow. The first task that we set for ourselves was to obtain analytical tools that would be adequate to the complexity and all-pervasive nature of fashion, and to establish a field of inquiry and determine a certain order, a list of aspects, on which to focus our observations. We cast our nets in all directions, seeking out signals of intelligent Fashion life, wherever those signals might originate. And the results of our observations are gathered in this book, subdivided into the four areas in which we feel that we have found persuasive evidence of forms of intelligence: fashion as a fundamental component of entertainment, and entertainment as a fundamental component of fashion; fashion as a form of the creation and communication of individual and social identity; the method of industrial design of fashion and its interactivity between the continuous variety and the demands of technical reproducibility of industrial mass production; and the economic aspects of fashion, and fashion's capacity to create wealth, an important aspect for countries such as Italy, but especially for Western nations,

for which fashion represents a major component of the economy. The complexity of fashion eliminates all strict and rigid definitions, and this is the reason why it is impossible to interpret all of the phenomena that are present and operative in fashion with the use of just one of the scientific disciplines that, over the course of time, have been used to study fashion.

We have referred to analytical tools derived from disciplines that are well tested in their work on the everyday: anthropology, sociology, cultural studies, communications analysis, and other, more rigorous fields, such as economic analysis. Each of the disciplines employed, however, frames a context that fails to consider a part of the image: the work of connecting and developing interpretations, which in some cases are merely hinted at, is left to the reader. Once the system of separate disciplines has been unhinged, the combination of information becomes infinite. This seems to us to be a method in keeping with the tendency toward variety that is typical of fashion.

We are not claiming to have made a discovery likely to change the course of human history, but we can say this: yes, there may be intelligent life on the planet Fashion. If nowhere else, then in the eyes of those who observe that planet.

Why brilliant fashion-designers, a notoriously non-analytic breed, sometimes succeed in anticipating the shape of things to come better than professional predictors, is one of the most obscure questions in history; and, for the historian of culture, one of the most central.

Eric J. Hobsbawm, *The Age of Extremes: A History of the World, 1914–1991*

Gianlorenzo Bernini,
Angel with Scroll,
Sant'Andrea delle Fratte,
Rome (detail).
Photo by Pino Guidolotti

FASHION AND THE SPECTACLE

G.M.

In search of a definition of fashion that was appropriate to the times, in which modernity had become a style, in 1933 Arnold Gingrich, the publisher of the magazine *Apparel Arts*, concluded, with the phrase quoted below, that the essential feature of fashion was the convergence of fashion and media. *Apparel Arts*, a magazine devoted to the economics and culture of the fashion industry that began publication in New York in 1931 and was modeled after *Fortune*, was the first publication to introduce an analysis of mass culture and its effects on the mass production and distribution of apparel and related products. It gave expression to a culture that was already quite widespread in terms of everyday operation (*Apparel Arts* was aimed at fashion designers, manufacturers, and retailers), and it viewed fashion as a phenomenon that could be understood and manipulated in accordance with an overall communications strategy. The articles in *Apparel Arts* cast light on a question that was crucial in the period when the American economy was struggling to emerge from the Great Depression, and when the

first manifestations of the mass media (popular press, radio, and especially the movies) had attained critical mass in terms of their influence on public opinion and the marketplace. Since there was less money in circulation, there was a general quest for ways of increasing consumption. The problem was how to get the merchandise out of the stores, where there was a backlog of stock. The solution included —aside from the birth of fashion design, on the model of industrial design, i.e., a specific manipulation of the aesthetic quality of merchandise—a continual and attentive pursuit of synergy between fashion and mass media, especially the movies: "Fashion in all fields, from home furnishings to automobiles, from clothing to making love, finds its lowest common denominator, for better or worse, on the silver screen." In other words, merchandise needed to be marked with symbolic value and conveyed through a symbolic system; for that reason, the mass media would play a fundamental role.

For the pragmatic culture expressed by *Apparel Arts*—without any pretense of theoretical profundity in terms of critical thought, but focused on the immediate and verifiable effect in terms of accounting at the end of each month—the mass media appeared as a tool with which to encourage a form of civilization of society in the direction of the market, the creation of an awareness of elegance in American men, an elegant way of promoting consumption. In the United States in the years immediately following the Great Depression, the media was seen to be important, not so much as a bearer of advertising messages, for which it was already widely used in this sense, but as an ideal model of reference for the redefinition of reality, as a social site for the creation of overlapping and interchangeable identities, whose circulation accelerated the cycle of manufacturing and consumption.

More than sixty years later, the pattern has not changed substantially. If anything, it has expanded in all directions and to every place on the planet that is affected by the global economy, which in turn corresponds to the reach of satellite television. Every fashion originates as an industrial product and, at the same time, as a form of mass communications, and every media phenomenon is the potential prelude to a fashion, and that fashion points to a series of products for mass consumption. The film industry produces movies that are financed by objects, which are promoted by the objects shown in the film. Retail outlets for the entertainment corporations stand side by side with fashion boutiques on the elegant streets of major cities around the world.

This is the case, among other things, not only for clothing but for dance, pop music, and the image of movie stars. After the war, from the 1950s on, for a countless and growing array of products at increasing distances from clothing, there were fads and fashions: food, tourism, and leisure time. The consumption of objects is prompted by association with a certain image of identity that these objects also possess, and not merely as a symbolic reference. The equivalence of fashion and novelty to novelty and news is not merely a play on words; this is an essential feature of modernity. And its ultimate version in the form of spectacle, i.e., the unbroken spread and diffusion of controlled images, is aimed at the creation of a common awareness and sensibility. Fashion has an increasingly important function in the creation of spectacle as an optical illusion, through which mass culture tends to triumph as a conception of the word. The recent, colossal media coverage of the death of Gianni Versace offers a fascinating demonstration of this—the definitive institutionalization of fashion and its stars, not only as divas of the entertainment world but as creators of the extant universe, since entertainment and reality, in the overall strategy of the spectacle, coincide, and not just for the "eight hours a day" that the American television network ABC, in its latest advertising campaign, asks the public to spend in front of their television sets.

The best definition that we can give you is this:
Fashion is, quite simply, the news.

Arnold Gingrich, "Add Vitamin E," in *Apparel Arts*, Fall 1933

MASS MEDIA AND RUNWAY PRESENTATIONS

Nadine Frey

On the face of it, most fashion shows—with their numbered seats, expectant audiences, codified sound tracks, and familiar cast of models miming a ritual as stock and familiar as any guignol—are deliberately inverted theater: a commercially targeted performance art where the tickets are free but almost everything on stage is for sale. Neither the broad theatrics of the fashion show nor the underlying economics of the event do much to advance the theory, almost universally accepted today, of the fashion designer as artist. As spectacle, they are both too showy and formatted to convey the subtleties of a designer's individual aesthetic. With all its trappings of performance—from the first raising of the stage lights to the spotlit entrances of the international cast of supermodels to the final bows of the designer—a fashion show, from conception to execution, is almost entirely orchestrated for the most banal of commercial aims. It is a sales show, a huckster's art, and it is quite straightforwardly played for monetary, not artistic, goals. Taken on their own narrow terms, the contemporary criterion for a fashion show's success is just how close it can get to a seamless sales pitch, a funneling of a designer's artistic message into something as recognizable and ultimately reductive as a Nike mantra.

Fashion shows today are staged for publicity, and in their hustle for editorial and television coverage, the clothes have taken a backseat to almost everything else. Buyers often shop the collections weeks before the shows, and even when they do not, the clothes they see in the showrooms afterward are usually much more commercial and wearable (the skirts are longer and those cellophane shirts have disappeared) than what they have seen on the runway. What the designers put on the runway is often just a high-glam, attention-grabbing version of the look they are staking their name on.

Though the hyper-media-ized fashion show is a relatively recent phenomenon, getting to this point was almost inevitable once ready-to-wear became the pan-global, multibillion-dollar industry it is today. In their initial conception, in the years before ready-to-wear, fashion shows were largely intimate affairs, where designers showed off their latest creations to potential consumers: for the most part, well-heeled society women and the occasional celebrity. Clients sat on tiny gilded seats, jotting down the numbers of the cards that the largely unknown models (whose role, unlike today's supermodels, was to efface themselves in order to better show off the merit of the clothing) carried primly in their hands.

Top:

Fashion show in a former House of the People in the Yakutsk region, in Russia. Photo by Franco Zecchin

Drawing by George Grosz (1893-1959)

Opposite:

Naomi Campbell, modeling for Gianni Versace. Photo by Marleen Daniels (Contrasto)

Overleaf:

Gucci fashion show. Photos by Claudio Vitale (Grazia Neri)

Photo by Ferdinando Scianna

With the advent of ready-to-wear, designers no longer showed to their final consumers but to an audience of buyers and press, neatly separated by the runway. The press is looking for ideas that will carry fashion forward. Buyers are looking for that, too, so that they will have a general idea of the season's fashion statement and therefore know what looks to emphasize in their buying for that season. But more important, they are looking for individual pieces that are likely to please their customers and attain the highest possible percentage of sales.

The absence of the final consumer at fashion shows meant that designers were destined to see their message ever interpreted, either in the pages of magazines—where film from the runway shows is clipped apart and rearranged, or where the clothes are simply reshot with an editor's own notions of styling firmly in the fore—or in stores—where only a sampling of the whole collection is purchased, with even that bit often merchandised in fragments (shoes in one department and sweaters in another). For a designer, that would be roughly equivalent to Steven Spielberg screening *Jaws* to an audience of film professionals who then reshuffle stills of the film in order to convey and explain its message to a final audience.

As a result, fashion designers, fueled in part by the high-octane energy of the 1970s, began conceiving fashion shows that were more about concept and message than clothes, shouting their message so loud that it could be heard over the heads of the inevitably interpreting buyers and press. What they were selling, after all, was a label—something ideally coveted enough to turbo-drive sales of everything from underwear to beach towels to perfume.

While the New York shows, with their bottom-line belief in the dollar-driven Seventh Avenue, tended to brook no silliness and still hew to a dryly commercial approach, and Milan strove to bully its way up the international fashion ladder on a can-do agenda of strict delivery times and an overtly earnest se-

riousness, it fell mostly upon Paris (where the notion of *être* versus *paraître*—being versus seeming—is a national ideology) to forward the notion of runway shows as a rollicking Broadway of international fashion. And the notion of molding fashion shows along a theatrical or cinematic model was almost unavoidable—you already had a bevy of pretty girls, music, footlights, and a stage. Given the democratizing nature of ready-to-wear versus couture, what more democratizing model to adopt than musical theater or cinema à la Busby Berkeley?

In Paris, fashion-show fever probably hit its height in the 1970s. While most ready-to-wear shows were staged for a thousand people, some, like Thierry Mugler's giant style extravaganza in the Zenith concert hall, were produced for an audience of five thousand. While the average designer hired about thirty models per show, a few went so far as to hire sixty. Star models, such as Jerry Hall or Iman, made a cool $2,000 per show (a bargain compared with today's supermodel rates of $20,000 and more). Lasers, deafening sound tracks, video screens, smoke, confetti, and bubbles were common. The freewheeling, free-spending French designers sent women out on the runways in carriages and sleighs, on bicycles, motorcycles, roller skates, stilts, and pogo sticks, often as not accompanied by French poodles, wolfhounds, cockatoos, Persian cats, and toddlers.

The harder shows worked to sell a message rather than clothing, the more entertaining they got. Think of Inès de la Fressange in the late 1980s, swanning down the Chanel runway in a pair of pajamas, pillow tucked under her arm, lying down for a nap at the end of the runway. Or Thierry Mugler sending Iman onto the runway kitted out as Sheena of the Jungle, warily promenading a baby leopard on a leash.

By the end of the 1980s, the supermodels themselves became the message. Designers packed their punch, and vaunted their wealth, by staging the runways with the likes of Naomi, Christy, Linda, and Claudia. Even when designers were not keen to pay the fees, they knew that the front page of tomorrow's *Figaro* or *Corriere della Sera* meant not the mono-kini of the youth-quaked 1960s, or any other design revolution, but simply sending out Naomi in something thigh-hugging or see-through, or Claudia in almost anything at all. And when the papers tired of seeing the same models in their pages, designers did not hesitate to pay Hollywood celebrities—from Madonna (who, pre-Lourdes, modeled in one memorable Jean Paul Gaultier show pushing a baby carriage) to Demi Moore to Elizabeth Hurley—to sit

new york

Drawing by Jeffrey Fulvimari

(Courtesy of Art Department, New York)

Nina Ricci, fashion show,
fall-winter 1996–97
collection.
Photo by E. Robert

Opposite:
Thierry Mugler,
fashion show, fall-winter
collection 1995–96.
Photo by Pierre Vauthey

Backstage at a Romeo Gigli
fashion show, 1995.
Photo by Armin Linke

ringside wearing their designs. If international press has become the stakes for which everyone is playing, then Paris's gamble on a no-holds-barred showmanship was right on the money. According to the Chambre Syndicale de la Mode Française, today there are roughly 850 journalists present at the Milan shows (which traditionally precede the Paris shows by several days to a week) versus two thousand journalists in Paris. One recent industry calculation held that the weeklong Paris showings generated two thousand pages of editorial and 120 radio and television shows internationally.

Yet one of the less sanguine results of the celebratory, self-congratulatory, over-the-top, cute, media-crazed frenzy surrounding the fashion shows is that veteran buyers and reporters—those who make the twice-a-year, month-and-half-long pilgrim-age from Milan to London to Paris to New York to see the major ready-to-wear shows every year—are beginning to feel wrung out before the marathon even begins. There are over a hundred shows in eight days in Paris alone, and the attempt to be heard above the crowd drives designers to hold shows everywhere, from abandoned subway stations (Martin Margiela) to deserted town houses (John Galliano) to seamy out-of-town warehouses (Walter Von Beirendonck). Even the invitations are exhausting. Show invitations today are disguised variously as mirrors, five-foot-square posters packed in unwieldy and outsized mailing tubes, holograms, vinyl backpacks, miniature stamps, tattoos, or items of jewelry—even telephone numbers in unmarked envelopes, numbers that, when called, provide show time and place: a floating rave for fashion initiates.

Model presenting for
Thierry Mugler, ready-to-wear
collection, summer 1991.
Photo by J. Donoso
(Sygma/Grazia Neri)

For the most part, vellum is a thing of the past, and it defies patience packing posters, backpacks, and T-shirts into a handbag for a day's schedule of dawn-to-dusk shows. Yet there are so many journalists in town during the ready-to-wear shows in Paris that the press offices of still-struggling designers will send out some 1,400 invitations to get four hundred warm bodies to a show.

Yet, however broad the theatrics, very often a show will contribute something to the changing way we see fashion and the way we are likely to be seeing fashion in the future. Somewhat less frequently, it even tells you something about the way everyone will dress and look and feel about what they wear at some point twelve to eighteen months in the future—depending on whether you are talking about people who wear the actual designer clothing or a street look influenced by a trickle-down of these designer flights of fancy (feather jewelry, spiked heels, body painting).

And it is an interesting truth that, every now and then, when designers want to say something about what they are doing as artists—as opposed to creating a message that is ultimately as recognizable as the shard of a Coke bottle in the sand—they inevitably eschew the theatrics. Instead, à la Giorgio Armani in his own low-key, in-house theater, they show to a reduced audience, get rid of the star DJs, cancel the supermodels, tell Sting and Elton to stay home, and just show the clothes.

COLORS OF THE MEDIA, COLORS OF FASHION

Peppino Ortoleva

For many centuries, a number of colors—such as royal purple or the dark blue of lapis lazuli—have preserved an elevated symbolic significance and were closely linked with certain of the upper classes. In the early nineteenth century, however, the situation changed: the growth of the chemicals industry and, first and foremost, the production of aniline and its derivatives allowed the development of a number of relatively cheap artificial dyes, which could be manufactured anywhere, with an array of colors that would previously have been difficult even to imagine. There were 14,400 shades of color classified in 1864 by Eugène Chevreul in his book *Des couleurs et de leurs applications aux arts industrielles*, which hardly seems like much now, compared to the sixteen million colors offered by any desktop computer.

The proper dyeing of fabrics had, by this point, become easy, both in terms of technical quality and in terms of responding to the tastes of the public: there was not a single shade that could not be created. According to the well-known interpretation of Gisèle Freund, the development of photography grew out of the widespread desire of the emerging bourgeoisie to enjoy the age-old aristocratic luxury of the portrait, with the help of a machine. In the same way, the development of the chemistry of colors and dyes allowed nearly everyone, whatever their income, to enjoy an array of colors that would once certainly have been clear signs of luxury.

Yet we know that in many European countries during the course of the nineteenth century, and through much of this century (and for men's fashion, practically up to the present day), there was no more than a partial appreciation of these new possibilities. In the prevailing styles of the European bourgeoisie, there long survived a tendency to limit the use of color, with a strong emphasis on what are generally thought of as non-colors, such as white, black, and gray.

Various interpretations of this phenomenon have been offered. Some have suggested that the emerging bourgeoisie wished to establish a different style, distinct from that of the aristocracy (which, however, contrasts sharply with other trends of the same period). Others have ventured that this two-tone or three-tone color scheme was directly linked to the values that were considered typical of Victorian culture, based on sobriety and strictness (as if black had an "objective" value of sobriety). Lastly, the idea has been put forth (notably by Thorstein Veblen) that the black-and-white look of nineteenth-century bourgeois style also—or even primarily—worked to sanction the sexual division of labor found in the "leisure class": the women of the privileged classes

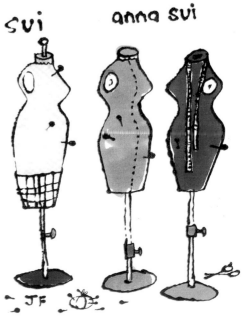

sui   anna sui

Outfit by Kenzo.

Photo by Ferdinando Scianna

(Magnum/Contrasto)

Artwork by

Jeffrey Fulvimari for Anna Sui

(Courtesy of Art Department, New York)

were transformed into status symbols in part through the totally impractical nature of their white clothing, which was entirely unsuited for hard work, while their husbands, dressed in black suits that "hide dirt," were better able to engage in practical activities. Perhaps insufficient attention has been paid, however, to a passage from the writings of Goethe, in his 1810 book *On the Theory of Colors:* "Educated people show a certain aversion to color.

This may in part be a result of a weakness of the eyes, in part an uncertainty of taste, which tends to take refuge from nothingness. Women therefore dress almost always in white, men in black." For Goethe, the obsession with black-and-white dichromatism was not the product of a mere issue of status but was linked directly to the level of education. And perhaps this is the most obvious and the simplest explanation. At the end of the eighteenth century,

vast and growing social groups—at first, the "learned classes," and later, with the development of mandatory education, sectors of the lower classes—began to find in the medium of the printed page not only a series of texts to read but also an essential reference for existence at large. Hegel wrote, during the Age of Restoration, that "the newspaper is the secular morning prayer of the modern man. Before, one got into touch with God, now one gets into touch with the world." This world was viewed as orderly and relatively uniform, a world "in black and white." This led to the idea of writing = rationality = production that confined images, especially images in color, to the emerging field of "art," which was understood as an essential activity but one that was essentially unproductive, while it assigned to the two-toned and orderly world of printed paper the role of a daily guide to existence. If this is true, the prevailing medium of the period, the printed page, had a profound effect—not merely on the color choices of individuals but also on the whole area of the organization of the chromatic taste of society at large, or at least of the ruling classes, in contrast with the very array of new possibilities offered by the technologies of chemistry and textiles. The prevailing taste in industrialized countries was dominated, until well beyond the beginning of the twentieth century, by dichromatism, a sort of binary obsession that may well have sprung, originally, from the black-and-white opposition of printing. The white and black of adults corresponded to the pink and light blue of children too young to go to school: these were indeed

colors, and they served to underline the fact that those who wore them had not yet acceded to the rational sphere. But they were pale, pastel colors, and above all, they were rigidly classified, with a neutral tone for males. In the political system, too, the counterpoint between left and right, which was to dominate European politics for nearly two centuries, was matched by another dichromatism: the red of the progressives and the black—so dear to Stendhal—of the reactionaries.

The obsession with the non-color colors of printing extended immediately to intimate clothing (the Italian term *biancheria*, literally meaning whitewear, is an eloquent indication) and to architectural style: even after the phase that could properly be called eoclassical, the white hue—upon which it was believed, wrongly, that the Greco-Roman style was founded—long remained the prevalent color in buildings of institutional importance. The industrial system was also affected by this line of colors, at least as late as the arrogant dictum of Henry Ford, who said of the Model T, "You can get it in any color you want, as long as it's black" (the most noteworthy confirmation of Marshall McLuhan's thesis that Fordism was a complete, and extreme, affirmation of the "Gutenberg galaxy").

Color found its own powerful presence in a number of ritual moments, almost as if to underline the need for an emotional bond. Goethe had classified several possible meanings for color, among which

Fashion on television.
Photos by Enzo

Michael Bevilacqua,
Life Is Sweet,
acrylic on canvas, 1997
(Courtesy of Jessica Fredericks Gallery,
New York)

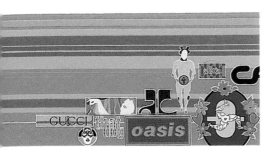

were symbolic meanings, based on a long accretion of customs and a number of principles of perceptions, and allegorical meanings, "which [contain] a greater share of happenstance and arbitrariness, I would even say of the conventional, inasmuch as, before understanding its significance, it is necessary that we should be offered the meaning of the sign, as is the case with green, said to represent hope." Throughout the nineteenth century, and for much of the twentieth century, these were the prevalent meanings of colors based on a conventional code. Flags are an example of this.

The symbolic power of black-and-white dichromatism continued to dominate the system of the media for many years, even after other revolutionary communications media had come onto the scene. Photography, for instance, was black and white, not only for concrete technical reasons (in the early decades of photography there was a remarkable array of work in color) but because of a conscious choice that at the time "appeared" entirely natural: the decision to base the new technique on the same chromatic system that already dominated the entire universe of information. The sole exception was the need, which still arose, for hand coloring the most valuable or important photographs. The same was true for the movies. Typographic writing, after having profoundly influenced clothing, was defining the entire chromatic system of communications.

And yet, at the end of the nineteenth century there

was an opposing trend at work, at first tentatively, and later more aggressively. Photography took roughly sixty years to obtain acceptable color techniques (color photography, a patent held by Louis Lumière, dates back to the 1890s), and it was not until after World War II that color photography was common in mass distribution. The movies took little more than forty years to bring color to the public. Television took even less time.

Color, in these new media of reproduction and illusion, appeared not only as an extra factor of truth and naturalness but also as an added pleasure, as a further degree of "desirability." "No! It is not the narrative object that generates the color, nor is it the photographic object. It is the music of the object." This statement by Sergey Eisenstein (one of the very few great intellectuals, after Goethe, to have examined the role of color in our culture) is decisive. The advent of color in photography (and consequently in offset printing) and, later, in the movies corresponds to a change in mentality: the system of colors has been presented ever since with the function not of imposing a single and uniform order but of allowing a variety of compositions—conventional, but based upon varied and shifting conventions.

One of the first outlets for this vast and often overlooked media revolution was in fashion magazines. With the end of World War II, it became common for women of all classes—in the United States and Europe—to seek in magazines not only their new outfits but the chromatic variety of reality: no longer just a pattern, for which they needed to choose a

color and a fabric, but a complete object with its color already selected. The color of illustrated magazines and of movies was probably a secondary—but not irrelevant—factor in the explosion of ready-to-wear clothing, and it had major effects on the history of cosmetics, beginning with the garish red of women's lips following the war, perhaps the most impressive and notable indicator of the end of dichromatism.

Whether it was these technological changes in photography and printing or whether it was the media devoting greater attention and effort—precisely because of the growing demand in society—that drove the widespread love of color is a matter to be explored separately. Media and fashion, in the years of television's rise, seem to have converged objectively and unnoticed into a new chromatic sensibility. With the advent of color television in the sixties and seventies, there was a further leap forward: television's color, in fact, is even less realistic than the color of film, since it is produced not by the projection of light onto an object, as is the case with photography and film, but by the same light that projects color onto us, the viewers. Television presents itself as a "window on the world" and at the same time depicts that world in colors that "do not exist." It was a chromatic system—still different, unstable, and counterintuitive—that was beginning to penetrate into everyday habits through the persuasive power of advertising messages, and precisely in television (especially in color television) it found its ideal medium, with a great variety of effects.

One of the first effects that emerged was the exact opposite of what we have described when talking about photography in the early years, when printing, the dominant medium, influenced the color sensibility of photography, calibrating it to black and white. In more recent years television, which is still the dominant medium for the majority of the population, has conditioned the medium of print. At the end of the sixties, while black and white seemed to enjoy a final triumph in op art, the world of "psychedelic" culture—which was hardly separate from op art—began to write in color, producing newspapers that were profoundly anti-Gutenberg. One example is the *San Francisco Oracle*, in which the violation of all typographic norms was the norm, and in which all the texts were in various colors, as if to suggest a different written dimension and a complete overthrowing of the relationship between text and image. Subsequently, the popularity of "acid" colors spread throughout the media. With the advent of the computer—a direct descendant of television in terms of its visual effects—we have seen the most radical transformation. We are becoming accustomed to writing on increasingly colorful screens, marking the words that we wish to emphasize with bright colors. Writing itself, which originated the two-tone, dichromatic obsession, now violates the alternation of black and white that for many centuries had endured as the unmistakable sign of the civilization of Gutenberg.

It is still too early to say exactly how popular taste in colors, especially among the young, is being modified in connection with these processes. One of the most interesting facts that emerged from an early study (by Laura Bovone and E. Mora) of the young people of Milan is their great sensibility in terms of choosing colors as a role in establishing identity. Moreover, these young people often insist on an idea that is commonplace in our time—that black and white are no longer non-colors but that they are colors to all effects (for that matter, "dark" fashion with its specific features would not otherwise be conceivable). Such an idea would probably have made little or no sense prior to the changes in sensibility (including visual sensibility) that have been encouraged by electronics. Another curious effect of the sensibility in terms of colors—a "cathodic" sensibility, as it were—is the variety of objects that are colored "as seen on television," such as those seen in advertisements with nuances of electronic luminescence. Examples of this trend are the bodies of many new cars and other metal objects for use in the home, or the use of synthetic fibers, such as latex, to evoke a sort of "cathodic" luminous effect.

On the other hand, as if to keep a symbolic circle unbroken, a number of different communications media have become items of apparel, from the Walkman to the portable CD, forming part of the circuit of fashions to the degree that they have systematically adopted colors that can be coordinated with clothing. Once communications equipment enters the realm of apparel, it conforms with the prevailing tastes in colors, in a clear convergence of fashion and media. In so doing, it provides a confirmation and, every so often, a slight modification of the chromatic system that constitutes one of the most difficult features to define with precision—and above all, to explain—in any culture.

W&LT's Fashion Show, fall-winter 1997–98 collection. Photos by Patrick Robert (Sygma/Grazia Neri)

Opposite: Poster from M. Farren, *Get On Down,* London, 1976

WORDS TO WEAR BY

Laird O. Borrelli

Laird O. Borrelli

Where would fashion be without literature? Diana Vreeland

While the potency of the fashion image—in both advertising and editorial—has long been established, the importance of the language of fashion has been largely glossed over. Roland Barthes, whose *The Fashion System* is the seminal work on fashion language, asserts that "it is not the object [or image] but the names that create desire." The seduction of the fashion image is immediate, but it is the language of fashion that perpetuates its romance, which is both ephemeral and organic.

Fashion magazines are primers of fashion language. The fashion magazine presents narratives that are built on the interaction of "image-clothing" and the "written garment." According to Barthes, the language of fashion (narratives) is "institutional." Barthes's research remains relevant because at its base the structure of fashion's rhetoric remains static. However, the narratives created in "*Vogue*-speak" by *Vogue* editors in chief Diana Vreeland, Grace Mirabella, and Anna Wintour between 1968 and the present reveal that the language of fashion (versus its structure) distinctively reflects the idiom of each editor, even as it reflects the times.

Particular emphasis is given to the visual, oral, popular, and emphatic aspects of fashion language in *Vogue*-speak narratives. Each editor personalizes her texts by the style in which she uses these ele-

ments. The visual aspect of fashion (image-clothing) is verbally conjured with adjectives and metaphors. Vreeland's use of adjectives tended to the baroque ("seraglio shimmer"), and her prose was especially rich in metaphor. Thus an evening dress could look "like something glimpsed in the Unicorn Tapestries . . . or in some *Très Riches Heures*." Vreeland's metaphors usually link fashion to the fantastic, while Wintour constructs metaphors that often relate to film and icons of popular culture.

Alliteration and rhyme are used in fashion texts to evoke the sounds and textures of spoken language. The "sixties pop of patent" syncopates Wintour's prose in 1990, while rhyme is used for emphasis when Mirabella writes, in 1977, of "wonderful new flings-of-things." A 1968 text in Vreeland's *Vogue* even mimics dialogue: "Drifty, Dreamy. Wow plus sigh." These examples are representative of what Marjorie Ferguson identifies as the "write-speak" style of women's magazines that is employed by editors to "personalize" the text in a friendly, as opposed to a dictatorial, manner.

Vogue's texts are made more accessible through the use of popular language, axiomatic expressions, and references to popular culture. This is particularly characteristic of Wintour's "faddist" texts, which are

On camera, Jean Shrimpton appears so with it, so much a part of the scene, that thinking about her overthrow is unthinkable. But in all truth, the real Shrimp rarely makes any scene. She hardly ever shows up at the discothèques, detests such fashionable occasions as movie premieres, doesn't smoke, drinks little—just an occasional Black Russian, at most—and owns a grand total of five dresses; her usual costume is blue jeans and a boy's coat.

Typically, when a British M.P. was told he had just passed Jean Shrimpton in a London restaurant last week, he exclaimed: "God! I thought it was just some girl trying to look like Jean Shrimpton."

Her 19-year-old sister, Chris, is engaged to Mick Jagger, the largest of the Rolling Stones, but the Shrimp prefers to quietly gather moss.

Karen Kilimnik, *The Shrimp*, 1994, crayon on paper

(Courtesy of 303 Gallery, New York)

Drawing for Moschino,
François Berthoud.

peppered with axioms such as: "Any woman worth her salt will . . . " New trends are made accessible in reference to icons of popular culture, as in "shiny leather motorcycle-style clothes with a rock'n'roll/Brando glamour," as opposed to Mirabella's straightforward and plain-spoken approach, which plugs, for example, an "attitude [that] is attractive, casual, nonchalant—the attitude of jeans and sweaters."

In the end, *Vogue*-speak only mimics popular language, for it is an editorial language. Its authority is often evoked through persuasive emphasis, which seems to allow only for bangs and never for whimpers. Emphasis (and enthusiasm) is achieved mainly through the use of hyperbole, repetition, and the superlative. Thus the coats of 1970 are "bigger, furrier, luxe-ier than anyone's, anywhere, ever," and the look of August 1968 is that of the "prettiest-girl-in-the-world," some of whose clothes are "tearingly romantic." Repetitive statements often rhyme or are alliterative. Sometimes a string of adjectives is used to describe an object, or a repetitive statement is fixed mantra-like on a single word as in "belt it tight, tight, tight at the waist."

There are fashions in language, even as there are

sartorial fads. "Groovy" and "swinging," which were once the superlatives of choice, have been morphed into "edgy" and "retro." In keeping with the fin-de-siècle tendency for review, there has been a recent bombardment of postmodern fashions. Perhaps more significant than the adjectives that designate the style of the moment is the origin of the words and references used in fashion narratives. These references reflect the editors' perceptions of their readers, of fashion, and of the time. I have observed a movement away from "high" culture and toward popular and media culture. Vreeland's texts, which are rich with references to literature and art history, are peopled with characters from Anna Karenina to housekeepers from Proust. In the long, sinuous line of a garment she sees a **"1970s nude descending a staircase, swinging through the streets, swinging all over the world."**

Vreeland's expansive perspective (which has sometimes been criticized as being elitist) stands in contrast to Mirabella's more democratic and popular appeal. Mirabella focuses on the reader as consumer, which is certainly in keeping with the recessionary economic climate of the 1970s and relative to the lifestyle of the working woman, whether she has the "credit of kings or [is] budgeted to the eyeballs."

Mirabella's "briefs" are countered by Wintour's "sound bites." Wintour has a journalistic, mix-master style that can result in somewhat kinetic advice: **"One bold stroke of ruby red lipstick creates forties glamour. In a few seconds a temporary tattoo provides downtown attitude."** Wintour expands the idea of global fashion to include "twenty-four hour" fashion. From 1968 to the present, *Vogue*-speak has moved, as Robin Givhans summarizes, **"from Proust to Madonna"**—both in the text and on the cover. Moreover, references in *Vogue* today are most often to electronic media, particularly television and cinema, which allows for and gives priority to statements such as: **"Leather still emerges with a tough, give-'em-hell attitude, which should satisfy the Thelma and Louise in every woman,"** rather than to the less accessible references to high culture preferred by Vreeland (**"Savile Row days, Walpurgis nights"**).

General fluency in *Vogue*-speak is ensured by the trenchant conventions of the largely static structure of fashion language. As we are bombarded with greater frequency by more fashion information, trends in fashion language will probably become more short-lived, but the form of the parlance of the designer, consumer, and editor will remain intelligible. An important and often overlooked aspect of this rhetoric is the enjoyment derived from the language itself. Ros Ballaster discovered that the very language of fashion was a source of pleasure to readers of women's magazines, reporting that "when talking about magazines, women endlessly and diligently parody and mimic them, displaying their own literacy in and mastery of its generic conventions." The perpetuation of fashion rests not only on the page but in the person-to-person dialogue that preserves the prom dress or the scandalous modernity of the mini. Through *Vogue*-speak, the splendor of the image-garment is translated into a jargon, indeed a purple prose, through which sartorial splendor is celebrated and shared.

Amico, pensa a guidare. Tanto non è roba per te.

SWISH

MODA MODA PER DONNE DONNE.

Advertising campaign
for Swish, 1994,
with Naomi Campbell.
Photo by Franco Origlia

(Sygma/Grazia Neri)

Asger Jorn,
L'avant-garde se rend pas,
1962

(Archivio Infinito)

COMPOSED BEAUTY

Laura Piccinini

Barbie models clothing by Christian Dior, advertising campaign for Mattel, Inc.

Mia, computer-generated photographic montage, by Enzo, 1997

A 100 percent virtual star. Absolutely virtual, but already famous—the model who never was. Idol of our time or cybermodel: pseudowoman in three dimensions, created to appear on magazine covers, to be seen and adored, loved and imitated. Or else hated because remote and untouchable: is it diet, plastic surgery, gene pool, a special mother? There is no answer; she does not issue statements. How could she? She does not exist.

She was created by clicking the mouse of a computer. She grew by bits and chips, her face and body manipulated until her image was perfect, the aesthetic epitome of everything that designers, advertising agencies, fashion editors, photographers, and potential consumers desire. She does not exist, but she has lots of names and lots of identities.

One of her names is Kyoko Date, the seventeen-year-old idol from Japan, with a body that is measured in inches, pounds, shapes, and colors, all extremely realistic but actually generated by computer, with an image comprising 40,000 pixels that shape a three-dimensional creature, on whose face alone ten people worked, the programmers hired by the prestigious HoriPro company, the leading modeling agency in Japan. Before the name is an abbreviation, DK-CG, which stands for Digital Kid generated by Computer Graphics. Thousands of fans adore her:

Kyoko, the part-time waitress and model, who is about to become a rock star when her new album comes out.

The other top virtual model of the moment is Lara Croft, a superheroine who somehow escaped from the *pistolero* adventures of a video game called Tomb Riders to become a cover girl for scientific, fashion, and style magazines, and even in the bastions of conservative business thought—*The Economist* praised Lara as an enchanting character, a heartbreaker who defies the law of gravity—is sailing to the heights of worldwide fame and success. Rock stars fall head over heels in love with her: Bono of U2 had her as the prima donna of the grandiose PopMart Tour, and she was wildly cheered by the crowds when she appeared on stage. She is a virtual Spice Girl, the big sister of the cyberchick Tamagotchi.

Lara is what was once known as "built" and wears an extra-large bra size (just like the outlandishly shaped Barbie, or any other Demi Moore–style actress): she, too, is about to release an album. Miss Croft is everywhere, but she does not take the Concorde, like her supermodel colleagues (whom she has already robbed of plenty of editorial pages and numerous fans), to get from the runways of Paris to those of New York. And whose creations will be modeled by Lara Croft?

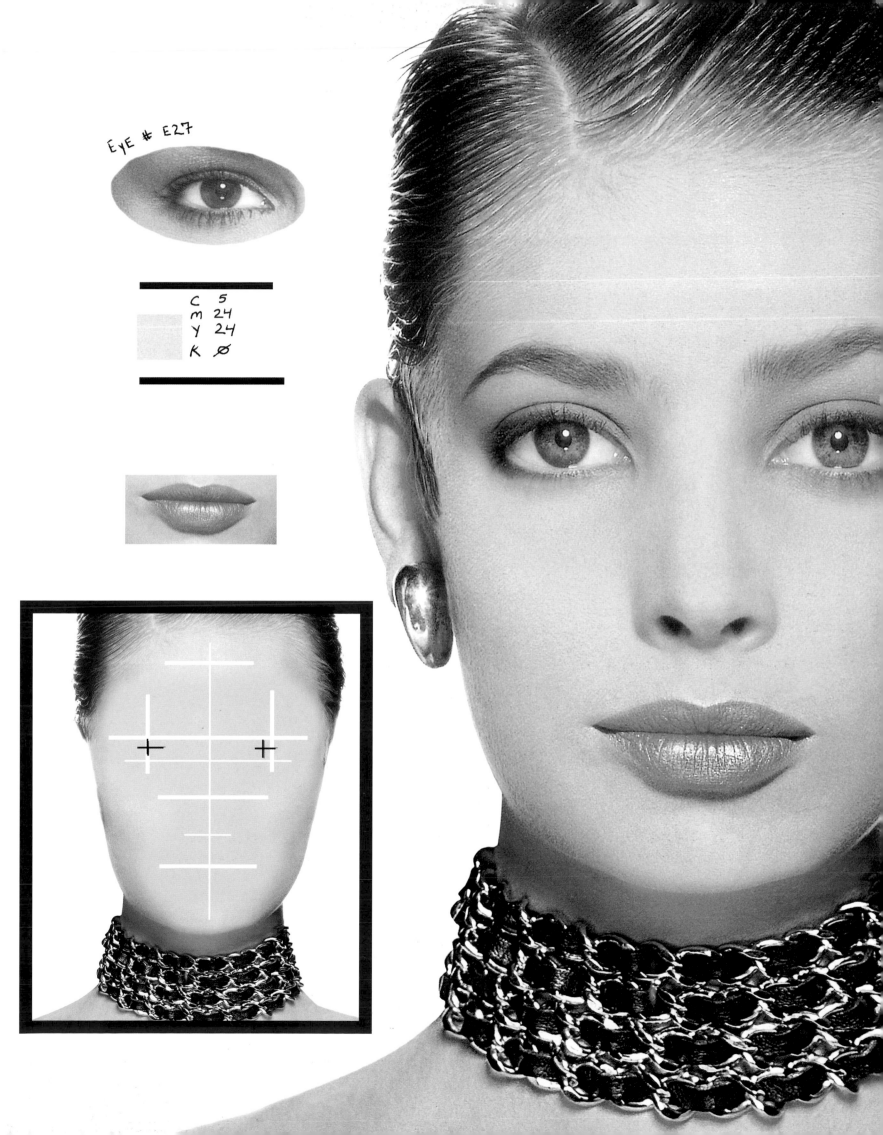

EYE # E27

C 5
M 24
Y 24
K ∅

Edland Man, Collage, 1996

Gabrielle, 18.18 17/11/95 U, Is fashion silly? 1

X-UIDL: 816876648.000
Date: Fri, 17 Nov 95 18:18:50 UT
From: "Gabrielle " <Gabrielle-AT@msn.com>
To: "'pittimmagine@softeam.it'" <pittimmagine>
Subject: Is fashion silly?

Fashion isn't just silly--it's DANGEROUS.

When fashion designers use models that are unnaturally thin, they set up a
paradigm of the female form that is specious, that is totally unattainable by
female youths. They drive young women to torture themselves and commit
harmful acts to their bodies in an effort to reach the unreachable.

This is a crime. Studies show that over 70% of high school-aged girls in California have some form of eating disorder. 70 PERCENT!

Why can't just one, JUST ONE fashion designer break free and do something totally crazy, like celebrating woman as she really is. The female form is beautiful, and the variety that exists among women's bodies is the essence of beauty.

I wish the industry that claims to enhance the beauty of the female form could acknowledge its past mistakes and love and support women for who they are. Sign the Thin Is Not Bitter

Edland Man, *Collage*, 1996

Mariko Mori, a flesh-and-blood model, takes pictures of herself, and then manipulates her image on the computer, in the same way that a normal model subjects herself to rigid diets, endless makeup sessions, and worse: a cyberprincess who has chosen to live in the borderland between the world of fashion and the world of art, strutting along futuristic runways—whether at fashion presentations or the Venice Biennale—always in settings that others only dream of occupying.

The bejeweled and imperturbable lady immortalized by Enzo, a New York photographer, is nameless: she has a classic, almost standard beauty, with no outstanding features, except that she is yet another of the increasingly numerous and sought-after 100 percent virtual women. Enzo was brilliant in his simplicity: he joined nose and ears, borrowed eyes from women's magazines and show biz rags, cutting and pasting in a free-form collage to obtain the features of an "ideal beauty."

"Okay, then, let's see what the computer can do," say the fashion photographers, putting their pictures through the new systems of image manipulation. You take a picture, and in a three-D simulation you can change the faces and bodies of anyone—even Claudia Schiffer and Naomi Campbell—or put them in enchanting, absurd, or hyperrealistic settings, like a beach in Malibu, but created at a console in a studio in London or Milan in the middle of winter (so as to save time and money). Everything is manipulated by computer, with paint box, electronic stylus, or digitized video image. Drawing life from and restoring life to diabolical Lolitas, shadows, and phantoms: they are so fake that they seem real or, on the contrary, devoid of all earthly characteristics. These are the new colleagues of paper dolls (like those clipped out by the photographer Edland Man), and they have other ethereal colleagues, so emaciated and drawn that they look like zombies, and they trigger debates on anorexia and heroin chic, so many addicts are posing (for photo shoots or runway presentations). We have not yet reached the stage of cloning models, but somewhere the umbilical fetus is already floating, head down, in a bottle of Calvin Klein perfume.

And if the computer does not do it, there are new artists who will. Consider the English painter Gary Hume, who deconstructs beautiful women, reducing to almost abstract splotches of color the renowned faces of stars and models such as Kate Moss, whose features were reproduced in an aluminum oval in which you can see your own features, a symbolic commentary on the role of the supermodel nowadays, an infinite mutant. At the far end of the spectrum, a French artist named Orlan manipulates her own body with actual plastic surgery done in art galleries. Once again, art synthesizes and depicts what fashion and beauty make of the identity involved in appearance. The shadowy phantom of a real model is transformed into a two-dimensional woman, a page of advertising, an entirely virtual icon, yet three-dimensional and realistic, moving well beyond the cyborg, which is a meeting place of technology and humans. This is the deconstruction of the identity of every model—either a rapturous cyberfeminism that hails the defeat of old standards with a new technological possibility of changing oneself, or the accusation of creating yet another, even more impossible ideal of a posthuman woman, while pursuing here on earth the obsessions with diet and the scalpel that create beauty, a threat to every unhappy adolescent girl. A denunciation of the post-Barbie mentality, an immaterial body for those who admire it from this side of the screen, even more dangerous than the ideals of celluloid. Contemporary beauty, whether real or virtual, follows a "fuzzy" logic, nuanced and undecipherable: the "fuzzy" lady is not human or inhuman—she is decidedly posthuman.

She is like the idoru, the cyberwoman from the book of the same name by William Gibson: a woman-idol, an array of software components, an industrial-strength combination of the faces of the last fifty or so women to dominate the mass media, seducing with a hypnotic gaze that generates holograms.

From top:

Measuring prospective
students for a Parisian
modeling school in 1957
(Courtesy of Farabola)

The French model Bibelot
being shaved bald by the
hairdresser Jacques Esterel
in August 1964
(Courtesy of Farabola)

Bibelot, with a lace mantilla
draped over her head
(Courtesy of Farabola)

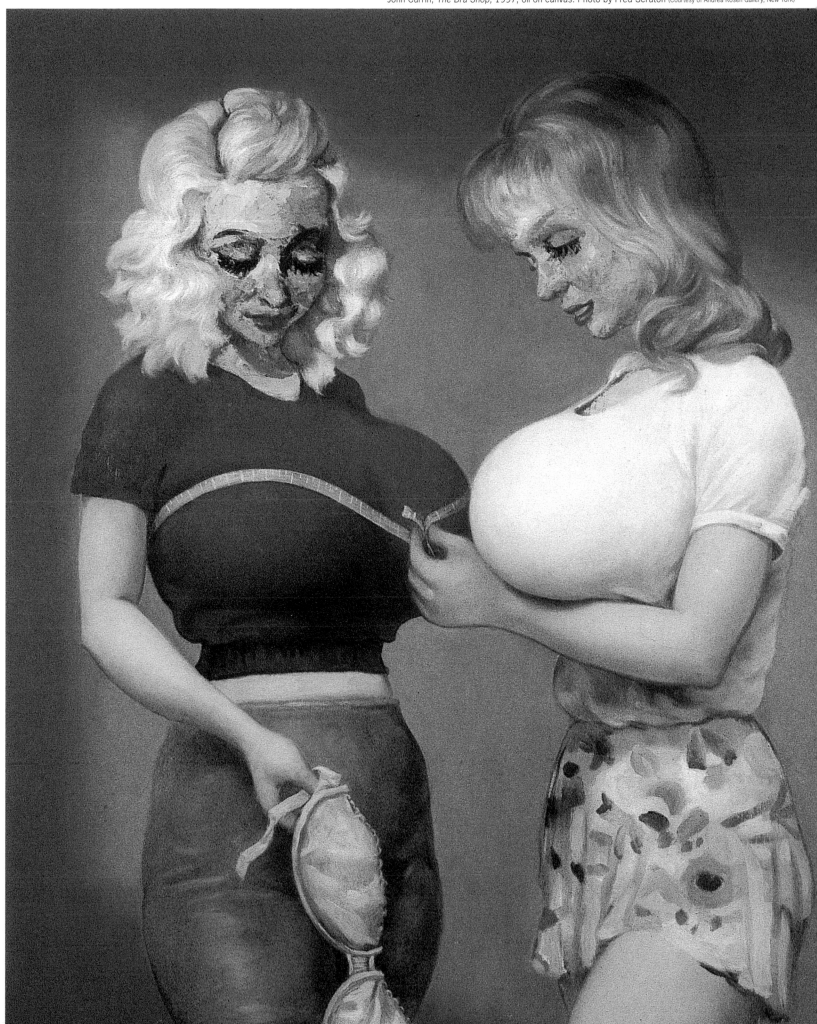

John Currin, *The Bra Shop*, 1997, oil on canvas. Photo by Fred Scruton (Courtesy of Andrea Rosen Gallery, New York)

FASHION,

Preceding pages:
Ijpont, Amsterdam, 1957.
Photo by Dolf Kruger

Scene from a Mexican fiesta
in Aguas Calientes. Photo by
Henri Cartier-Bresson, 1964

(Contrasto/Magnum)

WHAT DO YOU WANT TO "SAY" TODAY?
G.M.

The most distinctive expression of Western society in our time is the accentuation of mobility, both as a way of life and as a cultural attitude. Mobility and modernity have coincided throughout the century. This is the symbolic reference indicated by Microsoft's advertising slogan: "Where do you want to go today?" Rarely has a corporate mantra been selected with such messianic conceit as that of a corporation that does not produce vehicles or means of transportation, as the slogan might suggest, but operating systems and software for computers. Many of the new technologies that have entered into everyday life in the twentieth century (cars, planes, televisions, cell phones, the Internet) are called by neologisms that—logically enough—contain references to mobility and distance, and are continually moving from one place to another, enhancing the abolition of distances in time and space, creating a loss of the sense of place and everything that goes along with that, including style of dress. The long-term consequences of this progressive dissolution of one of the fundamental fulcrums of human culture are not yet clear, but this does not keep us from considering it to be quite normal to cross time zones and entire continents for pure fun, to visit seven world capitals in a week, to change our geographic and cultural context as nonchalantly as we change our clothing.

Actually, our mobility is more apparent than real. As the global economy unifies the economic structures of the most disparate countries, the worldwide spread of mass communications tends to eliminate the specific cultural differences of each place. There is a greater possibility of traveling and seeing different places; at the same time the depth of the differences among cultures diminishes. There remains a sense of disorientation, a general sense of not belonging, or—if we look at this from another point of view—the possibility of easily changing garb, of shifting among interchangeable images. There was a time when this was not possible, when clothing was codified strictly according to the cultural requirements established by tradition: every outfit and every decoration of the body had a well established and unchangeable meaning, and could be worn only on certain occasions or by certain individuals. This was the case when it was a slow and difficult process to travel or move from one place to another, when communications were costly and difficult, and certainly less powerful than tradition. The differences in clothing and decoration gave travelers a perception of distance, as did differences in cooking, language, and customs. If someone went to China, they would see Chinese people dressed in Chinese garb, and they would feel that they really were in China. They would meet true "others," different even in their dress. Fashion, then, has transformed clothing, making its laws and customs mobile, i.e., making tradition a thing of the past and replacing it with an endless array of continually changing possibilities,

determined by the interaction among individuals and the interaction of those individuals with the media. Fashion is, in this sense, the transposition of mobility into the field of decorating the human body. Fashion represents the possibility of moving among images of different identities, a system of expression in which everyone can choose what meaning to express through their own clothing.

"What do you want to 'say' today?" is the mantra of fashion.

Fashion represents what can least be explained; actually, the obligation that it presents of a renewal of signs, its continual production of apparently arbitrary meaning, its thrusting of meaning, the logical mystery of its cycle in reality—these all represent the essence of the social moment.

J. Baudrillard, *For a Critique of the Political Economy of the Sign*, 1973

THE THOUGHT OF FASHION

Peppino Ortoleva

Outside of the narrow milieu of the European court, it was not until the development of urban societies in the eighteenth century that it truly became appropriate to speak of fashion: the same context, and the same historical period, in which we began to see the formation of that mysterious phenomenon, modern public opinion. Through the development of means of communication, the opinions and convictions of citizens—or to be precise, of those citizens who knew how to read and write and who had access to the press—established themselves as a sort of independent power, separate from and in opposition to political power. Society, in part through the development of public opinion, presented itself as a separate entity—separate, but equally important to collective life, with respect to traditional institutions. And fashion was indeed an expression of society in those terms, of the spontaneous form of society's relations, but also of its complex network of conventions, unwritten rules, imitations, and differentiations. The development of public opinion and that of fashion, then, are not simply parallel: they are linked by curious, and significant, similarities. Just as the advent of public opinion replaced a body of unchanging beliefs with a variety of points of view that were diverse and changing over time, in the same way fashion replaced the relative stability of custom and

costume—which codified and prescribed the appearances and forms of presentation of different social groups—with a series of models that varied over time and required one and all to move as quickly as possible in adopting these new models. Just as public opinion eliminated the principle of authority in favor of the circulation of various ideas (but also of the unwritten practice that advises that we adopt as our own the prevailing opinion of the moment), fashion imposed no formal rules or obligations but pushed individuals to adopt as their own the dominant taste.

We might say that the advent of fashion presented itself from the beginning as a "light" version of the same process that was imposing the new power/non-power of public opinion: light, perhaps, but capable of seeming to some degree overdone and grotesque by its frivolity and its absolute inconstancy. If this is true, we can understand at least one of the reasons for the ancient and deep-rooted hostility of European and American intellectuals toward fashion. To them, fashion seemed (and still seems) to hold up a funhouse mirror, in which they could not help but glimpse something of themselves, but in which they also saw precisely the least acceptable aspects of their own condition, and in which, in particular, they saw a reflection of their own worst fears: that the

François Gerard,
Madame Recamier
(details), 1805,
Musée Carnavalet, Paris

Christian Lacroix,
haute couture collection,
fall-winter 1997–98.
Photo by Thierry Orban
(Sygma/Grazia Neri)

New Saints, Wilhelm Moser,
1993, silkscreen on metal
(courtesy of Charles Cowles Gallery,
New York)

Linda Evangelista.
Photo by Brad Branson
enhanced by Fritz Kok
(Courtesy of *The Manipulator*)

emergence of society as a relatively autonomous subject, separate from religious and political institutions, would bring with it not only a greater degree of freedom, but also a relaxation of moral intensity; that in modern civilization (the etymological link between "mode" and modernity is quite evident) there should be no space for solid ideas, certain truths, and authentic behavior, but that it should be a great vanity fair; that the tyranny of absolute power should be replaced by the capricious, but ultimately ironbound power of imitation and conformity.

We must necessarily take into account this attraction-repulsion of intellectuals with respect to fashion if we are to understand the ways in which the social sciences have treated fashion. Or perhaps we should say, the ways in which they have failed to treat fashion. It was not until the end of the nineteenth century (it is no accident that this was at a time of profound crisis for the very idea of public opinion) that a number of European and American intellectuals—few in number, to tell the truth, and generally considered "heterodox thinkers," from Gabriel Tarde, who represented an important but outnumbered school of French sociology, to Georg Simmel and Thorstein Veblen—began "to take fashion seriously," making it an object of study. It is also more than a coincidence that they all made a certain, precise decision, aside from differences in their interpretations: they all took fashion separately from its most typical and distinctive characteristics—superficiality and inconstancy. For the founding fathers of the sociology of fashion, the individual variations that were progressively imposed on clothing—in fact, clothing itself, as such—were purely secondary issues and frivolous; to attempt to explain them per se would be a fool's errand. To them superficiality was not the essence of fashion; on the contrary, it had to be discarded in order to understand the true fundamental substance of fashion. Moreover, it would have been useless to follow the shifting changes of fashion over time, because those changes were considered excessively rapid and substantially meaningless, given the inevitable cyclical returns to a certain sameness. What counted for all these thinkers was to understand the logic of the change, and this underlying logic was substantially always the same. The true essence of fashion, according to their analysis, was the interplay between the differ-

ent and the identical, the equal. In short, the interpretation is as follows. The need for identity, for equality, pushes the lower social classes to follow the example set by the upper classes, creating a so-called trickle-down effect, which leads fashions to spread from the top of society toward the bottom. This process prompted the American author Jane Addams, as she saw the rapidity with which young factory workers decked themselves out in imitations—inexpensive, but almost perfect—of the clothing of the high bourgeoisie, to wonder whether the United States was becoming "democratic only in dress." The same process, however, led the upper classes, in a quest for markers of their own distinction, to reiterate their class status from time to time, originating an unending series of trends and new styles. Fashion, then, was seen as a pure projection of the class system, its dynamic as purely a consequence of the fundamental social contradiction: an interpretation that remained dominant until very recently and that even now finds an articulate and authoritative—though singularly rigid—expression in the sociology of the French writer Pierre Bourdieu. The depiction of fashion as a social pathology (exemplified with extraordinary efficacy in a dialogue written by Giacomo Leopardi, one of the greatest Italian poets of the nineteenth century, in which fashion is described as the sister of death, inasmuch as they are both daughters of caducity) was replaced by an analysis of fashion as part of the physiology of society, and being a physiological function, it was considered predictable and translatable as a simple consequence of well-known rules.

After Tarde, Addams, Veblen, and Simmel, little changed for decades in the sociological interpretation of fashion: we may speak, to use the now classic terminology coined by Thomas Kuhn, of a full-fledged "interpretative paradigm" that has survived nearly the whole century unaltered. If there were any substantial new developments, we find them in the early 1960s in the new field of semiology, where the analysis of fashion was largely a matter of communications rather than a matter of social issues, and there was no real calling into question of the dominant paradigm. It has only been in the last ten to fifteen years that the social sciences have seemed to consider fashion from a partly new viewpoint. This is, among other things, a result of the radical remixing of cultural hierarchies that sprang, first of all, from the revolution in taste of the 1960s (with pop art and the triumph of camp) and, later, from the field of cultural studies: the distinction between intrinsically important cultural matters and other, unimportant cultural matters was abolished as unworthy of study; all cultural matters as such were considered interesting, at least as symptoms of something larger.

Underlying the new view of fashion, however, there is also, probably, a deeper and more solidly rooted trend in aesthetic and literary research and in the social sciences: from texts we can see that the attention of scholars is increasingly shifting to the behavior of the public, indeed of consumers seen as a potentially infinite variety of different subjects. Clothing becomes, in this context, not simply an object of study, just as worthy as other subjects more traditionally recognized, but it also presents aspects of specific interest that are, in certain ways, exemplary. We are in fact examining a complex system of signs in which there certainly are models and rules (but soft rules), but central to that system is the process of adaptation that each individual undertakes of those models. The consumer appears as a participant and, in part, as a creator of the act of communication, not in metaphorical or abstract terms (as is still the case for the reader of books or watcher of movies) but in a way that is empirically verifiable. After being a relatively secondary subject of sociological research for some time, fashion has become established as a proper field of endeavor and study that does not fit into the context of a specific discipline but seems to bring together different social sciences on a common ground.

We are not trying to say that a new paradigm has been established but that we are faced with a series of new signals. It is worth our while to examine closely three of these, in part because they underlie the origin of this book and in part because it may be useful to devote some critical attention to them.

❶ From the sociological viewpoint, typical of the research that established the dominant paradigm, the study of fashion has shifted to the anthropological viewpoint. There is a tendency to see clothing as a total social phenomenon, in which society manifests all of its values and conflicts. There is a tendency to see in fashion more than the narrow symbols of status: rather, a potentially limitless variety of symbolic universes.

One of the most significant consequences of this shift in outlook is the attention now focused on the transcultural aspects of fashion, the role that is played in shaping it and modifying it by the instances of encounter and even conflict between the different cultures that now coexist in the space of the metropolis. Moreover, the emergence of an anthropological analysis has focused attention on the variety of phenomena that can be ranked under the term "fashion," and on the existence in every society of stable differences among groups and subcultures. In effect, subculture is today a key word in the social study of fashions that tends to single out and classify the various "tribes" that circulate in the modern urban setting: perhaps a less radically new analysis than we might think, if we recall the gimmick used by newspapers at the turn of the century to identify the various groups of the "dangerous classes" of Paris—then mightily influential in terms of customs and clothing—by the names of the principal American Indian tribes. The preeminence taken on by the concept of subculture brings with it, we should add, a considerable risk: that the study of fashion should overlook the behavior that affects and interests the great majority of the population and focus only on new and radical values and looks.

❷ While in the classical sociological interpretations the cuts and shapes of the outfits were generally considered to be insignificant, nowadays many are beginning to wonder whether there might not be systems of meaning that can be found in the actual rules of clothing, in the very superficiality and visibility of articles of clothing and accessories. One thing is certain: these are systems of meaning that are unstable, understandable only in dynamic and evolutionary terms, and not according to the classic rules of the interpretation of texts. Or perhaps we should view fashion as an unbroken social "conversation" and individual articles of clothing as fragments of this long dialogue.

❸ If we look carefully, we can see that the newest aspect of the recent interpretations of fashion and clothing is that there is no longer an effort to identify changes with a stable system of laws. Scholars are beginning to pay specific attention to new fashions, indeed to fashions still in formation, and are trying

to understand their inner logic and dynamics. This new approach, which is certainly appealing, raises a considerable problem of method. The classic sociological interpretation considered fashion from without, not only in the sense that it denied that there was any interest to its objects per se but also in the sense that it set itself in a different temporal context, that of the long-term stratification of society. If we no longer believe in a stable social scheme, of which fashion is an expression, then what is the temporal context of the observer?

It is significant that precisely when scholars began to study fashion in the new context that we are describing, they immediately wondered whether fashion as such still exists. When one first examines a scene of change, one tends to wonder whether that change is transitory, like a fashion, or whether that change is epochal.

In keeping with the ideas of postmodernism—according to which the dichotomy of premodern/modern today has a new avenue open to it, in a certain sense synthesizing the two and in another sense eliminating them entirely—numerous authors now sustain that the "classical" opposition between traditional costume and fashion is giving way to a third possibility: clothing as a field of the expression of identities of individuals and groups, where fashion in its classical dynamic has a limited influence.

Basically, even though there are certainly changes in the social customs surrounding clothing, the dynamic of fashion—as it was described by the great sociologists of the late nineteenth century—is still alive and well. However one-sided their answers may have been, we may well wonder whether their basic question (what profound social contradictions create such an intense and distinctive cyclical movement) was not, in the final analysis, correct; and perhaps we should return to that question, with the remarkable baggage of new things that we have learned in the last few years.

Photo by Brad Branson
enhanced by Fritz Kok
(Courtesy of *The Manipulator*)

WHY PEOPLE HATE FASHION

Valerie Steele

Alexander McQueen
for Givenchy,
fall-winter 1997–98.
Photo by Thierry Orban
(Sygma/Grazia Neri)

Opposite:
Stockings by
Jean-Paul Gaultier and
shoes by J.A.D. Paris.
Photo by Claus Wickrath
(Courtesy of *The Manipulator*).

Perhaps "hate" is too strong a word, but fashion is widely despised and denounced. Antifashion sentiment goes back many centuries and continues to flourish today, especially in England and America, where many people are more or less hostile to the very idea of fashion. But even in fashion-friendly countries such as Italy, there exists an underlying ambivalence about fashion, expressed perfectly in Moschino's advertisement that depicts a beautiful but vampirelike woman and the slogan, "Smash the fashion system!"

Fashion is oppressive—especially to women. In popular discourse, fashion has frequently been referred to as a tyrant, just as fashion designers are called dictators. Conversely, those who obey are scorned as fashion slaves or, in today's terminology, fashion victims. Nineteenth-century dress reformers called fashion a "fiend" and "monster" bent upon the "subjugation" and "degradation" of humanity, and especially of women, who were said to be "groaning under the whimsical whip of Fashion." Although today's language is different, similar ideas are still popular.

"A saga of human frailty and vanity was unveiled in the Galleries of the Fashion Institute of Technology when a major exhibition, 'The Undercover Story,' opened yesterday," reported fashion journalist Bernadine Morris. "[This exhibition] vividly depicts how far women have gone in the past to distort their bodies willingly in the name of fashion." Notice how she says that women in the past were fashion victims, with the implication that modern women would never be so foolish. It is common practice in journalism to criticize fashions (like the corset) that conveniently happen to be out of fashion. However, high-heeled shoes are routinely described in the American press as instruments of torture, which create health problems ranging from corns and bunions to misaligned spines. Why then do women persist in wearing such items?

Fashion is an irrational form of female fetishism. The tyrant fashion is sometimes characterized as a female divinity, raising questions about whether women are the victims or the votaries of fashion. "Fashion is the goddess of woman, because she is like woman," declared one Victorian writer: *Varium et mutabile semper femina.* This image of the fickle goddess subtly shifts the emphasis away from the metaphor of power and toward the even more problematic issue of irrationality. Fashion is often linked

with "follics," a word that encompasses both absurdity and stupidity.

"Twin sisters ever are Fashion and Idiocy," declared another Victorian author. Simple clothing may be required for reasons of protection and decency, but extravagant, absurd, or capriciously changing fashions serve no useful function. Changes in fashion often seem mysterious, arbitrary, and senseless—except as part of a conspiracy to force people to buy new clothes.

Fashion is capitalism's favorite child. As Kennedy Fraser once observed in *The New Yorker*, fashion is not only viewed as oppressive and irrational, it is "additionally damned by being at the mercy of commerce at its most corrupt." Certainly, Moschino's ironic injunction to "smash the fashion system" implies the revolutionary destruction of a global corporate conglomerate. The exploitation of garment workers has long been a theme in Communist literature. As Friedrich Engels wrote in *The Condition of the Working Class in England*, "It is a curious fact that the production of precisely those articles which serve the personal adornment of the ladies of the bourgeoisie involves the saddest consequences for the health of the workers." Presumably the suffering of the workers would be more easily justified if they were engaged in socially productive labor rather than in the manufacture of useless trinkets. But the potential victims of the fashion system also include the bourgeoisie, who are coerced into buying new clothes long before the old ones have worn out. Why are they willing to squander their capital on fashion?

Fashion is associated with the sins of lust and pride. History demonstrates that long before the rise of capitalism—throughout the centuries when men dressed at least as modishly and extravagantly as women—fashion was already the object of opprobrium. According to Genesis, the origin of clothing is sin. As Saint Augustine explained, once Adam and Eve had experienced lust (or at least Adam did; Saint Augustine was unsure about Eve), they became ashamed. And although clothing became a necessary evil in light of humanity's fallen state, dress and adornment could all too easily become luxurious and seductive. The prophet Isaiah warned that the

Lord would "take away the finery" of the daughters of Zion to punish them for their pride and wantonness. Tertullian also argued that women should content themselves with "the silk of honesty, the fine linen of righteousness, and the purple of chastity."

Fashion is an incitement to immorality. "Sin led to the invention of dress, and now dress lures the souls of the weak and vain among women into sin," declared Lucy Hopper in her 1874 article "Fig Leaves and French Dresses." The relationship between fashion and prostitution was often cited by nationalists who self-righteously asserted that temptation came from abroad. Americans believed that evil fashions came "from licentious Paris and infidel France! Where woman stoops from her high position of virtue and morality, to mingle with the vicious and impure, to pander to the low passions and base desires of compeers in the arts of hell!" The "daughters of Puritan ancestors" should not imitate the "fashionable courtesan class in the wicked city of Paris." Meanwhile, in France, nineteenth-century treatises on confession emphasized that women's clothes were a constant source of danger. Priests were advised to tolerate women who merely followed the fashion in order to please their husbands, but to warn those who invented new erotic fashions or dressed to seduce that they were guilty of mortal sin. In 1954, Pope Pius XII instructed Catholic bishops to act against indecency in dress, stressing that summer fashions in particular were having "spiritually ruinous effects" on people.

Fashion is a waste of time and money. The Quaker William Penn called "excess in apparel" a "wasteful folly," and told his followers: "If thou art clean and warm, it is sufficient; for more doth but rob the Poor and please the Wanton." The rise of the modern work ethic ("time is money") also led to a denigration of anything as frivolous as fashion. Time and money should be spent on worthier projects than self-adornment, which has often seemed to epitomize the most egregiously "useless" activity imaginable. The greater utility of modern men's clothing (plain, simple, functional) has frequently been cited as an argument against fashion. There might be a

Thierry Mugler, spring-summer
1991 collection.
Photo by J. Donoso
(Sygma/Grazia Neri)

Opposite:
Kellie O'Bosky,
"Harper's Bazaar Cover,
Christy Turlington," acrylic
on magazine, 1995
(Courtesy of Jessica Fredericks Gallery,
New York)

B ZAAR

Is It Safe To Go Back ?

OH MY GOD

@KO95'

few "shallow-brained young 'society men'" who follow every shift of fashion, declared the writer Henry Finck, but most men "laugh at the silly persons who meekly accept" every style concocted by greedy tailors. As more women became educated members of the workforce, they, too, increasingly dismissed fashion's followers as silly and shallow.

Fashion is uncomfortable, unhealthy, and supports pernicious hierarchical distinctions. The negative social consequences of fashion are perceived to be wide-ranging. Most criticism focuses on the inconvenience and discomfort of women's clothes, but there are always a few men who complain about items such as neckties. Health hazards have also been associated with men's fashions. Tight briefs and trousers, for example, allegedly decrease the number and vitality of sperm; and men, as well as women, can fall off platform shoes or inadvertently strangle themselves with long scarves.

The business suit (so beloved by feminists) has often been attacked by male leftists as a sartorial straitjacket that reinforces the class system. "Because fashion ranks people, it is often viewed as suspect," observes journalist Christa Worthington, "especially in America where we can't admit to class." Meanwhile, in Third World countries the business suit sometimes comes under attack as a neocolonialist uniform, but much greater hostility is directed toward female fashions. In the Congo, for example, miniskirts and trousers for women have been outlawed as contrary to local standards of morality.

Fashion promotes the "beauty myth." Even more pernicious than physical pain are the alleged psychological effects of fashion. "For people with imperfect bodies, fashion can cause a lot of stress," adds Worthington. They feel (whether or not with good reason) that they will not be able to measure up, so they hate the fashions that they cannot wear successfully and envy the people who can wear them.

Many people today are convinced that fashion causes anorexia in young women by promoting images of slender models in skimpy clothing. In reality, this is about as logical as claiming that country-and-western music causes adultery and alcoholism. Nevertheless, it is now almost an article of faith among perhaps the majority of American women. As obesity becomes more common in the industrialized world, and particularly in the United States, such complaints about fashion are likely to escalate, since for many women, fashion is related to problems of body image.

Fashion is unnatural and artificial. In the contemporary world, the utilitarian ideology has increasingly dominated discussions of fashion. Yet this ideology is extremely problematic, because, logically, fashion, pleasure, beauty, and art are essentially useless. As Elizabeth Wilson points out in her brilliant book *Adorned in Dreams*, "the thesis is that fashion is oppressive, the antithesis that we find it pleasurable." Underlying the myriad criticisms of fashion there is a widespread sense that the "only justification for clothing is function—utility," which leads in turn to a debate on what is or is not natural. But dress, she argues, "is never primarily functional," and human beings "are not natural."

We live in socially constructed cultures, and it is precisely the artificiality and pointlessness of fashion that makes it valuable as an aesthetic vehicle for fantasy.

Fashion 1995.
Photos by Alfred
Wetzelsdorfer

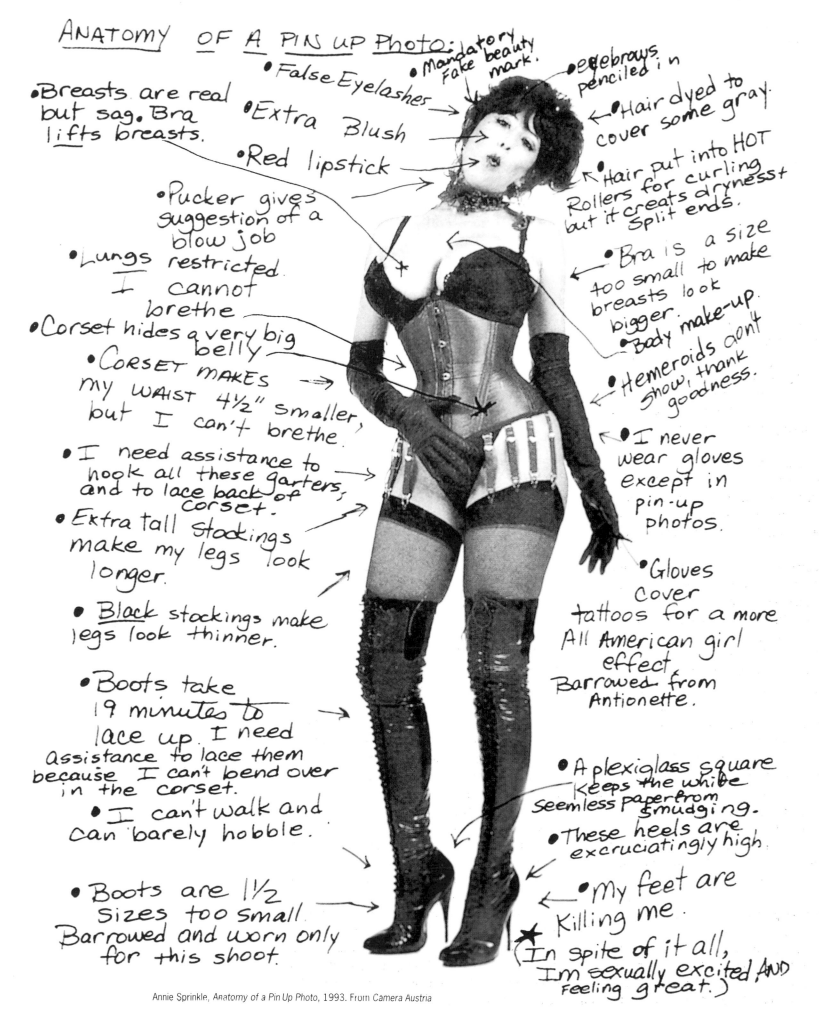

ANATOMY OF A PIN UP Photo:

- Mandatory Fake beauty mark.
- False Eyelashes
- Eyebrows penciled in
- Breasts are real but sag. Bra lifts breasts.
- Extra Blush
- Hair dyed to cover some gray.
- Red lipstick
- Hair put into HOT Rollers for curling but it creats drynesst split ends.
- Pucker gives suggestion of a blow job
- Lungs restricted. I cannot brethe
- Bra is a size too small to make breasts look bigger.
- Body make-up.
- Corset hides a very big belly
- CORSET MAKES MY WAIST 4½" smaller, but I can't brethe.
- Hemeroids don't show, thank goodness.
- I need assistance to hook all these garters, and to lace back of corset.
- I never wear gloves except in pin-up photos.
- Extra tall stockings make my legs look longer.
- Black stockings make legs look thinner.
- Gloves cover tattoos for a more All American girl effect. Barrowed from Antionette.
- Boots take 19 minutes to lace up. I need assistance to lace them because I can't bend over in the corset.
- I can't walk and can barely hobble.
- A plexiglass square keeps the white seemless paper from smudging.
- These heels are excruciatingly high.
- My feet are killing me.
- Boots are 1½ sizes too small. Barrowed and worn only for this shoot.
- (In spite of it all, I'm sexually excited, AND feeling great.)

Annie Sprinkle, *Anatomy of a Pin Up Photo*, 1993. From Camera Austria

BEYOND FASHION

Ted Polhemus

Unlike the leopard, we can change our spots. Indeed, the antiquity and universality of Homo sapiens' inclination for deliberate alteration of appearance makes it a unique, defining characteristic of our species.

How appearance is changed—the particular techniques and styling—is determined by culture rather than genetics. In the distant past (arguably going back to the origins of our species) the possibilities of appearance alteration were strictly limited by rules of tribal or group conformity, giving little scope for individual variation. As we prepare to enter the twenty-first century, however, we in the (so-called) First World do so with an unprecedented range of possibilities for modifying appearance—the postmodern body is extraordinarily promiscuous in its incorporation of the full range of styles and techniques, which were previously available only in one form in one society and another form in another society (or limited to a particular historical period). Only now can we have it all: an Eskimo labret piercing the lower lip, 1960s mascara, a traditional Thai sarong, "old school" trainers from the 1980s, a Maori tattoo, African jewelry, a *Wild Ones*–style motorcycle jacket from the 1950s, Amazonian hair coloring, and a classic Chanel handbag all worn as one "presentation set." It is insufficient to see the motivation for appearance alteration simply as aes-

thetic. (What of "war paint," which is deliberately designed *not* to look attractive? And is not our notion of aesthetics too rooted in our own cultural heritage to be useful in a cross-cultural application?) A view that sees appearance alteration as communication, on the other hand, is less problematic, since we have fieldwork from a wide range of tribal and peasant cultures that identifies the information communicated by body adornment, alteration, and garment signifiers (thus the New Guinea "big man's" tielike bamboo tail indicates wealth, the size and type of a Native American's feather headdress indicates political rank, and the embroidery design of a Slovakian peasant woman's blouse indicates marital status).

While it is typically verbal communication that is seen as *the* human achievement, the power, range, and subtlety of nonverbal, bodily communication remains largely unexplored and uncelebrated. It is clear, however, that possibilities of expression exist within nonverbal, bodily communication that are not achievable with verbal language (and of course, vice versa)—a fact that becomes enormously important in an age such as ours, which has debased and sucked meaning from the spoken and written word. (Hence late-twentieth-century art's rediscovery of the body as a medium of expression and the ever increasing demands on the appearance industries—

This and following pages:
Pictures of a publication
party for Ted Polhemus,
London, 1997.
Photos by Steve Lazarides

fashion, makeup, hairstyling, etc.—to create products that make a "statement.")

Appearance has always been communicative but what has been "said" has varied enormously. There have been three distinct systems of body appearance modification, and each has been focused on a different—often contradictory—set of meanings.

Within tribal and peasant societies a highly conformist and (perceived) timeless traditional style served to signal group identity and the immutable stability of the cultural system. The principal problem faced by such societies was, and still is, how to identify vividly the boundaries of tribal membership and promote social stability. Traditional styles of appearance modification—fundamentally social and conformist in nature and seen as timeless and beyond human volition—effectively resolved this problem (at the same time, establishing the most important of all human metaphors: that analogy of the individual's subjective body and the shared "social body" of the community). As an ever present reminder of social control ("Everyone in our society paints their bodies with blue stripes") and cultural immutability ("We have always painted our bodies with blue stripes because that is what our ancestors did"), traditional style played a key part in realizing tribal and peasant societies as more than the sum of their parts and their cultural systems as intergenerational, stable constructs—thereby greatly assisting the unique development of our species.

Stretching across the vast majority of human history, such traditional styles were only supplanted by the fashion system, which from the Renaissance to very recent times reflected and celebrated the prochange, antitraditional presumptions of modernism. To define a lineal and progressive timeline, fashion strove to produce an endless succession of "the new" that, ipso facto, would be seen as improved and desirable—in the process vividly defining a single, agreed direction of history in the broadest sense. (The differences of each era underlined, symbolized, and in a very real sense, were created by their distinctive fashion looks.) Like the timeless stability of traditional cultures, the perpetual progress of modernism is a fiction—one that, like its predecessor, served to alter the perception of time as well as the body. At least as conformist as traditional style ("Next season skirts will be worn two inches below

the knee"), fashion was differentiated from its precursor by its diametrically opposed signification of change—defining it as desirable progress rather than, as in traditional societies, pernicious threat to sociocultural stability. Once started up, the engine of modernism (and its primary signifier, fashion) seemed unstoppable—a production line of "the new" (improved), which season upon season provided irrefutable proof of progress (while filling a graveyard with instantly passé and suddenly worthless old-fashioned corpses). Within this system only one message mattered: the perpetual triumph of progress. While traditional style distinguished between those inside and those outside the tribe, fashion's dividing line was between those stepping into the future (the avant-garde) and those stuck in the past (the old-fashioned).

Perceived from within, the world of perpetual novelty that fashion created seemed as real and everlasting as the world of timeless stasis created by traditional style had. By the 1980s, however, the seemingly endless roller-coaster ride of fashion (and therefore of modernity) was showing signs of going off the rails. Questioning both the reality and the desirability of progress, for the first time since the Renaissance, fashionable change for its own sake became suspect. Suddenly, someone who reflexively followed the latest look was branded a fashion victim, and the word "trendy" became a put-down rather than a compliment. Suddenly, those who could well afford the new proudly boasted "I've had this for ages" in an attempt to signal a personal, antifashion,

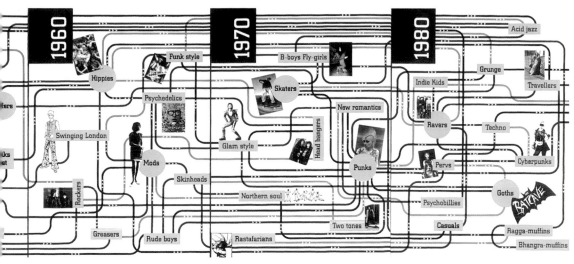

Supermarket of Style, 1994,
map of street styles;
concept by Ted Polhemus,
design by Italo Lupi

classic stability—to be a dedicated follower of fashion was to undermine one's authenticity. Suddenly, unable to sustain a single consensual direction, fashion (like the wider world around it, which all systems of appearance alteration inevitably, dramatically, and concisely reflect) fragmented into a plethora of designer "signature styles," which, despite an increasingly frantic hyping of fashion change tended to remain much the same from one year to the next (the difference between Armani 1986 and Armani 1987 being less significant than the difference between Armani and Versace in any given year). Suddenly, appearance modification was focused on personal identity rather than on the "next big thing," and as the zeitgeist switched from modernism to postmodernism, fashion as a system of perpetual novelty went out of fashion. Style, however, did not go out of style. Indeed, it was reborn. And for a time it seemed that everything had simply come full circle: timeless, tribal style (à la youth subcultures like the punks, goths, or the modern primitives, or à la designer tribes like those lead by Gaultier, Westwood, or Armani) would be resituated within the context of the global village. It is now clear, however, that postmodern alterations of appearance constitute a distinctive third system rather than simply a return to the first.

Postmodern style differs from tribal style in at least three key respects. First, rather than being timeless it is synchronic—offering up any time (or a collage of various times) within an ever expanding instant of past-present-future. Thus, we can listen to 1990s techno while wearing 1960s mod clothes and sitting on 1850s Shaker furniture. Second, instead of being strictly contained within a particular cultural place (Masai, Maori, punk), postmodern style is geochronic—leaping across all cultural-geographic divides. Thus, we can eat sushi and watch a Brazilian soap opera on cable while wearing a Peruvian peasant costume, African jewelry, and Indian sandals. And third, while tribal style is emphatically conformist in nature, postmodern style is just as emphatically an expression of idiosyncratic, personal difference. Thus, while the message of tribal style is "We are," the message of postmodern style is "I am . . . "

Post-tribal and postfashion, postmodern style demands that we each fill in this blank in our own way. Sampling and mixing from the synchronic, geochronic supermarket of style, the postmodern stylist (which now includes everyone except the dwindling ranks of the fashion victims and neotribalists) assembles an ego-specific statement. Unlike the fashion victim who wears the work of one designer from head to toe, the postmodern stylist might bring together a classic Armani jacket, an Indian shirt (bought on holiday in Goa), a pair of Levi's 501s, a Vivienne Westwood–designed Swatch, Dr. Martens boots, Dior lipstick, a mod haircut, Diesel wrapfront alien sunglasses, and an Ed Hardy tattoo.

Perpetually surfing and zapping through all lifestyle universes, the postmodern stylist may effect a completely different appearance the next day. And the next. And so on. The message, however, will remain the same: "I am a complex, unique inhabitant of the postmodern world who cannot be stereotyped, categorized, or target marketed."

Each appearance style says: "I am *this*." We cannot satisfactorily translate "this" into words. Verbal language was never well suited to statements of personal identity (consider the futility of a written summation of self in a lonely-hearts ad) and this is why appearance communication is so crucially important. Especially now that verbal language has been debased by advertising and stockpiled in ever growing mountains of surplus data. Especially now that we and the world around us are so complex, contrary, fragmented, and beyond labeling. Especially now that nothing is black or white. Postmodern style allows us to say: "I am a bit of a feminist but not that kind of feminist," "I'm a subtle blend of sensitive new

man and old-fashioned Latin lover," "I'm both a party animal and an intelligent lifeform," "I'm rich but also streetwise," "I'm a new gender," and so on.

In a recent issue of *The Face* magazine, an article about inventions for the future proposed an "intelligent badge" into which information about ourselves could be fed and which would beep and flash when we near someone else's badge that is programmed with similar lifestyle and ideological information. Of course such an invention is completely unnecessary, as we have already devised and every day make use of precisely such a system. It is called style, and it is perfectly capable of flashing and beeping similarities and differences of personal identity, lifestyle expectations, and ideological information.

Style is our identity badge. And it is completely, instantly reprogrammable. All we have to do is surf the style universe for a different presentation set. No longer constrained by either tribal or fashion conformity, able to pluck our wardrobe of style adjectives from everywhere and every time, we have succeeded in proving yet again the problem-solving potential of that extraordinary signification system that is appearance. In the traditional world what was needed was a visualization of tribal identity and cultural continuity. In the modern world it was a matter of providing a ticking timepiece of change and progress. In the postmodern world what we need and what we have is an infinitely generative signification system that is powerful and subtle enough to transmit between those distant, self-contained parallel universes that we all now inhabit.

Implications for the Appearance-Alteration Industries

❶ Within the appearance-alteration industries I include clothing, hat, footwear, jewelry, eyewear, and sportswear designers; hairstylists and makeup artists; exercise and body-building specialists; body piercers and tattooists, among others. Altering appearance is not and never has been simply a matter of covering the body with garments. While different industries draw on different techniques and expertise, all (or many) are integrated into a total look. As in the production of, for example, an automobile, the appearance-alteration industries should be working together rather than separately. The product is a look, and fabric, leather, feathers, chemicals, and so forth are only a means to this end.

❷ People today buy clothes, cosmetics, etc., on the basis of what these products "say." Semiotics rather than aesthetics is the raison d'être of today's fashion industry. The more packed with reference, allusion, and symbolism, the more valuable and desirable the product. Such signification can be achieved either by the use of color, cut, design motif, fabric, etc., or by value added by marketing and advertising. The consumer wants and needs to buy a new vocabulary rather than a new dress, necklace, lipstick, or haircut.

❸ What is being said by appearance grows ever more complex. If in the past a look was intended to say "I'm rich," "I'm respectable," "I'm sexy," a look today is intended not only to say "I'm interesting" but to specify in precisely what way that person is interesting. The juxtaposition of opposing—even completely contradictory—styles and meanings is one way of accomplishing this. Irony is another. The more multifaceted, layered, and downright confusing a look, the more likely it is to be perceived as authentic.

❹ In order to make a unique, idiosyncratic appearance statement, a person must assemble the component parts (the adjectives) that will work together to express just how that person is "interesting." As with music, appearance today is "in the mix."

❺ The day when the designer or stylist could (and was expected to) dictate a "total look" is long gone. This is not, however, to suggest that designers are less important than before—just that their role has changed. Designers are now semiological component manufacturers for a self-assembly product (the "style statement").

❻ Seasonal fashion change for its own sake is no longer valued by the majority of consumers. (Indeed, it risks signifying a lack of personal integrity.) This is especially true when fashion journalists strive to cram many looks from different designers into a singular direction (mistakenly thinking that is how they should do their job). Brown is not the new black—every color is. The consumer wants to have information about the full and glorious range of what is

This and preceding pages:
Pictures of a publications
party for Ted Polhemus,
London, 1997.
Photos by Steve Lazarides

available. The "next big thing" is that there will not be a "next big thing."

❼ The importance of the designer as visionary grows ever greater. Realized in the form of fantasy garments, which could never be worn in real life, or in extraordinary photography for advertisements, these visions of how life might be are what the consumer wants to buy into. (The signified—the dream, the vision of how life might be—rather than the signifier—the shirt, pair of shoes, eyeshadow, etc.—is the product.) Compressed into a logo, these visionary signifiers can be sold in the form of accessories, T-shirts, perfumes, and wearable garments. That people are buying a logo rather than, say, a dress is not at all to devalue the process, it is simply to underline the extent to which appearance is a communication business. A logo that radiates the right lifestyle messages is a valuable product in and of itself—that is, valuable for the consumer who wishes to incorporate it into their presentation of self. (Thus, insofar as one can put these things into words, the Benetton logo gives its wearers the possibility of communicating that they are socially responsible, nonracist practitioners of safe sex, while the Diesel logo gives its wearers the possibility of communicating that they are wacky, fun-loving, off-the-wall, ironic, surreal, psychedelic, knowing sort of people.)

❽ Nothing sells like signification. But at the same time no properly postmodern person would want to be seen wearing just one signification. It is much more interesting to juxtapose oppositional meanings within one presentation set. (For example, a Benetton sweater worn with Diesel trousers, suggesting a personal identity that balances social responsibility with an off-the-wall sense of fun—e.g., a person who uses condoms and ecstasy.) Designers who refuse to allow their work to be shown (for example, in editorial magazine photography) with work from other sources give the impression that their work is not amenable to do-it-yourself sampling and mixing—thereby devaluing it in the eyes of today's postmodern consumers. (For the same reason, the importance of the catwalk show where the work of only one designer is on display needs to be questioned. Just as furniture manufacturers now use catalogs to show their products in use in a "real" situation, so those in the appearance industries must display their products in use in the "real" world.)

❾ It used to be that being able to afford someone to style your appearance (or to decorate your home) was a mark of status. Now to do so just signals a lack of authenticity. To be real is to do it yourself. Those involved in the business of fashion must now take this onboard. The appearance industries are more important than ever before, but to be successful the professionals need to let their creations became a starting point for something else and not a fait accompli. The consumer wants to be treated like a creative partner rather than like a mannequin.

❿ Whether we call it fashion or style (or whatever) is not as important as recognizing that what people want from their clothes and accessories has radically changed. Fashion is not what it used to be because the world we live in is not what it used to be, and appearance alteration has an almost magical ability to express and shape itself to the zeitgeist of an era. In the 1950s or 1960s (as in the Renaissance), people wanted clothes to say "I'm avant-garde." Now that modernism has given way to postmodernism a key change is our attitude toward change—namely, like our tribal ancestors we fear change at least as much as we welcome it. Instead, our postmodern age is focused on exploring all the possible parallel universes that can and do exist within the here and now. Such pluralism and heterogeneity, however, make it ever more important to find a way to cut through the buildup of alternative white noise to proclaim "I am here." This is what people today need their clothes to do: to signal where they are in an ever more confusing world. Luckily, appearance is a rich, multifaceted, subtle, powerful, and instantaneous communication system that is fully capable of saying anything we want it to.

What do you want to say today?

Here's looking at you.

BARBÈS: VISIBILITY AND CONTAMINATION IN THE LABORATORY OF FASHION

Franco La Cecla

Your attention is attracted by the heels of a woman. You follow the rhythm of her shoes. Her feet move elegantly, firmly held by the brightly colored strip of cloth that encloses her toes. You turn the corner and take a closer look—sure enough, her heels poke out of her shoes. Then you look around and realize she is not alone. Other women are doing similar curious balancing acts on their heels, which poke out into the air, free of the tyranny of the sole. And those heels appear at the bottom of long colorful outfits, glittering with batik patterns. It must be a coincidence of some kind. Then you see two tall women wearing purple turbans. Each is carrying a child slung in a length of purple cloth clutching their mother's shoulder. The children's heels also emerge from the hem of the "wax," the long colored cloth that envelops them.

It is Sunday in Barbès and there is a festival in the air, the Fête de la Goutte d'Or, the fête of this much discussed quarter of Paris, home to the latest waves of African immigrants from Senegal, the Ivory Coast, and Mali. Here, the taxi driver who takes you home from the station is a one-time Peul shepherd, and the travel agencies offer the cheapest possible flights to Bamako or Dakar. The Goutte d'Or festival is today because it seems appropriate to devote one day in July to this strange mixture of Africas that

somehow manage to hold together. Alongside cultures from the heart of Africa, there is the desert dreaming of the songs of Um Khalsoum and the aroma of mint tea brewing. Berber bridal shops offer gowns and special confectionery; in the same street, Algerian women model bolts of red cloth and white shoes studded with sequins. Not far off, there is a boutique specializing in belly-dancing outfits and a Caribbean *comptoir* where grandes dames from the Antilles cast fortunes and sell protective herbs.

And here we rediscover those heels that we had lost sight of. Two vast black women each reveal a bare shoulder between the folds of cloth slipping down onto their arms, and the inevitable exposed heels. Why? I make an effort to understand the interplay of attraction, and I venture a hypothesis, well aware that the rules of attraction are fundamentally contextual and are linked to things that may have origins and triggering factors that are impossible for me to grasp. The hypothesis that I come up with is this: these exposed heels, so clearly objects of pride and flirtation, are part of an interplay between the dark skin of the ankle and the lighter skin of the sole of the foot, a special marker of nakedness. There seems to be a certain thrill, a shiver of delight in tracing that line of separation, not unlike the thrill that, in other cultures, can be sensed along the line

Etching for
Jean Paul Gaultier,
by François Berthoud

80

between the tan and white flesh. These are mature women, women who here. in Barbès, in the Goutte d'Or, have regained a complete mastery of a fashion that originated elsewhere. amid the lights of Bamako or Ouagadougou. but that here finds a proud new venue in which to appear, to show off. Those heels are the clue that informs us that Barbès and the Goutte d'Or are the site of a remarkable laboratory of fashion.

"Paris entre deux amours," Paris as a destination, as well as a point of departure: that is how Josephine Baker sang of Paris, and though things may change, it is still the city where things with distant roots find a new setting. What is happening in neighborhoods like Barbès is a completely new phenomenon. After decades of uneasy and incomplete coexistence—while the city government of Paris clearly wished chiefly to conceal the principal immigrant quarters, pushing them as much as possible toward the farthest outskirts of the city, the *banlieue*—there is a sudden and vast rebirth of "visibility." The African presence has a powerful, confident new look; the quarter has become a showcase for new styles. If you happen to stroll along rue Mihra, rue de Poissonniers, or the thoroughfare of boulevard Barbès, you will immediately sense that people are beginning to dress for show. It is as if they had finally shaken off the timidity of newcomers; now it seems that the very difference of their origins is what is being shown off. Even the hairdressers, the shops selling beauty creams. and the restaurants and bistros—only a few years ago relegated to a minority. immigrant clientele   are now Afro-Parisian, and the exteriors stand out with an exceedingly self-assured style. The hairdressers, especially, are operating in an ambiguous or gray area. Visible from the street, the heads of Nigerian or Senegalese women are hard to tell from the piles of braids, curls, and wigs that are imported from Africa or the Antilles. Inside—though it may not be easy to get in—all sorts of things take place: parties, fashion shows of hairdos and lingerie, and there always seems to be a little crowd of men and women, until the wee hours, as if it were a place of entertainment. People go to the hairdresser twice or three times a week, to change their *couleur*, the feel of their hair. to get towers, cascades, and lace doilies of hair. Truckloads of wigs arrive, and the teenage girls—teetering on

stacks and high-heeled gym shoes—play at being silky and blonde.

Just a few years ago, straightening hair or lightening skin was a way of "asking permission" of the host culture, which had a fairly rigid set of aesthetic criteria. Nowadays, doing the same things has an aggressive and even daring meaning. a self-aware form of coquetry. which makes use of the great fraud that underlies differences. Perhaps this is the same game that is being played with the exposed heels, that thrilling borderland where the display of the edge of difference itself becomes an element of seduction, as if to say: can you see how skillful we are at dressing as whites, and how at the same time we explode the illusion that we are white? It is not unlike the game of androgyny. which sometimes proves to be a more powerful weapon than femininity. Fashion here plays with the ambiguous nature of distinctions.

Though they may not be easy to enter. these temples of hairdressing are central points of reference for a funnel cloud of dressmaking and tailoring, retouch artists, fabric shops, shoe stores, and even full-fledged fashion designers. This year there were numerous competitions among the new Afro-Parisian fashion designers, and they no longer seem to be shackled into a single quarter or a narrow circle of ethnic clientele. They are now a regular feature on the city landscape. There are African weeks, organized by Radio Nova and the art magazine *Revue Noire*, and a Rive Gauche crowd flocked to the runway presentations of new Afro-Parisian creations. with the setting for the shows designed by African industrial designers. The chief difference from the past lies in the fact that this is no longer an "ethnic wave" phenomenon. These are no longer exotic oddities, nor is this a quest for "ethnic authenticity." Rather, this is a thriving workshop of cultural mélanges and contaminations. What is happening now in the area of clothing and looks has already taken place in the field of music. There was a progression from an initial attitude that was keen to preserve differences—akin to the zeal of purists or collectors—to the confident practice of contamination and boundary hopping. emerging from ethnic fashion to an array of new styles.

Barbès is, however, the point of arrival for a process that began in the 1950s, when things first

Fashion in the street.
Barbès, Paris, 1997.
Photos by Piero Zanini

Overleaf:
Moroccan bride in wedding
dress.
Photo by Pino Guidolotti

began to stir in the major cities of Africa. Exhibitions by various portrait photographers working in Bamako in the 1950s show a construction of identity in display windows that, even then, mixed original styles with Western styles. And in fact, this is the crux of the matter. We are too accustomed to believing that contamination is a one-way street, and we are astonished when places like Barbès overturn this view of things. We think that the West and its invasive, overbearing fashions have eliminated all resistance among local styles, tastes, and forms of behavior. And yet we cannot understand how the young London Pakistanis described by Hanif Kureshi manage to appropriate and modify fashions for their own use, or how, here in the Goutte d'Or, the street is a laboratory in which to experiment with new mixtures.

There is a logic between the center and the outskirts, or between the colonizers and the colonized, that is never quite linear. Marshall Sahlins and other anthropologists who have worked on the concept of contamination are quite clear in this regard. It is not obvious that, say, an Indo who wears gym shoes, each one a different color, or an Aborigine who wears an alarm clock around the neck are "victims" of poor Western taste, their culture devastated by the intrusion of the West. Quite often, there is something far more complex going on. These are ways of taking possession of the alien in order to overturn it, in order to "personalize" its efforts to contaminate. And for that matter, clothing, hairstyles, and ornaments exist for precisely this reason, in order to facilitate the interplay of masks and disguises.

We are accustomed to thinking of fashion as something created by famous designers and glossy magazines. The work being done by Ted Polhemus and others shows us that fashion takes as much from the streets as it gives. From this standpoint, the logic of visibility that is being developed at Barbès turns it into a remarkable workshop and laboratory of visibility and contamination. Here, we are in the presence of a true avant garde situation—a composite population, with distinct roots of origin, is living in a quarter of a European city with strong "traditional" features. This is close to Montmartre, where there is a solid tradition of open-air markets and supermarkets selling cheap clothing, like Tati and Kata. The quarter has developed the typical potpourri effect of multiethnic neighborhoods, with a further mixing effect in the case of clothing shops, food stores, and restaurants. There are Vietnamese running Antillean grocery stores, Pakistanis operating African video shops, Tunisian Jews who sell Arab pastries. This is certainly the most advanced level of coexistence and tolerance. And over the past few years, increasing prosperity has allowed a growing expenditure on appearances, on "looks." This flow of prosperity has created greater prosperity. There is a substantial flow of money spent on imported fabrics, "ethnic" goods, products used by hairdressers, and special brands of shoes that let the heel hang out.

Let us come back to the question of heels. In order to comprehend how little we understand the effects that people have on fashion—aside from the effects that fashion has on people—we can find an excellent example in the case of the heel. A recent film had the title *Clothing, and the Effect It Has on Those Who Wear It and Those Who See It*. Whenever we talk about fashion, we should take into account two subjects that are relevant to every change in style. First, the street is a showcase, where the relational nature of showing off develops. In a logic of visibility, the most creative sites are likely to be those where one can glance quickly at a series of new appearances. If you see me today and then again tomorrow with the same hairdo, how can I amaze, provoke, and interest you? A street style requires the desire to be commented on by one's neighbors but still maintain the anonymity required to keep from becoming familiar to them. In this, there is an everyday construction of meaning, the limits of which lie in the capacity of subjects to accept the exaggerations and paradoxes of display without losing the delicate taste for scandal. Street fashions should cause you to turn and stare, start in amazement, laugh or whistle in approval or rejection. Second, the rules of indoor fashion shows have caused us to forget that the street constitutes the primary condition of use. And this is one reason why the new borderlands of identity, the multiethnic quarters, are now remarkably interesting laboratories of fashion. There is, in the everyday condition of a multiethnic quarter, sufficient distance and sufficient proximity that one needs, on the one hand, to define one's identity and, on the other, to undercut it. Contamination is a rhetorical figure of the proximity and linkage between contrasts. Fashion loves to be

Christian Dior,
haute couture collection,
spring-summer 1997.
Photo by Ben Coster
(Camera Press/Grazia Neri)

86

infected by things that until the day before were worlds apart, and the next day become successful provocations.

Multiethnic quarters like Barbès have, out of sheer necessity, gone beyond the condition of pure and simple "ethnicity." For this reason, what happens there is never "politically correct." For they constitute a condition in which identities are on the boundary, set out on a balcony of comparison, in the zone of transition where place and culture of origin can only be invoked as stereotypes, not as a means of support or comfort. And this is why the quarters in which there is cultural and stylistic contamination are the borderlands, where many people find themselves passing among two or more identities. This makes these particularly rich and controversial areas less ideological and rigid than the rest of the city.

Fashion—fashion as the daily negotiation of the paradox of identities and differences—helps identities in transition in the sense that fashion represents an area of play, just as a key has a margin of "play" so that it can easily fit a keyhole. Fashion makes the borderland of identities livable, exercising those identities in the masquerades of the stage play of visibility.

Moreover, it shows that there are different areas of seduction that can be represented but not understood (at least, not all at once). The heels, the necklines, the hair pulled back, the pointed shoes, a certain way of walking—all these things represent horizons of male or female provocation, whose point of view is hidden in more exclusive settings or in other geographies or combinations of geographies.

The Fête de la Goutte d'Or continues, punctuated by local rappers, graffiti, African and Maghrebian fast food, and all of the problems, of course, that are intrinsic to being foreign but no longer just foreigners. It is a foreignness that must carve out a difficult equilibrium, a cultural space—as well as a physical abode—in which those who are beginning to be integrated (and who, therefore, begin to become strangers to themselves) can find a moment to observe themselves in the reflection of the curiosity of others. And to this purpose, fashion—human, concrete, of the street—can offer its services.

THE PUERTO RICAN DAY PARADE

Richard Martin

Miss Puerto Rico 1997,
Puerto Rican Day Parade,
New York, 1997.
Photo by Luis Martinez

Opposite:
Man wearing boa
constrictor, acrylic on film,
by François Berthoud

New York City, June 8, 1997

If you believe Paul Poiret or most designers who have followed him, along with Elsa Klensch and many fashion writers, the fashion show is supposed to be the medium's most spectacular procession. But even the most extraordinary runway show cannot match the real thing, the forty-block-long runway of the Puerto Rican Day Parade along Fifth Avenue. It is always New York's largest and finest runway show.

The gala and gay-friendly Greenwich Village Halloween Parade with its drag queens and lampoons, the family-imbued Macy's Thanksgiving Day Parade, and the St. Patrick's Day Parade following a green line along Fifth Avenue all pale beside the Puerto Rican Day Parade. After all, the Irish entered with the Kennedys and others into the American elite; even gays and old Greenwich Village liberals have come to see considerable tolerance and welcome in New York. The struggle is over when everyone tries to wear green on St. Patrick's Day and butch guys from the suburbs think the Village Halloween is convivial. Even Disney has been treating Manhattan like a big theme park with the spectacular opening of *Pocahontas* in Central Park and this year's *Hercules* light parade.

The Sunday of the Puerto Rican Day Parade is different—more vibrant, more alert. It is not about

consensus and assimilation, the great traditional American dreams. It never gives up its salsa sense of defensiveness and difference. Spanish-speaking Puerto Rico, American but not one of the fifty states, is defiant: there are no pretty shamrocks or subtle ironies in this parade. It is still about politics, and most important, it is about people. More than any other parade, it can seem insolent and unruly to many New Yorkers. In fact, the week before the parade, the president of the Madison Avenue Business Improvement District urged stores to remove expensive merchandise or to close for the parade. The day after this pronouncement, amid vehement protest, he resigned, but the spirit of his request is standard among the stores near the Fifth Avenue parade route, from midtown shops to the Metropolitan Museum of Art. "Establishment" New York often disdains the Puerto Rican community. Ironically, doormen at luxurious Fifth Avenue apartments, very few of whom are Hispanic, ferociously protect their entrances and sidewalk gardens from the parade watchers who camp out along the avenue for the day. In the aftermath of the parade, haughty gossip columnist Taki complained in *The Spectator* (London, June 14, 1997) that his weekend in New York was "ruined [as] two million Puerto Ricans invaded Fifth Avenue for their annual Puerto Rican

pride parade. Never have I seen a more motley collection. They were fat, squat, ugly, dusky, dirty and unbelievably loud." Obviously, I saw a different parade, which I perceived as a more clamorous, glamorous, kaleidoscopic democracy.

The Puerto Rican Day Parade is colorful and confident. But the spectacle is not only in the street, it is also among the spectators, and the effect is not specific costumes, but the splendors of street style and often of self-invented clothing. For the most part, parades have become commercial cavalcades, but the Puerto Rican Day Parade is the real thing, something genuine and naturally ebullient in a world of simulated, stimulated emotions: real spectacle.

The red, white, and blue of the Puerto Rican flag are everywhere. In America, where Ralph Lauren and Tommy Hilfiger have already done seemingly everything one can to bring flags and red, white, and blue into clothing, the Puerto Rican flags that are waved and worn add to the sea of colors. And on this day, clothing is dramatically altered. Puerto Rican flags are sewn onto $4 T-shirts, with the result that they look like $18 Tommy Hilfiger shirts. (For the most part, middle-class Americans do not modify or transform their clothing, preferring to settle for the facile authority of Ralph Lauren or Calvin Klein.) A number of women wore slashed jeans or tops, not carved by the designers but homemade. Not since the popularity of the movie *Flashdance* has the mainstream seen so much slashing of clothing. In some way Shakespearean, these resplendent cavaliers and ladies of slashed doublets and hose are self-fabricated, self-created figures, intuitively striving for something out of the historical pageant.

T-shirts and cropped sweatshirts—again, the efforts and ideas of home industry, not of the designer or anonymous manufacturer—are often worn inside-out, deliberately subversive to the mandated, popular fashion. Among men, in particular, sleeves are torn off, generally not in the styling of the designer but in the inventions of home sewing (or home ripping). The baring of biceps, in many instances featuring tattoos, warrants the gesture of shredding at least the sleeve of a store-bought shirt. The results are shirts that take on the shredded aspect of movie superheroes, the Schwarzenegger or Van Damme type of bodybuilder who survives minefields and senseless brutality with only a shredded sleeve, the better to manifest bulging biceps. Scenic and vulnerable, narcissistic and contrived, the gesture gives an unaffected macho impression that is even more powerful than a John Bartlett runway show.

On floats and in bands, little girls strut with the glitter of preteen cheerleaders and fairytale princesses. These girls might have been those of any American group that exalts little girls paraded as beauty queens. Bare midriffs, obviously a particular pride of Puerto Ricans among both men and women, flatter youngsters but are almost as popular among older celebrants—even, surprisingly, those with ballooning bellies. Cultures of the beach and of poverty do not admire only the gym-toned and svelte.

But the real distinction of the Puerto Rican Day Parade is the men. In the June heat, New York suddenly becomes Latin, tropical, and macho for a day. Menswear and male vanity strut Fifth Avenue as on no other day of the year. The informal Easter parade's finery is restricted to women; even the Gay Pride Parade is sporadic, with its contingents from the Chelsea Gym and a few other narcissists, along with groups dressed in campy disarray or displaying significant AIDS messages.

At the Puerto Rican Day Parade, whole families have turned out in their casual best, even if they are bringing barbecues and planning to picnic along the Central Park side of the parade

Puerto Rican neighborhood
baseball teams, the Bronx,
New York.

Photos by Luis Martinez

route. Clothing is practical, and though generally based in washable whites, there is also a display of colorful abandon seldom seen by the chic legions of New Yorkers who dress in black. Among these families, men announce themselves not with suburban decorum but with malta-drinking dandyism—as men of natural authority reinforced with a cocky style. Teenage boys and men in their early twenties among the spectators constitute a testosterone parade of their own, flaunting new muscles and old-fashioned manliness. And to judge from this year's parade, in the Puerto Rican community tattoos are still the sole province of men and, fairly standard in format, are generally confined to the arm. The grand decorative designs of Indian and other Asian tattoos for young men and women were absent in this crowd, as was any notable instance of body piercing. Perhaps the solid, unquestioning body vanity, which is so evident in these men, does not need superficial decoration or minor articulation, so confident are they in their machismo and dandyism. According to Carlyle, "A dandy is a Clothes-wearing Man, a Man whose trade, office, and existence consists in the wearing of Clothes." The dandies of the Puerto Rican Day Parade are not self-conscious Beau Brummells, yet their clothing is equally well chosen to the effect of articulating the male body, not in cravats and breeches but in tank tops, immaculate tight white jeans, or nonchalantly oversized blue jeans. The one accessory frequently seen at the parade that might be envied by a Regency dandy was the snake, worn by some dozens of men at

this year's parade. Oozing casually over a bare torso, or providing color to a white T shirt, the live snake is a version of fashion's less animated boas and stoles, making an exotic combination of the virile image of a conqueror and the coquetry of fashion accessories. Prim Fifth Avenue ladies are not accustomed to the circus-like atmosphere of men wearing snakes, but the effect is mesmerizing to children and others who dream of Tarzan and semi-naked machismo. A few iguanas on shoulders seemed wimpy, minor amusements, lesser masculinity in a fashion system that prizes torsos with serpents.

Animals played the role at the Puerto Rican Day Parade that whippets and greyhounds once played in society portraits of the jockey-club variety. If not the torso-clinging snakes of the boldest dandies, many men were accompanied by their dogs, beautiful and/or ferocious. Pit bulls and other warrior dogs on a leash testified to the manliness and toughness of several of the strutters, while some of the more domestic men, accompanied by wives and children, settled down with dogs of gentler breeds. For many spectators, the trip to Manhattan is an exceptional one and part of a long day, so the family dog has to come along rather than be left home alone.

In addition to the colorful spectacle, there is the political reason for the Puerto Rican Day Parade. Some demand statehood; others promote employment and opportunity; yet others call for recognition of Spanish as a first language. But freedom's most poignant and effective sign is the liberated expression of clothing.

In April and November for womenswear, and January and July for menswear, the fashion shows appear on New York runways. But the longest, brightest, boldest runway of the year is always Fifth Avenue's Puerto Rican Day Parade, when New York is jolted from its usual discreet sophistication and urban, swanky, elegant modishness into a place where fashion really happens, literally on the street, and people invent their own clothes and dream the dream of freedom, which is where fashion begins.

THE CIRCULARITY OF PRODUCTION AND CONSUMPTION, OR THE REFLEXIVITY OF FASHION

Laura Bovone

In any process of communication, we consider both the significance that we assign to things and our definitions of the situation in a process of coordination and negotiation that never leaves things as they were originally but modifies to some degree the position of everything and everybody, i.e., all the meanings in question. That is what we mean when we use the term *reflexivity*.

Writing about fashion in this context means considering fashion, in all of its moments and aspects, as a phenomenon of communication. By that I am not emphasizing unilaterally the immaterial aspects of fashion, nor am I considering fashion as the locus of abstract cultural development; rather I am referring to a display of the cultural contents of a production that has its reason for existing in its evident material nature. We may consider fashion as a typical setting in which to study the intertwining of culture and economics that is so typical of our era—the way in which culture becomes a material of economics, how economics affects culture, and how culture becomes of economic interest. Publishing, telecommunications, tourism, entertainment, and advertising are, like fashion, cultural industries.

The fashion system is a cultural industry in which a variety of highly differentiated subjects are at work, with variable commitments of time and differing levels of remuneration. These converge around the material object of fashion and, entering into communication—i.e., coordinating—they establish for it a value on each specific occasion, a value that is at once economic and cultural.

It is practically impossible to name all of these categories in a thoroughgoing manner, but it is reasonably easy to distinguish among three major aggregate areas: production, consumption, and communications. The first area is where the fashion idea finds concrete form: whether that is a knitting mill or a leather-crafts workshop, a traditional dressmaking shop or a famous atelier. In certain cases the fashion idea is developed within the manufacturing structure; in others it occurs outside of that structure, and therefore, the category of the creatives (fabric, pattern, etc.), whether broad or narrow, may or may not belong to the structure in question, but will certainly be economically dependent upon it. From that point on, there extends an array—in part hierarchically arranged—of technicians and skilled workers, numerous in the larger structures and limited to a small group of workers with only slightly differentiated tasks in the crafts workshops. Certainly, from the entrepreneur to the fashion manager, from the directors of the sales divisions to the employees and the more or less specialized workforce, there are radi-

Young Rocker, Hamburg, 1950s.
Photo by Jurgen Vollmer
(Rapho/Grazia Neri)

cally different cultural worlds converging in a single company, bringing with them different ideas of what is beautiful, salable, proper—all with different outlooks as to the future of the product, its imaginary setting in different contexts, its use by various potential clients, and so forth.

The level of quality of the product, its placement on the market, the stylistic and organizational decisions, and the marketing approaches are all products of a coordination of the various cultures of the company, a negotiation among actors with different skills and degrees of power, but in any case a decision that can scarcely be laid to a single decision maker. For instance, the quality of Italian fashion is not merely a policy that is decided by top management—it is a result of the availability of a qualified labor pool. It is no accident that the managers of the multinationals that export around the globe from northeastern Italy withstand the apparent temptation to export their manufacturing facilities as well, since they are keenly aware that the skill of Italian seamstresses at reaching unparalleled levels of refinement in finishing articles of clothing is not the result—or not the result alone—of specific professional training, but rather a product of the fact that they live and communicate in a specific context, and their diffuse familiarity with well-made things, i.e., a cultural tradition. (And this is already one of the points where we see the unbroken circle of production and consumption.)

Thus, the brilliant fashion designer, set within the context of a major corporation, must take into account the costs of producing a set of bright ideas, defend or renounce those ideas entirely, or else reach a form of compromise. It is evident, then, that the creative beginning of the manufacturing process is, in reality, closely linked with the merchandising of the product, which marks the final step in that process. The marketing, for that matter, like the design, lies within the manufacturing structure only if we are talking about a more or less crafts-based manufacturing process; outside of that structure, in accordance with the most up-to-date organizational

styles, the commercial history of a fashion product may be quite lengthy and complex (from wholesale to retail, from the trade fair to the small shop or boutique, and so on) and may follow a variety of paths. Again evident is the degree to which the contraction of meanings in all these various passages must be laborious.

The second area is the less structured one of consumption, which ranges from the purchase to the use of an item of clothing. Here company choices find their testing ground. An article of clothing may be used in unexpected ways and in surprising combinations by the "wrong" subjects. Consumption, in fact, as has been made clear by the British anthropologist Mary Douglas, is anything but a purely passive social practice, guided by such simple instincts as need or envy. One may state, in fact, that the consumer plays a role in the cultural industry of fashion, and not merely the economic role of purchasing—which justifies the activity of manufacturing—but rather the diverse cultural and material roles of someone who decides to spend their money in a certain manner: of someone who purchases an article of clothing with the intention of wearing it and with the intention of modifying it or mixing it with other objects, thus continuing the material production of fashion, to display a certain image of themselves, as a political banner or as a tent behind which to hide.

In fact, designers and manufacturers are well aware of the need to treat the consumer as a competent counterpart, i.e., to come to an agreement with him or her concerning the meanings to be attributed to purchases and forms of behavior. To that end, two complementary strategies are employed. On the one hand, what sociologists call participatory observation: the professionals of fashion move among consumers and act as fashion hounds in order to understand what specifically is fashionable, and in reality suggesting, once again, in the form of a testimonial, their own fashion choices. (Here is a specific aspect of the circularity of production and consumption—the sphere of production itself consumes a vast portion of what it produces, and induces consumption, both by producing and consuming.) On the other hand, through market research: the systematic gathering of data concerning the demands and ideas of consumers. The development of such strategies is already a first indication of the reflexivity of fashion and its continual insistence on an exploration of meanings. This reflexivity reaches its highest value when the subjects involved are aware of the process in which they take part; this, we know from recent research, is true for all subjects involved in the area of production, who see themselves as synthesizers of the

Evolution of women's style from 1929 to 1959, from *Fashion & Anti-Fashion*, by Ted Polhemus and Lynn Procter

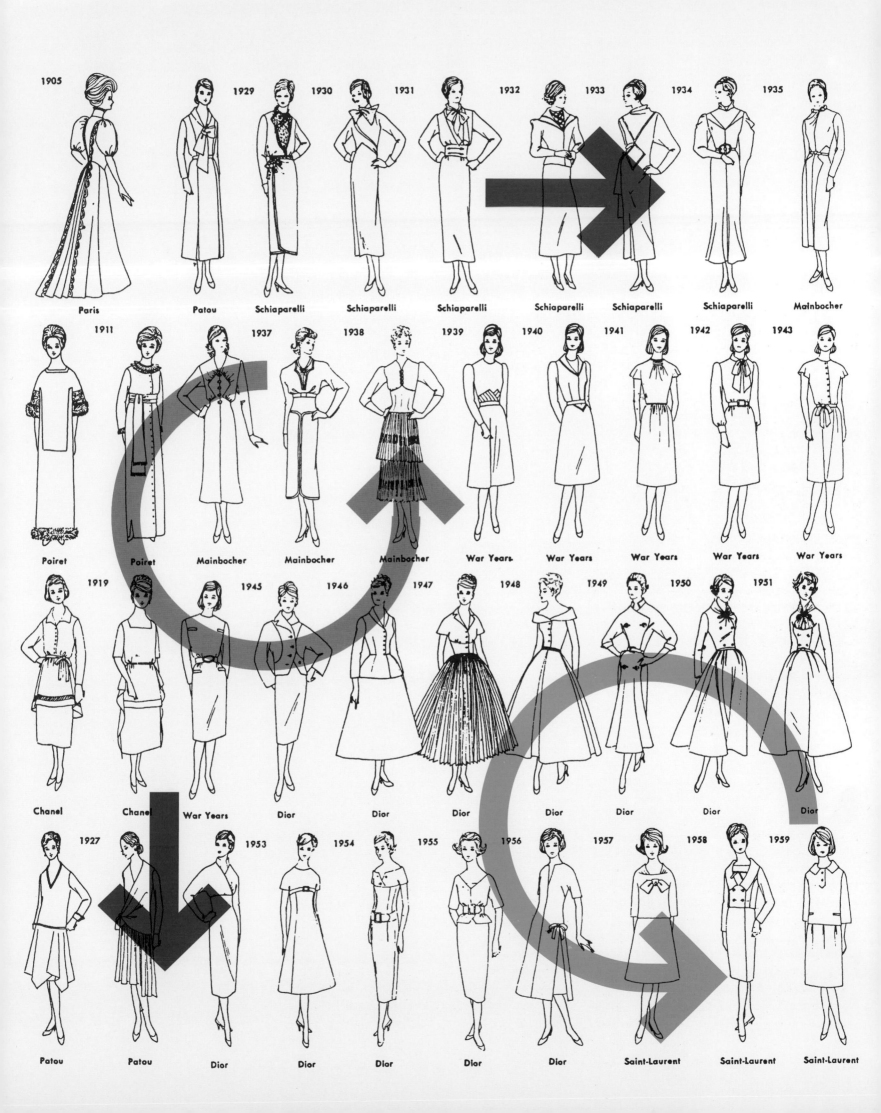

1905	**1929**	**1930**	**1931**	**1932**	**1933**	**1934**	**1935**
Paris	Patou	Schiaparelli	Schiaparelli	Schiaparelli	Schiaparelli	Schiaparelli	Schiaparelli	Mainbocher

1911	**1937**	**1938**	**1939**	**1940**	**1941**	**1942**	**1943**
Poiret	Poiret	Mainbocher	Mainbocher	Mainbocher	War Years	War Years	War Years	War Years	War Years

1919	**1945**	**1946**	**1947**	**1948**	**1949**	**1950**	**1951**
Chanel	Chanel	War Years	Dior	Dior	Dior	Dior	Dior	Dior	Dior

1927	**1953**	**1954**	**1955**	**1956**	**1957**	**1958**	**1959**
Patou	Patou	Dior	Dior	Dior	Dior	Dior	Saint-Laurent	Saint-Laurent	Saint-Laurent

many "signals" that punctuate life in the city.

And so the professionals of fashion state that they take inspiration from nature and from stamps, from shop windows and from world travel. Above all, however, they know that they are copying existing forms of culture, perhaps to offer a new synthesis of elements of the past. "With our culture and with our information, we repeat an up-to-date formula that already exists," according to a fabric designer. These professionals, then, participate consciously in the reflexivity that typifies our era and are well aware that they are manipulating culture, i.e., acting as creators of meanings and designers of urban settings much more than producers of objects for everyday use. According to one young fashion manager, the heir to a family of entrepreneurs: "An individual surrounds himself or herself with various objects out of a need for a certain setting; we provide one of these settings, portable and wearable".

With market research, we have already entered the third major area of the cultural industry of fashion—in my hypothesis no less important than the other two—that is directly involved in the commercial transaction. The third area has to do with organized communication, the area in which official links and contacts between the other two areas are arranged, aside from the many informal and individual contacts that constitute the circuit of communications of fashion.

Scholars and interviewers involved in more or less marketing-oriented research, advertising people, fashion journalists and photographers, events organizers—they are all working solely to interpret and to supply interpretations, to juxtapose diverse items in order to suggest specific (or unspecified) lifestyles, to disassemble and to reassemble cultural frames (with reference to Erving Goffman) within which to set dramatic or ironic (or preferably, ambiguous) definitions of the situation. The continual fluctuation of meanings is sought out as a strategy by which to reach a variety of different audiences; the allusive attraction of iconic communications disproportionately accentuates the characteristic of instability that has always been associated with fashion. If fashion designers and manufacturers have shown that they are keenly aware of their roles as cultural intermediaries, then that is even more the case for advertising people and photographers and, in general, all communicators, whose task it is, in practical terms, to serve as middlemen for the fashion product, which they reinterpret.

The younger generations are evidently witnesses and actors with respect to these characteristics of the fashion system, less-inhibited actors than those adults who—rightly or wrongly—recognize for themselves a major role in the construction of fashion, demanding in some sense to set the boundaries.

Casting for an Italian
television variety program,
Bellissima,
Gabicce Mare, Italy, 1995.
Photo by Armin Linke

The young Milanese whom we interviewed feel that they are citizens of the world, because they purchase their clothing near their homes or in flea markets all over Europe, because they follow in the footsteps of American graffiti artists and English rockers. They are perfectly aware of the ambivalence of images, or the contamination of meanings placed in different contexts, of the provisional nature of their choices and the choices of others. They understand the reflexive interplay of fashion in the frenetic ricochet of fashions: Italian rappers smile, tolerantly, having always ignored the fashion of the major Italian designers, and they now begin to mention in their songs the names of Armani and Dolce & Gabbana, imitating American rappers who are taken with Italian style.

AND STYLE

(Courtesy of Archivio Infinito)

THE METHODS OF FASHION DESIGN
G.M.

This is art, that is industrial design, and here is fashion. Our culture feels bound to distinguish among certain entities; we are accustomed to thinking in categories. On the basis of specific categories, we build theories, we establish hierarchies of value. The fact remains, however, that things, in the final analysis, in objective reality, are far more intricate, articulated, and complex: that distinctions blur; that mental categories overlap and intertwine; that values flip, switch, and fall between the cracks. At this point—which is the point that we have reached now—the distinctions that bracket the disciplines we recognize have, in effect, become grids that force our interpretations into a certain preconceived framework. What is fashion design nowadays? It is not considered an art, because its final purpose is to design objects to be mass produced and sold in large numbers. Fashion design must take into account all of the tricks demanded by marketing and media. But can we seriously claim nowadays that wiliness, marketing, and media savvy are incompatible with art?

Fashion has in common with both art and industrial design the need for a source of creative energy that can process and elaborate the signs of the present. Fashion design is not even accorded the cultural legitimacy of industrial design, because it does not strive to create a pure, functional, definitive form. Fashion design is always excessive, interchangeable, variable, and ephemeral. Even when it is minimalist—i.e., when it tends to reproduce the formal vocabulary of modernism—fashion lasts for the space of a season, and this aspect demonstrates the lack of depth that disqualifies fashion design from joining the ranks of real disciplines. Well, then, what should we say about the increasingly numerous series of industrial objects—manufactured in varied, arbitrary forms and in garish colors, with decorations and flourishes—from wristwatches to motor scooters to sound equipment? And for that matter, what are functional forms, if we also count among the functions of objects the representation of symbols? We might well point out that the many new products derived from the newest technologies—products with exceedingly high coefficients of functionality (such as cellular phones), developed long after the end of the cultural hegemony of rationalist design—are, in terms of appearance (and perhaps in terms of the conception of use), already quite similar to fashion accessories.

The fact remains that fashion is produced (or is reproduced, if we wish to attribute greater value to the spontaneity of individual choices) in factories on assembly lines, precisely like other objects for which design is judged, instead, in terms of industrial design. When cars had fins, in the 1950s, their design was called styling and was considered to be a vulgar subspecies of industrial design. Fashion is, perhaps, a far more sophisticated form of styling, capable of developing continually new—yet equivalent—forms, which allow the market to absorb new products each season. In this way, fashion design must solve a vast array of problems, and is required to consume an avalanche of creativity in exceedingly brief periods. The design of a fashion collection is a process of creative, organizational, and manufacturing interaction that is quite as respectable as the design of a refrigerator or a spoon. The problem is that there is no discipline to define that process, inasmuch as the activity of fashion design lies outside the boundaries and borders of other disciplines. Fashion design stands in the same relationship to industrial design as the overall design approach of rational culture of the machine age stands to the result of the postmodern demolition of ideological certainties. In order to understand the meaning of fashion design, it is necessary to push the envelope of disciplinary schemes, reshuffle the cards, and relaunch the practice of expressive research, without prior constraints.

First and foremost, it is necessary to ignore entirely all market research. Achille Castiglioni

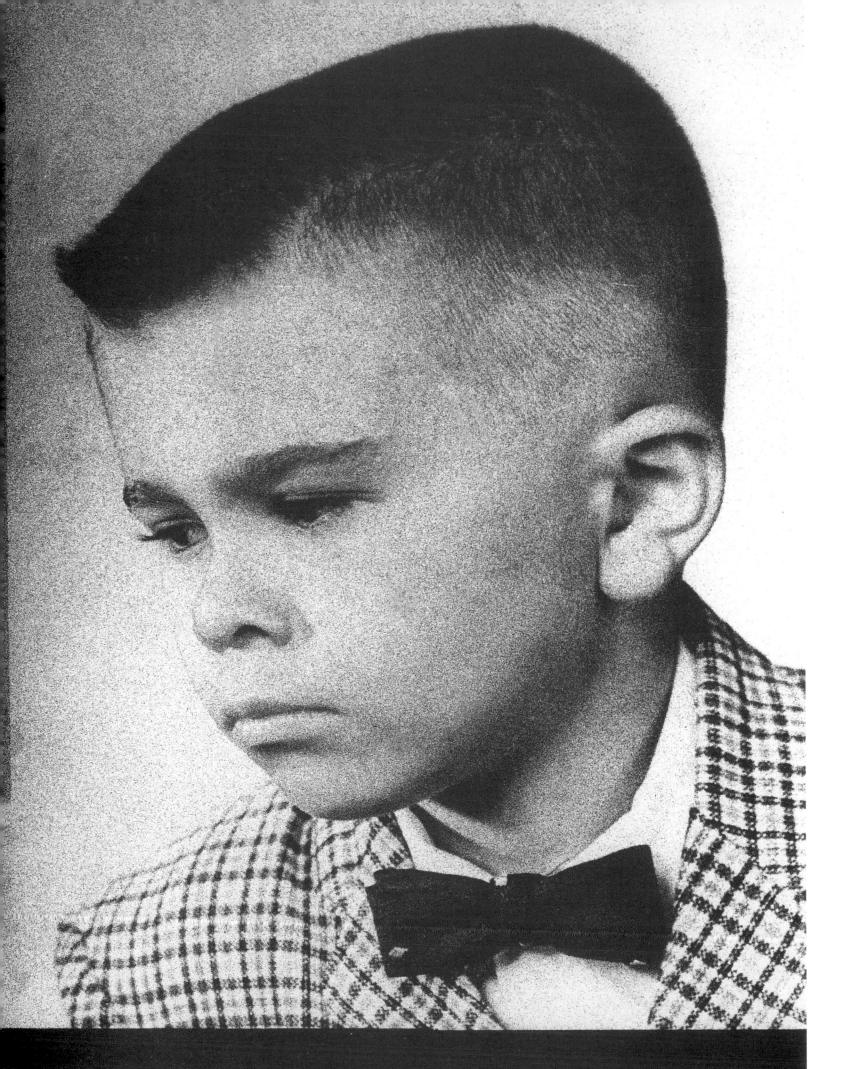

CREW CUT OR BRUSH CUT

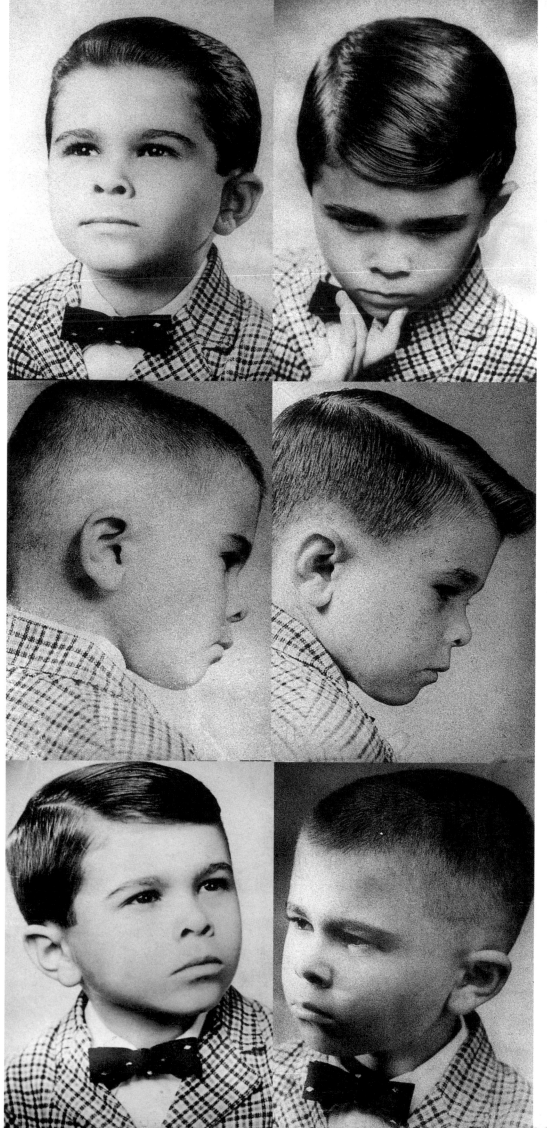

Posters of boys' hairstyles on barbershop wall, Miami, 1992.

(Courtesy of *The Manipulator*)

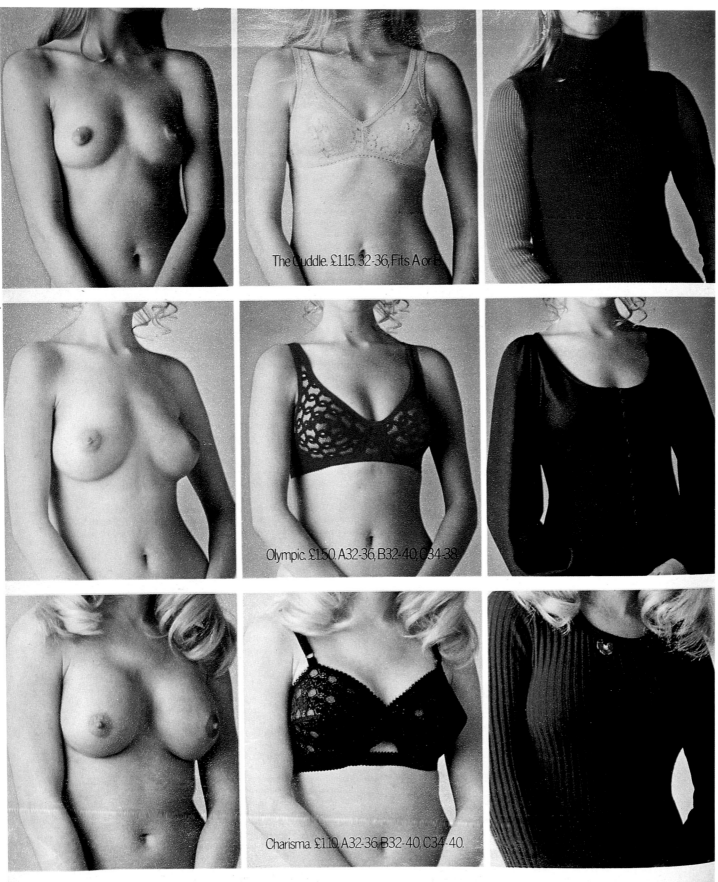

The Cuddle. £1.15. 32-36, Fits A or B.

Olympic. £1.50. A32-36, B32-40, C34-38.

Charisma. £1.10. A32-36, B32-40, C34-40.

Lovable makes the best of what you've got.

Variations on a theme: advertising campaign for Lovable brassieres, from *Nova*, 1972

Opposite:
Styling of eight new Italian scooters, 1997

FLA10
FLA23

FLA11
FLA22

FLA09
FLA27
FLA97
M390

FLA39

ME18
ME20
ME29

ME07
ME24

MEO9
ME30

ME33

MEO7
ME28
K212

MEO9
ME27

MIX
MATCH

FLA16
FLA25
W104

Melon Smoothie

MIX & MATCH

GREEN FLASH

FLA17
FLA30
LM80

FLA47
FLA44

FLA37
W110

FLA18
FLA21
FLA96

ME35
ME37
ME97

ME17
ME23

ME11
ME22
M320

Royal Blue

VENUS
SWIMWEAR

RB11
RB22

GEO33
LP15YEL

GEO18
GEO21
K233

-07
28

RB18
RB20
RB29
K201

GEO
GEO
GEO
GEO

MIX MATCH

Venus

RB35
RB37
RB96

RB09
RB30

GEO16
GEO25
GEO96
K231

GEO11
GEO22

Preceding pages: Swimwear styles from Venus Swimwear catalog, 1997

Italian styling of the 1950s: Twenty versions of the same model of car, the Alfa Romeo 1900 (Courtesy of Archivio Storico Alfa Romeo)

VICINITIES: FIBER, FABRIC, CLOTHING

Nancy Martin

The art of weaving probably began seven thousand years ago as an elaboration of the technique of basket making. The practice of weaving is strictly related to the agricultural revolution. A fixed habitat necessary for growing crops could only come about when human beings could trust each other enough to live close together in small communities. Life in enclosed spaces, in the vicinity of other human beings, encouraged the development of a new sociability and the art of weaving, an archetype of group work. The weaving of myths and symbols could ritualize the natural hostility and aggressivity that form the fearsome dark side of human nature. Agriculture brought humankind into close contact with the plants and animals that would later become the raw material of weaving, once the process of spinning was developed. Weaving provided metaphors clarifying the relation between the natural and the supernatural in every culture where it was practiced. The grass farmers of ancient India celebrated the coming into being of their world through songs, many of which use the weave as metaphor, as in the Upanishads (Sanskrit for "a session"), ancient books written between 800 and 200 B.C. collecting Indian wisdom and ritual. The following is a question-and-answer excerpt from "The Famous Debates in the Forest." Gârgee, a young girl, asks Yadnawalka, a sage, to explain to her how the world was made: "Since everything is woven on water, please tell me on what is water woven, warp and weft?" Yadnawalka replies that water is woven on wind, wind on sky, sky on the region of the celestial choir, the region of the celestial choir on the sun, the sun on the moon, the moon on the stars, the stars on the region of light, and the region of light on the region of spirit. But when Gârgee asks to know more, Yadnawalka replies: "Gârgee! Do not transgress the limit or you will go crazy!"

Seven thousand years later, a different person describes Western men's clothing, as seen by a fictitious Samoan chief on a visit to Amsterdam: "The men always keep their chests covered completely. From their throats down to their breast glands the alii (gentlemen) wear a chalkstiffened loincloth the size of a taro leaf. On the top of that rests a white ring, also stiffened with chalk and wound around the neck. Through that ring he draws a piece of coloured cloth, plaited like the rope of a boat; it is pierced by a golden needle or a pearl and it hangs down the white shield. Many Papalagi (white man) also wear chalk rings around their wrists but never around their ankles."

The first passage treats weaving as a cosmic metaphor. The second, instead, is a complex pas-

Giorgio Armani, spring-summer 1998. Photo by Pino Guidolotti

Woman of the Tarahumara
tribe, 1981.
Photo by John Running
(Courtesy of *The Manipulator*).

Opposite:
From the fall-winter
1997–98 Guy Laroche
catalogue.
Photo by Katerina Jebb

Advertising campaign
for Gommatex, 1980s.
Photo by Tyen
(Courtesy of *The Manipulator*).

tiche using the stance of the primitive to cast moral
doubt on the sense of Western fashion. The debate
continues today, and cloth still makes itself useful as
the building blocks of the fashion system. While the
first citation denotes a profound understanding of
the weaving process, the second was obviously written long after the Industrial Revolution, and the
feigned ignorance of cloth is, indeed, genuine.

In India, cloth weaving, dyeing, and embellish-
ment are inherited professions. Textile culture
revealed the scientific relation between textile fibers
and other natural substances (dyes) without the
assistance of the scientific method. In the West, centuries would pass before science cleared the way for
the Industrial Revolution and the mass production of
textiles, its most important product.

Water and manpower are fundamental prerequi-
sites of the modern textile factory. In Italy, one still
finds textile factories clustered around a water
source. The older factories are grouped according to
fiber type (Como for silk, Biella for wool), but today
practically all fibers are imported. The factories tend
to remain in fiber areas for technical reasons:
trained workers are more likely to be found, as well
as technology.

The fiber limits the image of the final garment,
just as the leaf contains the limits of the tree. Each
fiber has a specific relation to water: cotton is highly

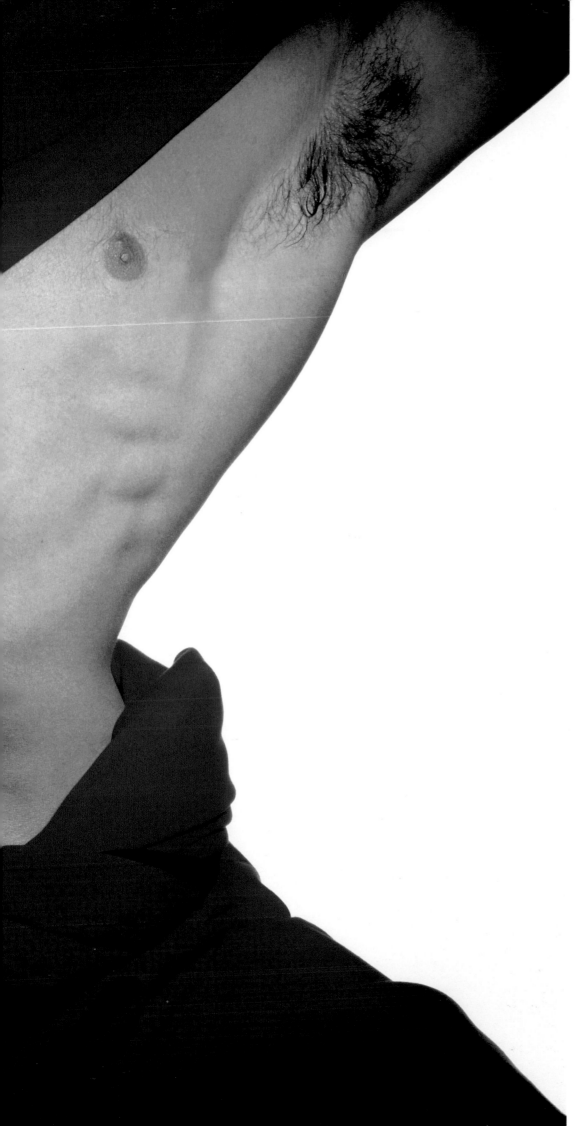

absorbent, and that same quality makes it one of the easiest to dye. Linen, an indigenous European fiber, has a built-in cooling system that draws moisture away from the body, creating a dry sensation. Wool, another indigenous fiber, is even more absorbent than cotton. Silk, inversely, can provoke perspiration. This is a fragment of a series of qualities, physical and chemical, that determine the future behavior of each fabric. Human-made fibers, however, are not designed to contain water. In Italy, for reasons of taste, tradition, and economy, noble and rare fibers are preferred to human-made fibers, but all fibers are used, producing a great variety of mixed yarns to work with. For the last few years elastic yarns have been used to create fabrics with built-in fit, which are now used in every sector of the market.

In the development of weaving, the loom predated spinning. Spinning is suggested in myriad ways in the natural world, from the galaxy to seashells. Spinning is a coiling and stretching motion that allows chaotic fibers to become cohesive yarns. Some fibers are so tiny they can hardly be seen, let alone grasped by the hand (such as polyester microfibers). Others are weak and must be coaxed into parallel systems before becoming usable. The Italian verb for spin, *torcere*, has a more sinister meaning: torture. The enclosure that occurs when fibers are twisted and stretched around each other

is made of a mixture of air and substance. The yarn appears, with its characteristic tubular shape, elastic and flexible. The spiraling strategy of the growing plant is copied by the yarn and continues when it is coiled onto cones for transport.

Not all of the processing that fibers and yarns undergo is healthy. The exquisite boredom produced by millions of miles of plain fabrics, identical replicas of each other, cannot be cured by a clever logo. The outer edge of the fashion planet demands fabrics that are mutilated, distressed, diseased, fractured, and irregular—in short, unique and nonreplicable. The Anvers Group of Six is the prime perpetrator of these textile homicides. They oppose the regular, the standard, the normal, as do most young fashion students who have no idea of how fabric is made and therefore ignore what constitutes a plus-value in a fabric. They grace it instead with a minus-value by overpainting, staining, or overlaying trash fabric on noble fabric.

This is a spontaneous testimony to how little students know (or rather, are taught) about raw textile material. Lack of perception becomes lack of sensitivity. Here there exists no vicinity: apparel and interior designers, with a few brilliant exceptions, know little to nothing about cloth and the vast formal

potential it offers (but they know what they like!).

When cloth is woven, threads will crisscross each other and bind themselves into a three-dimensional plane called fabric. At this point they will receive a name. The name once served as a code for reproducing an identical replica. Sometimes the name indicates the place the fabric was first made (marocain, ottoman, Vichy, madras, Harris), sometimes its physical aspect (piqué, filasse, homespun, givrine, spugna, pelo d'uovo), sometimes its function (mattress ticking, regimental stripes), and sometimes the inventor (Bemberg, Jacquard, Raschel). The most poetic names for fabric are Indian. Dacca produced a rare muslin that when laid wet on the grass was indistinguishable from the evening dew and was called subham, "the dew of evening." Another was called ab-rawan, "running water."

Fabrics are as modern as the period in which they are made. But the textile factory remains essentially as it was two hundred years ago. The wonderfully soft, clean material issues from a dreary grid of iron machines chattering endlessly at supersonic speed. Bits of fibers float in the air and an occasional human being or robot passes by to check a loom that is not functioning. This person is not a weaver, but a mechanic who has no relation to the

Samples of special decorative effects on fabrics, by Domus Academy/Nancy Martin Studio in collaboration with Limonta SpA

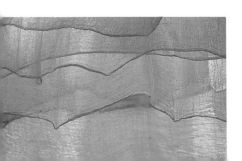

design of the fabric, the guardian of the machinery.
There is not a weaver in sight. Fabrics are made in
solitary confinement and rarely are touched or
caressed by the human hand. The designing and
planning is done elsewhere by the technical adminis-
tration. Mechanical weaving is as remote from hand
weaving as Dairy Freez is from mom's ice cream. As
Anni Albers admonished fifty years ago: "As an antidote for an elated sense of progress, [retrospection]
shows our achievements in proper proportion, and
makes it possible to observe where we have
advanced and where not . . . When we examine
recent progress in cloth making . . . the momentous
development we find is limited to . . . the creation of
new fibers and finishes while the process of weaving
has remained . . . unchanged for centuries. Textile
chemistry has brought about . . . greater changes
perhaps than even those brought about by the fast
advances in the mechanics of textile production during the last century."

Although the factory remains unchanged, conditioned by the unforgiving linear architecture of the
textile process that can neither bend nor run backward, the fashion system has given new life and new
soul to fabric production and design. The friendly collaboration between stylist and fabric producer is a

unique quality of the Italian fashion system. Whether
the client is a master stylist or a beginner, Italian
companies are highly receptive to unedited fabric
proposals. They churn out, at considerable cost in
research and development, new collections twice a
year. The new designs are prototypes, and many will
never go into production. But continual trial and
error keeps the eye, the hand, and the mind keenly
concentrated on the new, the other, the next big thing
emerging in the textile vicinity. The close and confi-
dential relationship between stylist and fabric manufacturer becomes a private language, refining the
textile ideology of both. Every stylist has an ideal
fabric, and Italian weavers are often enthusiastic to
take risks on new ideas: in any case, if it works, both
sides win. Beautiful as it may be, cloth is, from
another perspective, just another raw material.
Textiles are rarely signed, even though the "feeling"
of the final garment is imprinted in the cloth itself.

Cloth has two faces: one facing inward toward the
body, the other outward. Between the two lies a
space where the two elements, skin and cloth, are
continuously moving toward and away from each
other. Aldous Huxley tells us of "something that he
had seen earlier in the morning and when later, looking down, he stared at his crossed legs, those folds

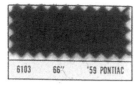 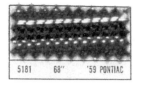 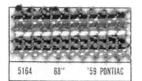 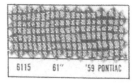

 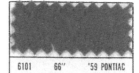  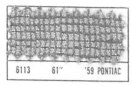

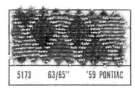 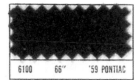 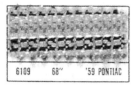 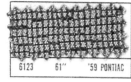

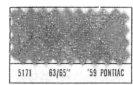 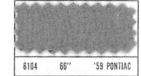 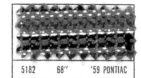 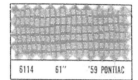

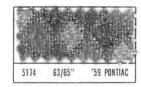 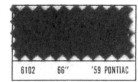 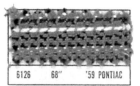 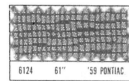

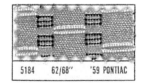 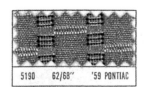 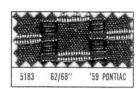 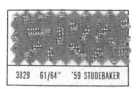

 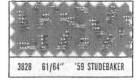 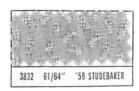

"NYLON STRETCH
BROADCLOTHS ON
PAGE 1"

STUDEBAKER

in his trousers—what a labyrinth of infinitely significant complexity, the gray flannel fabric—how rich it was! How profoundly, mysteriously sumptuous!" What Huxley saw in the folds of his trousers was an image of natural law: the image of the ripples and saddles that occur when material is evolving in space. The interruption of the smooth, even surface of his trousers became a panorama of craggy mountains and shady valleys. It was at that moment that he understood the obsession of Renaissance painters for drapery, the "inexhaustible theme of linen and wool drapings," the "historical serenity of the drapings of Piero della Francesca." Huxley concludes that through observation of the draping in art one can understand the feeling of a particular period.

Beyond the statistics of commerce and the welfare of the economy lurk more insidious realities. Cloth is a perfect medium for the observation of natural truths. Cloth allows the nonexpert in scientific subjects to observe the magic of its mathematics. The vast distances that separate human beings from the manufacture of the things they use separates hand from head and dulls the senses. Stronger and stronger stimuli are needed to induce feeling. Fashion is a unique antidote to the poverty of aesthetically available events. Having a style, a look, means today what having a place in society, a job, a knowledge or a personal experience once meant. The place of fashion today goes far beyond the notion of gorgeous fabrics exquisitely made into garments. Fashion defines the locus and contours of a natural need for aesthetic events. The observation of clothing—on ourselves, on others, and through the vast media landscapes—is, for many, the only vicinity in which the beauty of human and natural behavior can be experienced. Getting up, getting dressed, looking at clothes on ourselves and others can breed virtual colonies of taste and style. We might conclude that fashion is the exclusive expression of "art" in a popular democracy.

Page from a swatch book: automobile upholstery for Pontiac and Studebaker. Photo by Irving Solero
(Courtesy of the Fashion Institute of Technology Museum)

Opposite:
Advertising campaign for Faliero Sarti, 1980s
(Courtesy of *The Manipulator*)

HOW TO DO IT: AN INTERVIEW WITH PAUL SMITH

Nadine Frey

NF: As a designer, you are moving from designing menswear to womenswear to children's and secondary lines throughout the year. Is the process of creating a collection the same for all of them?

PS: Well, certainly the same principle applies to all of them. The hard thing in designing seven lines twice a year is dipping from the feeling of one to the other without losing the grasp. I work hard at making sure that all the lines have their own identity.

NF: For simplicity's sake, let's narrow our discussion to the creation of your top menswear line, the Paul Smith collection, a line you launched in 1976 and have been designing for over twenty years now. When are the first ideas put together?

PS: Actually, straight after the show you are starting to put your mind to the next collection. The crazy thing about fashion is that you never really stop. If you are an actor, you can work hard and have a year off. In a lot of other professions there is time out. But in the world of fashion you are always involved in your next collection. The first step takes place right after your last show. What you want is to develop the general feeling of the next collection, and that can come from anything, really. It can come from the history

of what has just happened, the show you've just had, and what the atmosphere is like politically, or the feeling of what's going on in the world. For instance, coming out of the eighties, there was a lot of rejection from youth of what the eighties stood for—the stock-market boom and materialistic values zooming through the roof. In the early nineties, the youth rejected that. So you feel what is happening around you, and if you are bright enough, you then start to play down fashion. So in the last few years, fashion has been a lot more simple and classic. That's why my July 1997 menswear show was important; it was a more attention-seeking collection.

NF: How do you evolve your feeling for what is happening in that sense? Where does your information on that come from?

PS: You've got to be very proactive and lively to witness that. A lot of designers surround themselves with subservients and travel in limousines and hide themselves in ivory-tower studios and lose touch. They forget who's paying their wages—the customer in the street.

NF: Once you are sure of your general direction, what are your first steps in translating that into a design message?

PS: You're starting to think about silhouette and

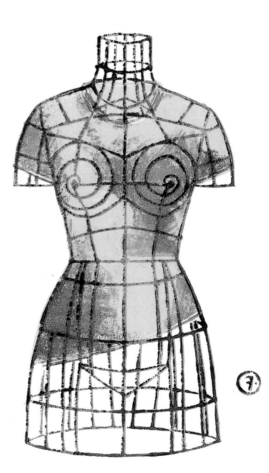

Fashion illustration by François Berthoud

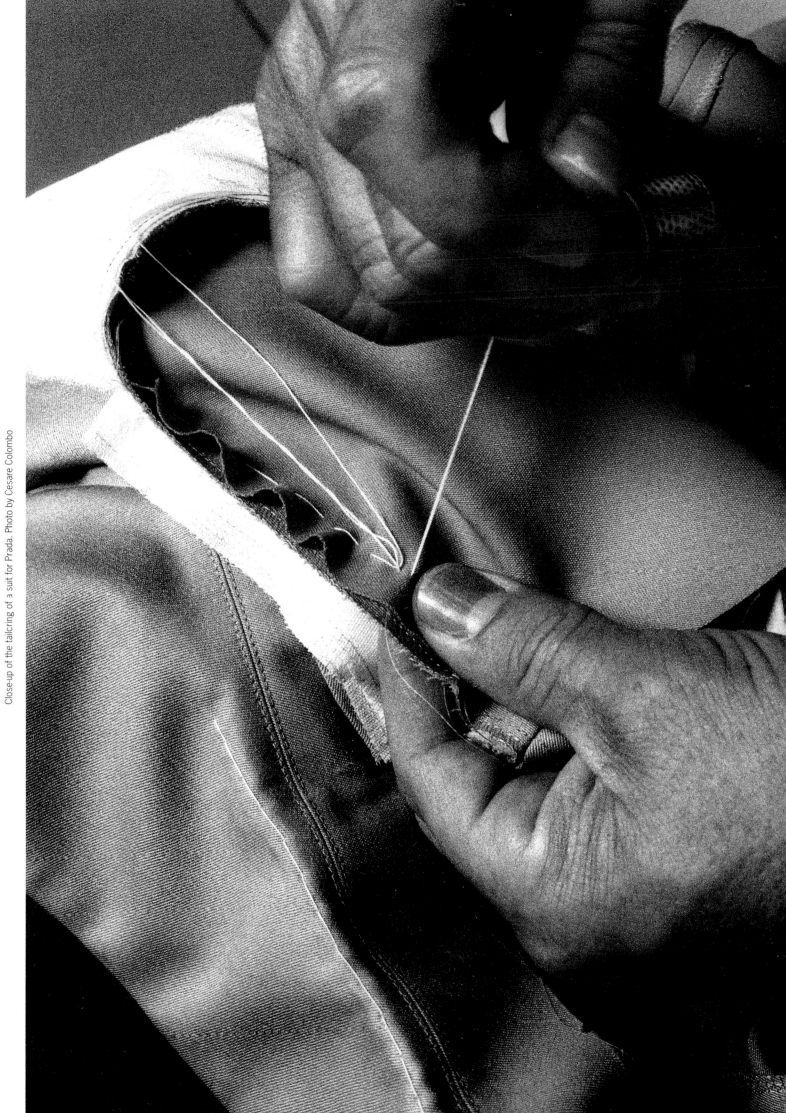

Close-up of the tailoring of a suit for Prada. Photo by Cesare Colombo

shape. If the silhouette has been slim, fitted, and shaped, then there really is only one way to go, to something looser, softer, and more relaxed. The feeling or direction is the first thing you think about, what the look of the main line is going to be, which is why the main line is what the Americans call cutting-edge. It's the line that is provoking and pushing the customer forward. The other lines tend to follow the main line from the previous season, they're slightly more commercial.

NF: When do you actually start to work on sketches?

PS: If I'm working on the winter collection of the next year, by the latter part of July and August. You have more of a feeling of where you're going. The way I begin is to start filling my notebook with words and ideas and sketches. It could be the words "white trousers" or "dandyish" or "Savile Row," or the name of a movie or an actor.

NF: When you begin thinking about actual pieces, what part of the collection do you begin with?

PS: Actually, the next process is to start considering things that take a lot of time. You start looking at yarn for T-shirts, knitwear, or jerseys. The Pitti Filati fair has already happened, so you've got some pieces of yarn from manufacturers and you start to decide which yarns would be relevant to the look you are building up in your head. If it's a chic collection, you're looking at a high-gauge, fine yarn, like a 25 to 30 gauge yarn, which will be very chic and simple. Or it could be a 5, 4, or 3 gauge for a heavier chunky yarn, or a shetland or a bouclé for a rugged look.

NF: Do you work with the mills in any way to develop the yarns?

PS: Once I've chosen the yarns they are dyed to my specifications. Generally speaking, we are dealing with simplicity, and color is especially important when you are designing a collection as opposed to a range. There is a hell of a difference between the two. Instead of a selection of jackets and trousers, which you would have in a range, in a collection all the individual parts go together and something ties them, whether it is color or texture or silhouette. After the color and the yarn selection, you're starting to get a general feeling. You are thinking generally about texture, then you start thinking about if you want prints.

If you do want prints, then you have to think about inspiration. Like my recent collection in Paris [spring-summer 1998], it can be flamboyant and outrageous as a particular statement about the blandness of the past few seasons. Other seasons you might find that prints aren't relevant. For this, I work with my textile designer and give her ideas: classical, neat, small, flamboyant—whatever.

NF: Where in the design process are you at this point, and how far along are you in understanding what the final collection will actually look like?

PS: I've decided on the general appearance. If it's dandyish, forties, Savile Row, then those messages that you're getting go into the fabric design, what sorts of prints. By that time the fabric fairs are starting—Ideabiella, Moda In, and Première Vision are all in early fall. The mills come to you with pre-collection ideas. Sometimes their ideas are not fully formed, but there's a hint of what they're thinking about. They'll say, "We're thinking of geometrics; what are you thinking of?"

NF: You work with a variety of Italian, French, and British mills. How closely do you work with them, and are you only interested in exclusive fabrics?

PS: You can do an exclusivity—you can enlarge the scale of a design, or add some colors, or change the fabric in some way so that you get some exclusivity. You have favorite mills that you work with for various reasons, and there is a constant relationship with them. Recently, I was working with a British mill and I spotted a French yarn I liked. I advised the mill to buy the yarn and mix it with the British wool. It was very successful. Fashion is transient, always on the move. The job of a designer is to be innovative and always on the move. In the fall you go to the fabric fairs. Some designers get ideas from fairs, but I know what I'm looking for: crepe, or drape or shiny—I'm quite clear by the time of the fairs. So you travel around the fabric fairs for days and days, and start to order swatches that you like. If you really love something, you'll order ten or twenty meters to make actual samples from them. You come back from the fabric fair with cuttings of the fabrics in your notebook, and after

Close-up of the tailoring
of a suit for Prada.
Photo by Cesare Colombo

two or three weeks the swatches start coming in. Then you start designing the clothes more specifically. You start working with your toilists to get the shapes into reality. And they make the toiles.

NF: Not all ready-to-wear designers make toiles as part of the design process. That's essentially a couture process.

PS: I have no formal training and by working from a toile you have a clear visual reference as to what you are looking for. If you haven't got a patternmaker who does it well, a slip of the pencil changes things. A toile lets you see quickly what the final product is going to look like. After you have the basic shapes, you hang flaps on pockets. Pocket details, lapels—those can come later. And then you start to make some of those shapes in real fabric instead of as a toile. You make them in fabric similar to what you have ordered—perhaps in the correct fabric but not the right color, so you can see how that fabric will behave in that particular style. By this time some of the sample lengths will have begun to arrive, and you start to build up your collection more carefully, based on the fabrics. You select the swatches that you want, and at this point the price, the availability, and minimum quantities become important. By the end of October, you finalize all fabric, prints, and yarn selection, and make sure the fabric can be delivered in six to ten weeks, depending on the type of mill. Obviously the yarn and prints are a longer process, so you order those earlier. By the end of November all prototypes of actual garments are made, and in the lull before receiving fabric you are starting to think, out of the fabrics you have ordered, what styles they can go into and how they work with the jerseys, shirting, and knitwear you have chosen. You're matching the pink stripe in a shirt with the pink of a tie, or the fullness of a shirt will have the same fullness of a suit. You start to get a harmony. One of the best ways to describe it to a layperson is, if you are making a cake that needs six ingredients, it won't work if you only have four. You have a set number of ingredients and it will only work when they all come together in a harmony of shape, texture, and color.

NF: There was a lot of talk in the eighties of computer-aided design and cost-saving technological changes in fashion design. How much of that is important in your design process?

PS: Computer-aided design in my business does not work. It works for print or stripings, or for a shirt or a jersey. My design work is more about lateral thinking and lateral notes—you can't get more creative than a notepad. On the manufacturing end, there is laser cutting, or pattern grading. You can get computers that will cut all the fabric for you, laying it up in the most economical way. There are now completely computerized machines for manufacturing pockets and seams. In our warehouses, all of the designs are recorded on a computer. You know that when fabric letter A comes in, you'll make it in style 2, 3, 7, and 8. After specifying which fabrics are for what pieces, the fabrics then go to factories. You'll have decided what types of lining, undercolor, button, and thread you'll be using. This information all goes into the computer in the design room. Once I've decided on fabric A for style 2, then I have to know that there's a certain color zipper, lining, and thread, and this all goes into the computer. Then when our salesmen sell to shops around the world, they put in the design and fabric the customer requires, and the computer already knows what lining and zippers are needed.

NF: At some point you need to produce a sample collection to show on the runway. When is that completed?

PS: At Christmas you send sample fabrics to the factories, sometimes hundreds of samples, and the factories send them back finished. Then you can take your samples to your various showrooms to see the buyers from the shops from all around the world, and they will place their orders. In Paris, for example, we have the whole collection there. We set up a showroom and put on a fashion show, which is—if we're talking about having the show around the twenty-eighth of January—selling fall-winter clothes that will be delivered in August of that year. After the fashion show the buyers come to the showroom. A fashion show is about seeking attention, so runway is for the more attention-seeking pieces. In the case of Paul Smith, we only show what we

make, unlike a lot of designers. But in the showroom the buyers see a bigger selection of other things that we make, and they pull out their collection based on price and on the location of their shops. A seaside shop doesn't want heavy clothing during the summer season and Los Angeles doesn't ever want anything that is too heavy. We put the orders into the computer—which will tell you that you need a thousand meters of this fabric or buttons of this type—and the production department takes the order, then orders all components.

NF: Retailers are quick to complain about delays in shipping. How much time elapses between the runway show and when you have the collection ready to ship?

PS: After the buyers have placed their orders, there is an eight-to-twelve-week lead time before buttons and fabrics start coming into our warehouse. By that time there are work dockets to match up with the fabric, so that when the fabric comes in, the zippers and buttons are sent along with the various fabrics you have chosen to make the clothes. The patterns will have been graded into the sizes—we grade the patterns in-house. Then factories make up the clothes and we receive the garments back ready to ship out during August and September. The warehouse starts to collate the customers' orders—we sell to forty countries around the world—until there are enough goods to be sent out. Usually you can make 90 percent of the orders, due to some letdown by mills. Then it is the job of finance to chase payment. By this time it's August and the design process will have started again.

NF: Of course, in the time since your January showing, you have designed an entirely new collection for spring-summer and for the July runway show.

PS: Yes, but the process is, as soon as I have made a fashion show the production department takes over and I start the next season, with a view to showing in Paris six months later.

Paul Smith, mental map of the process of industrial production of fashion. Drawing on paper
(Courtesy of Paul Smith)

P. S. organisation (menswear)

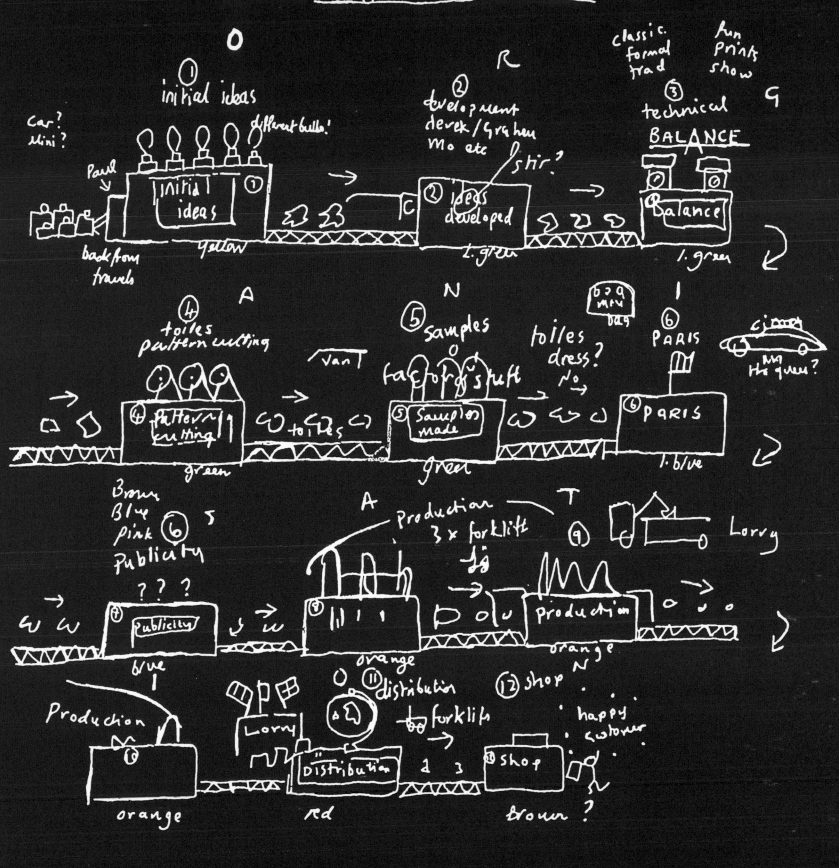

O

① initial ideas

car? mini?

Paul

different bulbs!

initial ideas

back from travels

Yellow

R

② development derek/Graham Mo etc

stir?

C ② ideas developed

l. green

classic formal trad

fun print show

③ technical

BALANCE

Balance

l. green

A

④ toiles pattern cutting

van

④ pattern cutting

toiles

green

N

⑤ samples

factory stuff

⑤ Samples made

green

toiles dress? No

6 × 9 men bag

I

⑥ PARIS

⑥ PARIS

l. blue

God save the queen?

Brown Blue Pink ⑥ S Publicity

??? ?

⑦ Publicity

blue

A

Production 3 × forklift

⑧

orange

T

⑨

production

orange

Lorry

Production

⑧

orange

O

Lorry

⑪ distribution

forklift

Distribution

Red

1 3

N

⑫ shop

⑫ shop

trouser?

happy customer

← 32 ft →

O R S A N I S A T I O N
1 2 3 4 5 6 7 8 9 10 11 12

CREATIVITY IN THE FASHION SYSTEM

Domenico De Masi

Let us imagine, to some rough approximation, a commercial system of fashion that is probably not far from reality. In Milan, let us say, a certain fashion designer, who is already quite famous, feeds this fame through a growing investment in advertising, in all the media. It is of no importance whether the commercials or ad pages allow the viewer or reader to appreciate the details of the no-doubt excellent apparel that bears the designer's name: the purpose is not to use advertising as a "showcase" for these products, as is the case with automobiles advertised in *Car and Driver* or the personal computers seen in *Microcomputer*. The purpose is much simpler than that: to mention, insistently, a certain label, reaching the greatest possible number of people around the world through emotional appeals that are designed to do no more than to confirm an atmosphere of refinement or daring, casual ease or youth, which that label has chosen to evoke and monopolize. All it takes is an excuse—the belly button or ankle of a famous model, the biceps or neck of a male model, or even a villa, a party, a divorce, or perhaps a murder—to assemble a page of advertising or a television spot and gain a space in the newspapers or on the evening news.

The great fashion designers—much like Giovanni Agnelli for Fiat or Bill Gates for Microsoft—are primarily interested in this "persistence of atmosphere" that, linked to their products, makes them desirable, encouraging the portion of the mass of customers that has been chosen as a target to buy those products. To a similar, if lesser, degree, this is also true in the system of industrial design and for certain groups orbiting such prominent figures as Renzo Piano.

And what products is our designer selling, and through whom? The designer succeeds in selling collections of "body furnishings," designed in Tuscany or in the Molise region by task forces of "creatives" (for the most part, exceedingly young designers). The prototypes of these "furnishings" will then be shown in Paris, Milan, or Rome in the seasonal presentations, created through the efforts of directors, advertisers, publicity agents, journalists, composers, musicians, choreographers, and models. Once they have been selected, the outfits will be produced in series of short runs, again in Molise or even in Tuscany, by intricate networks of technicians and craftspeople (cutters, tailors, packers, and shippers).

Our fashion designer then sells these products through a chain of stores that bear the designer's name, but which he or she does not own, scattered across the globe and designed in Milan, down to the tiniest details, by other "creatives" (architects, industrial designers, experts in persuasive behavior), who have planned out the settings and modes of sale, then scrupulously assigned to other "executors" (display-window artists, representatives, salespeople). The system of industrial

Color Reference Chart for 1935. From *Apparel Arts*, Summer 1935

HAT....PORK
FELT...LIGHT WEIGHT FOR
SPRING AND SUMMER
USE....RESORT AND COUNTRY

TOP VIEW

FRONT ELEVATION

SIDE ELEVATION

HAT....HOMBURG
SPECIFICATION...STITCHED BRIM
USE....TOWN WEAR

FRONT ELEVATION

SIDE ELEVATION

COLLAR....LAUNDERED
SPECIFICATION...WIDE SPREAD
OPENING

USE..TOWN WEAR
WITH COLORED
OR WHITE...SOFT
OR STARCHED
SHIRTS

SHIRT....FOR TOWN WEAR
WITH NECKBAND

COLLAR...SOFT TAB
TO MATCH SHIRT

SHIRT....FOR TOWN OR
COUNTRY WEAR
SPECIFICATIONS....ROUND
COLLAR ATTACHED .. IN
SOLID COLORS AND PATTERNS

SHIRT....COUNTRY WEAR
SPECIFICATION...2¾" POINTED
ATTACHED COLLAR
PATTERNS...DEFINITE

TIES
1 MACCLESFIELD STRIPE
2 ¼" CHECKED
3 PLAID WOOL
4 WHITE GROUND
SPITALSFIELD

#2

#3

DETAIL PATTERN TIE #4

#4

"Illustrierte Sittengeschichte"
Eduard Fuchs   (wie E. 239 - reference)

Vol I
Plate 481
Page 51
Plate 224 (the 3rd of the engraving on the right
            hand side is what interests me)

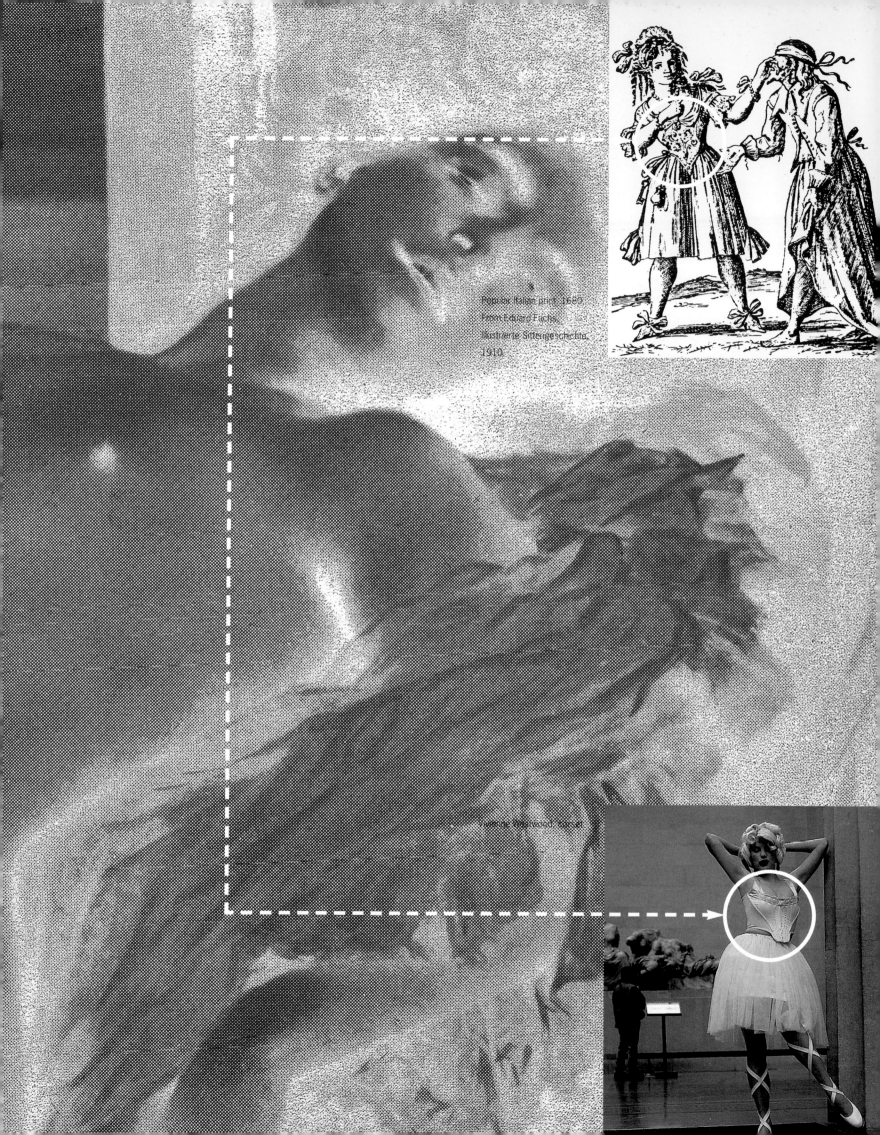

Popular Italian print, 1680
From Eduard Fuchs,
Illustrierte Sittengeschichte,
1910

Vivienne Westwood corset

design is partly different; here runway presentations are replaced by furniture fairs, and where it is the manufacturer (Cassina, Frau, Driade, etc.) who controls the system, commissioning the design of objects as needed from the designers that the manufacturer prefers. Let us now return to our famous designer. He or she has a central office in Milan (or Paris or London), where financial and commercial strategies are developed, along with joint ventures, aesthetic directions, advertising campaigns, spectacular social events, and various scoops. Here, the creativity has to do with strategic marketing, obtaining and investing financial resources, allocation of packets of stock shares, acquisition of models, the liturgy of fashion shows, communications, image creation, hiring concept people and technicians, and originality of the network of distribution.

A number of links in this chain (advertising, publicity, financial management, and organization of distribution, for instance) can be outsourced, mostly to Milan but also to New York, Tokyo, or other postindustrial cities. The conception and design of the clothing, shoes, and purses, however, increasingly takes place in Molise or Tuscany (just as in France it takes place in the Auvergne or Provence, and in Great Britain it happens in Scotland or Wales), next door to the factory where computers optimize the cutting of the fabrics, experts ready prototypes, and organizers handle the increasingly dense and vast network of contracts and subcontracts, all the way down to piecework done in the home.

As is evident, in each of these phases the creative aspect and the implementation intertwine, but the need for creativity increases as we move upstream through the processes that drive the entire system. Save for a very few rare cases—such as the incomparable Roberto Capucci, who still designs and shapes his creations alone, creations that are perhaps destined more to biennial festivals and museums than to runway presentations and wealthy matrons—behind the major labels there are no individual designers, only teams with processes of invention that reiterate (admittedly with some variants) the characteristics that are generally found in the organization of creative groups of artists or scientists.

Established in the same years in which the methods of industrial production were being developed, these groups inaugurated types of organization that, at first glance, might seem to have more to do with craftsmanship than with industry. But—when examined carefully—they are entirely original when compared to either craftsmanship or industry. Between the 1850s and the 1930s—while the United States, with Taylor and Ford, was developing brilliant methods for organizing workers into units of mass production—Europe was developing its own original methods for organizing creative groups

in the arts and sciences: the Institute Pasteur in Paris, the Stazione Zoologica in Naples, the Wiener Werkstätte in Vienna, the Bauhaus colonies of Weimar and Berlin, the Bloomsbury group in London, the Institute for Social Research in Frankfurt, the group of physicists working in Rome under Enrico Fermi. There are many excellent examples of this European approach to creative organization, which is in some sense a descendant of the glorious tradition of Renaissance workshops. These groups were the first to organize as networks, projects, integrated systems, or lobbies, and they took extreme and very modern care of image, production, distribution, their public relationship, and their own reputations.

The creative groups that work nowadays at various points in the chain of the fashion production system, though they are tempted by the siren's song of the traditional techniques of organization of industrial Taylorism, are nonetheless forced by their very nature to pursue a different sort of efficiency, with different techniques. In order to justify this statement I should illustrate, in general terms, just what I mean by "creativity." Silvano Arieti, who has written what is thus far the most persuasive exploration of the origin of the individual act of creativity *(Creativity: The Magic Synthesis)*, believes that the creative process consists of a synthesis between primary and secondary thought.

The *primary process*, for Freud, is a way in which the psyche functions, especially its subconscious portion. It prevails in dreams and in certain mental illnesses, especially psychoses. The primary process functions in markedly different manner from the secondary process, which is the way in which the mind works when awake and using ordinary logic. The mechanisms of the secondary process appear again in the creative process, in strange and complex combinations with the mechanisms of the primary process and in syntheses that, though unpredictable, are nonetheless subject to psychological interpretation. It is from the proper coupling of the mechanisms of the secondary process that these primitive forms of cognition, generally limited to abnormal layers or unconscious processes, become forces of innovation.

From my studies of teams of the past and those of the present, there emerges the need to enrich the creative process described by Arieti as a synthesis of primary and secondary thought through the addition of a further variable: it is, in fact, not merely a synthesis of conscious (secondary) and subconscious (primary) thought, but also a synthesis of the rational sphere and the emotional sphere. The intersection of the axis that links the emotional with the rational and the axis that links the conscious with the subconscious gives rise to four areas, two of which are of interest in this context: the area involving the emotional sphere and the subconscious level, i.e., imagination; and the area involving the rational sphere and the conscious level, i.e., concreteness.

Creativity, unlike what is generally believed, is not just imagination; it is, in fact, a synthesis of imagination and concreteness. A creative genius, then, is someone who manages to embody both a powerful imagination and an exceedingly concrete command of things. Most people, however, have different components of imagination and concreteness, but fail to develop them to the same degree: some people excel in one area, and some excel in another. In working groups, however, the disparity increases, because some groups (for instance, a group of artists) tend a priori to select only highly imaginative people, while others (for example, companies) tend to select only very concrete people.

The creative groups that worked in the late nineteenth and early twentieth centuries, assembled by such remarkable organizers as Dohrn, Gropius, Guccia, Hoffmann, Horkheimer, Pasteur, etc., opened unimaginable horizons of creativity, leading to the transition from small art and small science to big art and big science. In accordance with the basic underlying concept, sometimes tacitly and even subconsciously guiding these great leaders, there is no need to rely on individual geniuses (who are quite rare), each complete with equal amounts of imagination and concreteness. It is quite enough to assemble groups of individuals, some endowed with enormous imagination, others endowed with great pragmatic capability, so as to make "creative wholes" that generate ideas and solutions: collective geniuses, comprising a number of individuals who, taken separately, would not be considered genius material. Therefore, producing creativity in organizations involves the formation of finely balanced mixes of imaginative individuals and concrete individuals, each of them true to their nature and to themselves but willing to cooperate with profoundly different personalities.

Our famous fashion designer, by increasing his or her fame, increases the incandescence, the level of excitement in this climate, attracting a growing number of shareholders and consumers, creating an aura that makes his or her products the great fetishes of our time, and making his or her label a great church, with mani-

fold phantasmagoric rites. One can obtain an increase in creativity, especially if the variegated group of imaginative and concrete individuals is also cross-class, anti-bureaucratic, internationalist, universalist, attentive to the aesthetic aspect of things, with a bent for modern technology, inclined to work in a playful manner, solidly rooted in history but with an eye to the future, and capable of transforming limitations into opportunities, conflicts into stimuli, and competition into contribution.

All of these characteristics can easily be found in the creative links of the chain that constitutes the fashion system, a sphere distinguished by its atmosphere of enthusiasm, the charisma of its leaders, its freedom of expression and action, its destructured organization—in terms of time and space—its intellectual curiosity, its refined aesthetics—all found in the styles and places linked to the headquarters of the fashion designer—its public relations, and the array of locations in which its products are conceived and designed. And these "noble" phases of the overall process are sharply distinguished from the rough productivity of the "vulgar" phases (production, distribution, financial control), still bound up with the Taylorism that is traditional in industrial manufacturing. The method of industrial manufacturing still sets the rules wherever work—reduced to mere repetitive execution—can be done even by illiterates. But when a company insists on extending this approach to phases of the process that are distinguished by high levels of creativity, the result is nothing more than a loss of innovation, competition, and independence.

In postindustrial companies, the workforce—increasingly educated and cultivated—has growing analytic and intellectual skills; machines can perform nearly all repetitive tasks; the market especially values sophisticated and personalized goods and services. Everything, then, contributes to placing value on creativity, at least to the same degree that, in industrial society, mechanical labor was valued. At this point, the lead organization, the organization that is copied in practical terms by all other organizations, can no longer be the factory as Ford conceived it, with its most eloquent symbol in the assembly line. This preeminent role should be something related to scientific laboratories, film troops, or artist's ateliers. And the system of fashion, which cunningly succeeded in combining phases of implementation with phases of creativity, represents in an exemplary manner the transition from old industrial models of organization to new, postindustrial models of organization.

Fitting a corset in the
Ateliers Thierry Mugler
(detail).
Photo by Sebastião Salgado
(Contrasto/Magnum)

Overleaf:
Fitting a corset in the
Ateliers Thierry Mugler.
Photo by Sebastião Salgado
(Contrasto/Magnum)

FORM FOLLOWS FASHION: INDUSTRIAL DESIGN LOOKS TO FASHION

Stefano Casciani

Fashion prescribes the ritual by which the fetish of merchandise is adored.
—Walter Benjamin, *Paris: The Capital of the Twentieth Century*, 1939

A mass phenomenon by origin and genetically linked to the economic revolution of the postwar period, when Italy emerged from its underdeveloped condition, industrial design has been for many years a fundamental tool in the creation of an image of the Italian nation, bent on the achievement of its "magnificent and progressive destiny": products for everyone, mysteriously linked by a substantial degree of industrial beauty (efficiency was a secondary consideration) and developed by the experimental pioneers of remarkable materials and technical solutions. Unfortunately, in the face of this overdose of creativity, the theorists and stars of a design culture that was—much to its eventual surprise, about to become a world leader remained tied to strictly modernist viewpoints, a sort of demo-aristocratic idea of design: every product and every design was set forth, ideally, as a universal archetype, as a virtually unchangeable model of a closely linked form of behavior. The object itself was thought in some way to create this behavior, along with performing its function. Objectively (and the term is used advisedly), this approach produced models that now form the core of

collections in design museums around the world, representative of a period in which industrial design could actually be a form of invention: the lamps of Achille and Pier Giacomo Castiglioni, the furniture of Gio Ponti, the children's games of Enzo Mari, the typewriters of Marcello Nizzoli and Ettore Sottsass, the chairs of Vico Magistretti, and so on—these are all fossils of a golden age of industrial design, an age not likely to dawn again. All the same, these very objects are still fully valid, and in some cases are still produced and used.

An important issue, central now to any possible new prospects for industrial design, is the idea that a product may also be ephemeral—bound up with a passing taste, pop culture more than ethics. This is an issue that has emerged only recently, and even now encounters widespread resistance: on the one hand, from dogmatic academics who continue to perpetuate the demo-aristocratic ideology in teaching and in critical discussion, and on the other, from an illusory pretext of quality, infinitely improvable over time, that industry is obliged to support instead of openly avowing its role as a manufacturer of formal variants.

The structural factor that, in some sense, both approaches attempt to cover up is that of a historic transition, already complete, from the industrial system of production to that of virtual industry—i.e., a

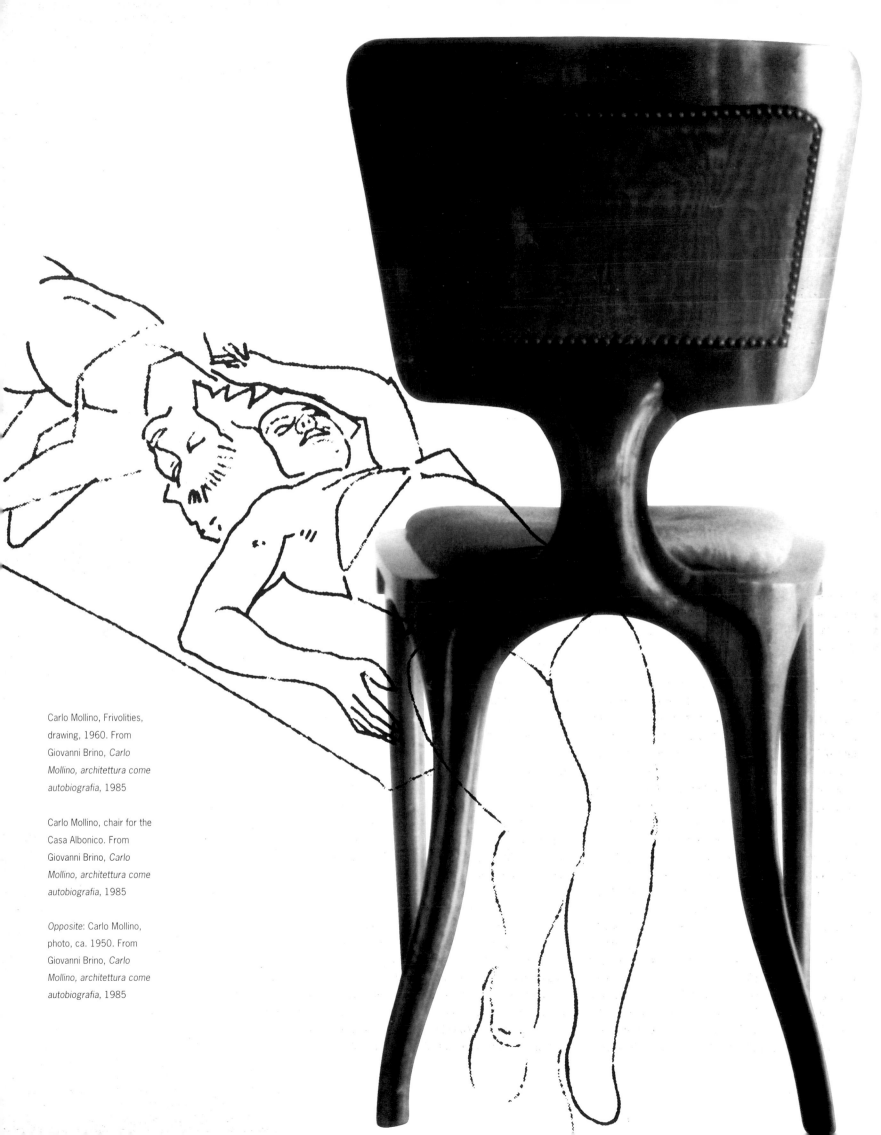

Carlo Mollino, Frivolities,
drawing, 1960. From
Giovanni Brino, *Carlo
Mollino, architettura come
autobiografia*, 1985

Carlo Mollino, chair for the
Casa Albonico. From
Giovanni Brino, *Carlo
Mollino, architettura come
autobiografia*, 1985

Opposite: Carlo Mollino,
photo, ca. 1950. From
Giovanni Brino, *Carlo
Mollino, architettura come
autobiografia*, 1985

system in which image, technology, design, and communications are organically intertwined, with the sole purpose of providing the consumer with products that are always "new" or, perhaps we should say, different, but which in any case create an image of a parallel universe, distant from the real universe, where to some extent the rules of the marketplace and mass psychological mechanisms become the rules of a perfect spiritual equilibrium, the engines of a virtual reality in a constant state of development.

Evidently, the fashion industry was the first to understand and adopt this new approach to design and manufacturing, articulated on the one hand in terms of classical financial and economic strategies, and on the other hand in the form of a number of essential rhetorical figures, such as the fashion designer, the collection, and the revival, figures that, already present in embryonic form in industrial design, were relegated to a secondary role, until it became necessary to adapt to a market moving toward globalization and cultural standardization.

Fashion Design and Industrial Design

It is no accident that for many years (certainly, throughout the period in which the concept of design was developing in Italy) the cultural debate over the problems of design furiously spun its wheels over the issue of the "definition" of design and designer: in the 1960s, theorists such as Maldonado were acclaimed as great thinkers merely for succeeding in formulating such a definition (though in truth, somewhat tautological), reconciling the opposite positions of aesthete and functionalist. Anyone who had dared in that period to define a designer as a *stilista* (from the exceedingly American term "stylist") would immediately have been banished from the collective discourse of design. And yet no one objected when a fashion designer was described as a "designer" (according to common use in non-English-speaking countries—in Germany, Jil Sander is a designer) or when the counterpart in the automotive industry is called a "stylist." In a singular sequence, the word that dared not say its name was rehabilitated by none other than the fashion system: fashion designers have become the new heroes of contemporary mythology, untouchable beings, capable of turning everything that they touch into gold, including mature industries of all sorts, provided that these industries decide to entrust the designers with their eyeglasses, bicycles, dishes, cups, and every other sort of antiquated knickknack.

The secret of these miraculous, miracle-working abilities, capable of sweeping away in just a few years all the religious fetishism of modernism, lies clearly in the patient insistence on the transformation of a system of action and thought capable of renewing itself every six months, staging on a daily basis an inimitable spectacle of communications through those silent actors we call models: always different and always the same, performing only and always a single myth cycle—that of beauty. Whether this myth is one of sadomasochism, dark style, grunge, street smarts, piercing, classic, or otherwise is of little or no importance. What matters is the allure that it exerts, the suggestion of an ideal world in which everyone is young, beautiful, and elegant. Anyone who purchases a suit, an accessory, or even just a soup tureen designed by Dolce & Gabbana, Romeo Gigli, Versace, or Gucci is buying a little piece of this dream.

Dressing Oneself and Furnishing Oneself

The important thing was to feed this system continually with new personalities (if not new ideas). The "high" model of the Italian furniture industry may well be the only industry capable of withstanding the impact of designer thinking, precisely because some time ago it borrowed its rhetorical figures, just as there has always existed a star system of Italian industrial design, against which the schools and the general critical discourse (and in a few rare instances, even the protagonists themselves) were largely helpless to find an alternate response, which might be more in keeping with their very demo-aristocratic ethic. Still, today we see no one capable of taking the place of the maestros—Castiglioni, Magistretti, Mari, Sottsass—with the possible exception of a plethora of fashion designers. It is perhaps indicative that the most spectacularly successful phenomenon of the last few years within the context of the star system is Philippe Starck, who did nothing more than amplify as much as possible the background noise generated by the cult of personality, so that the objects he designed—any and all critical judgment aside—in their perpetuation of a system of signs and forms typical of styling emerge as nothing more than incidental notes to a single and unified elegy, an elegy that proclaims the qualities of the hero Starck, a mighty chorus, comprising all of his manufacturers, wholesalers, retailers, and purchasers, all ready to take, as a spiritual communion, every last little sign that Starck distractedly jots on a sheet of paper. Even if we leave aside the effects of this mystical phenomenon on the psyche of the designer in question

Masanori Umeda,
Rose Chair, 1990

Opposite:
Outfit by Roberto Capucci,
set in an architectural design
by Gio Ponti.
Photo by Pino Guidolotti

138

Paco Rabanne, haute couture collection, spring-summer 1996: The Paco Rabanne catwalk show. Photos by Eric Robert (Sygma/Grazia Neri)

(first and foremost, the loss of a certain irony that had redeemed him in the past), the fact remains that Starck blazed the path to a strong identification of industrial design with fashion design, or between the industrial designer and the fashion designer.

Originating from the joint efforts of manufacturers, designers, and marketing managers—who all work in concert on a remarkable experiment of design genetics—the virus of fashion design is engendering an interesting array of hybrids. One typical case is the revival of British industrial design. Held in hibernation by years of repressive Thatcherism, overwhelmed by yuppie tastes (which tended to favor a sort of eclectic miscellanea over the feeble modernist expressivity of the British tradition), industrial design in the United Kingdom regained the spotlight through the emergence of a new generation of minimalist eccentrics. A group of designers that was welcomed en masse from the late 1980s on by Giulio Cappellini in the collections of Cappellini International (the most authentic, full-fledged equivalent in the world of furniture of what the fashion system is for the world of apparel and its derivatives)—Tom Dixon, Constantin Grcic, Matthew Hilton, James Irvine, Ross Lovegrove, Jasper Morrison, and Marc Newson—became the new stars of international industrial design, hastily drafted into the ranks of the industry hardest hit by crisis: the furniture industry. The result is a series of objects that are terribly repetitive in their literal fidelity to stylistic principles (however diverse they may happen to be), but for that very reason unquestionably successful, at least in terms of media. And it was precisely the mass media, completely agog over the fashion system (which ensures simple, modular, inexhaustible contents), that treated these industrial designers like so many fashion designers, as long—of course—as they were willing to adhere faithfully to the rule of self-imitation.

The phenomenon, however, proved uncontrollable. Reinforced by a great and eccentric alternative tradition, a number of young British designers have set themselves up as the true heirs to the idea of styling, designing outfits that are intentionally neopop, neo-minimalist, or whatever in a specific phase constitutes newness or simply a sufficiently unexplored revival (or a revival that has not been revived for a sufficiently long period of time) just like in British fashion, which cannot be worn by any "normal" human being but is terribly alluring in terms of media image. To what degree the Italian furniture industry has been helped by these fashion designers has yet to be shown, especially in the light of cases such as that of the Motò, designed by Philippe Starck for Aprilia in 1995: an effort to reconcile the formalism of the designer with the system of signs typical of the mystique of motor-

Styling from the 1950s
(Courtesy of Archivio Infinito)

Nuvola, Alfa Romeo prototype, 1996. (Courtesy of Archives Alfa Romeo)

cycles. It was largely rejected by the larger public of aficionados, who saw it is an affront to the fetishistic spirit, replaced by a vague visual "normalization" in a vortex of curves and countercurves. Even Starck's personal love for motorcycles, enhanced by the *Easy Rider* look, must not have been much help. (It seems that Ettore Sottsass, in describing a designer that he disliked, once said: "He is a motorcyclist.")

Style and Engines

In the new virtual dimension of the market, there is a particular episode that perfectly summarizes all of the contradictions of the fashion system, and it is that of the automobile: *the* product, almost by definition, and yet a holdover from an industrial phase of economic development, almost prehistoric in the context of the lifestyle of the society of information technology. The automobile is a piece of functional and ethical nonsense in the age of networks, of the end of resources, of commuter aircraft and high-speed trains. It is a genuine living fossil, kept alive on life-support systems by huge financial and industrial groups, flying desperately in the face of all human logic. The cost in fatal car crashes and pollution-engendered cancer is clearly not justified by the profits that can still be squeezed out of this object. A ridiculous caricature of a horseless carriage, especially in its low-horsepower versions, the automobile came close to extinction in the years of the energy crisis. In fact, it was during the energy crisis that the chassis scraped the aesthetic bottom. And cars have never really risen from that nadir, not even with the enormous quantity of industrial design that appears to have been added from the late 1980s and throughout the 1990s. What could have produced such a disparity between the use of intellectual and economic energy expended in this effort to preserve and mummify, and the formal result? Comparison with the fashion system may provide an answer.

Once upon a time (at least until the 1970s) there were cars built by Ford, BMW, Jaguar, Mercedes, Lancia, Alfa Romeo, Peugeot, Volvo, and even Fiat and later the Japanese: terrifying scale models of American cars, as if horrible cramps had crushed them down into mutant shapes and sizes. Meanwhile in Europe there glittered the stars of Italian body designers and manufacturers, saviors of the world auto industry (as in the case of Peugeot, ennobled by the tireless efforts of Pininfarina), who were treated snobbishly by their cousins, the architects and industrial designers, because they could never quite adhere to the demo-aristocratic logic. Blithely ignoring that logic, the manufacturers preserved their image and their market with questionable but certainly original models, with one quite distinct from the other. The

beginning of globalization spread panic and, in certain cases, extinction for these industrial dinosaurs. Aside from the recurrent jokes about the unification of major European companies (or even with Japanese companies—for example, let us not forget the case of the remarkable Fiat Arna), the rules in this field originated in Japan. Brilliantly turning the very weapons of European body design against their inventors, the Japanese manufacturers created the iconography of the turn-of-the-millennium automobile in a supreme exaltation of the rankest styling. Independent of any structural logic, the automobiles of every engine displacement and category have become rounded, organic, apparently inoffensive, and in short, user-friendly, a slogan in whose name the worst crimes are committed, such as making a Mercedes resemble a Ford Scorpio, a Volvo resemble a Fiat Marea, and a Fiat Brava resemble a refrigerator.

The code of recurring and inevitable signs, the possibility of disguising and personalizing one's own vehicle (as is the case of the new Smart, an offspring of a Swatch and a Mercedes), the exponential multiplication of colors—all of these things seem to be accessories in comparison with what seems like a nihilist thought: eliminating the idea of the automobile as a beautiful and useful object. And yet the reactions of the consumers, especially women, who seem to be favorably impressed by little monsters such as the Ford Ka, begin to make us wonder. If the design codes and the aesthetics of the end of the millennium are those of fashion, and if the intentionally ugly has full citizenship in this form of aesthetics and in these codes, then why should the industrial design of the automobile not have its own indulgence in a period of trash?

The Death of Versace

The great books have all been written, the great designs have all been sketched, the miniskirt has already been invented by Mary Quant. Like the Borges character who spent his life writing a chapter and a half of *Don Quixote*, like aging rock bands and operatic tenors who continue to cover old hits, for fashion designers as well (real ones) nothing remains but to attempt all of the combinations and references imaginable, or in the best case, to perpetuate a sort of manneristic autism, by means of which the recognizability of one's own product is assured.

While, however, the perfect compatibility between

Piero Fornasetti,

tie and dish

(Courtesy of Archivio Fornasetti)

Opposite:

Marc Sadler, Bap, safety

jacket for motorcyclist,

Ricerca e Sviluppo Dainese

Spa, 1994

(Courtesy of Archivio Dainese)

Alessandro Mendini,

Clothing Furniture,

performance, 1979

(Courtesy of Archivio Infinito)

the commercial system and glamour, between cash flow and high society—which distinguishes the experience of Italian fashion—has led Italy to seize economic leadership from other countries and to maintain that lead (if not in terms of creativity, then certainly in terms of the world market), the other areas of production of traditional consumer goods that have tried to adhere to this model have done so slowly and quite awkwardly. The attempts at styling in transportation and consumer electronics have been less than felicitous: even the case of the Swatch watch, now that the unquestionable innovative distinction of its beginnings has dwindled, is no longer an example; the owner, SMH, must now undertake other types of manufacturing diversification, such as the risky Smart car. The distinction of operations from gadget marketing is often a fine one, as is shown by the case of Alessi, obliged after a long phase of light production (various sorts of plastic figurines for domestic use) to return to the solidity of steel, though still with the design of old masters, from the late Aldo Rossi to Richard Sapper. And that is not to mention such absurd operations as that undertaken by the German industrial designer Dieter Sieger, who continues to offer things he creates to various manufacturers—from Arzberg to Ritzenhoff— while copying from Alessandro Mendini, Alchimia, and Memphis the idea of group creativity, functional decoration, and seasonal collections.

The true model of reference for the domestic object (the true test ground for the *solidità di uno stile*) still seems in many ways to have been the experience of Versace, in a certain sense rehabilitated by the death of the designer himself. Entirely aware of its transitory dimension, based purely on the reproduction of the motifs and ornaments of clothing on objects and surfaces (whether "design objects" or not is of no importance), the operation undertaken by Versace in the world of home furnishings had, if nothing else, the merit of sincerity, of wishing to declare nothing more than its own repetition, the statement that a Versace style (kitsch, obvious, garishly simplistic) exists, in any case, and can survive, even after the death of its creator. With the death of the physical person—the purification of the myth of untouchability, unattainability, of a heroic life lived beyond the reach of all earthly pain and suffering— this design experiment appears as exemplary and consistent. It restores to the virtual dimension of fashion—and of design that looks to fashion—its most basic qualities: ephemerality, mortality, joyous uselessness.

From top:

Mercedes Benz Class A

vehicle, 1997

(Courtesy of Mercedes Benz)

Prototype New Beetle

Volkswagen, 1997

(Courtesy of Volkswagen)

Prototype

Mercedes Benz-SMH, 1997

(Courtesy of Mercedes Benz)

Styling of the 1950s.
Development of the tailfins
on the 1954 (right) and 1959
Cadillac (left)
(Courtesy of General Motors)

Right:
Benelli K2 Scooter, 1997 model.
Detail of the bodywork
(Courtesy of Benelli Spa)

Raymond Loewy,
Coca-Cola vending machine,
1940
(Archivio Infinito)

ONE-TO-ONE ON-LINE: FASHION, THE INTERNET, AND THE ROLE OF DESIGN

John Thackara

"Only connect," said the English novelist E. M. Forster. "Everything is in connection with something else," echoed Goethe. "That which separates, is sin," thundered Nietzsche. Europeans are natural networkers, so we should not be surprised that they gave us the World Wide Web, which was developed at CERN, the particle-physics research facility in Switzerland.

But Europeans have not always been so good at exploiting their own inventions. Americans tend to be quicker on the uptake when they encounter new ideas. So when the first issue of *Wired* described the Internet as the "most important invention since the discovery of fire," Europe did not take it seriously—but Americans immediately went to work.

A few years later, various ways to exploit the Internet for business are being investigated and developed. The best way to think of the Internet is as a direct-to-customer distribution channel, whether it is for information, goods, or services; it bypasses the middlemen and fosters new relationships among producers, suppliers, and customers.

These new relationships are changing business processes and long-standing financial arrangements in profound ways. In the short term, connectivity, by allowing parties to communicate better with each other, squeezes out cost inefficiencies. But in the long term, consumers will perceive as "cost inefficiencies" the revenues and profits of many players in today's fashion system. The high profit margins enjoyed by distributors, communicators, publishers, and retailers will certainly be undermined by connectivity.

Electronic commerce is already gathering momentum. In the mid-1990s, forecasters believed that electronic commerce would total $20 billion by the year 2000. By late 1997, that figure had risen to $50 billion. My own view is that electronic commerce will grow even more dramatically once it builds momentum: the only unknown element is how long it takes for the boom to begin.

Electronic commerce will be delayed less by technological factors than by organizational and cultural inertia. And therein lies the danger for traditional industries such as fashion: by watching each other, rather than being on-line pioneers, fashion companies (and designers) may be taken by surprise when competitors enter "their" market from outside.

Outsiders have already penetrated other traditional markets by using the Internet. Take flowers: 1-800-Flowers, a very popular on-line enterprise in the United States, has grabbed a huge slice of the market in less than two years. This happened quickly because new benefits to consumers and business

Photo by Brad Branson.
Enhanced by Fritz Kok
(Courtesy of *The Manipulator*)

cost efficiencies interacted. Customers give the company a list of important anniversaries concerning friends, family members, and loved ones. A week or so in advance of each date, 1-800 Flowers e-mails customers a message like, "Do you want to send your mother flowers for her birthday?" Can you guess how they answer? The florist already e-mails 200,000 reminders to clients in a single year, and figures that its on-line customers spend three times as much on flowers as others; they also spend about $10 more per transaction. The whole operation is sublime.

In Great Britain, the supermarket chain Tesco created an on-line catalog of 20,000 products that people can order by phone, fax, or through the Internet, even specifying whether they would like their bananas yellow or green, and tomatoes firm or soft. Initial skepticism that consumers would not take to the new service was confounded by the rapid growth in popularity of the service. The Web site, which only serviced one part of London, quickly became one of the most visited Web sites in the country. Tesco now expects between 10 and 30 percent of such supermarket shopping to be done from home within five years. This has startling implications for retailing and urban planning—even the nature of home.

Research and development of the electronic-commerce infrastructure is picking up pace. Microsoft is just one of many developers creating systems that connect customers, suppliers, and producers. These so-called merchant services and supply-chain integration tools enable goods that were produced and distributed traditionally to be available via the networks in completely new ways.

Old Business, New Bottle

It is important to think about the Internet not as an exotic new business but as a new way to do old or existing business. This is certainly true for fashion, with its many small producers of textiles, shoes, accessories, and clothes. If these small companies, working alone or in clusters, can find a way to sell directly to the customer—which they surely will—then the whole fashion system will be transformed.

Any industry involving small companies working together stands to benefit from connectivity. There are nearly sixteen million companies in the fifteen countries of the European Union, for example.

Ninety-eight percent of these companies have less than fifty employees, but these small companies account for over two-thirds of all jobs in Europe and create the bulk of national wealth. And they do so locally. The vast majority of small- and medium-sized companies around the world operates within a radius of thirty miles.

Most of the early hype and rhetoric surrounding the Internet stressed its miraculous conquest of distance—"Wow, you can look at someone's home page in Australia"—but the likelihood is that the Internet will actually be most useful at a local level.

"Farm-to-Market" Fashion?

It is early to predict that some kind of on-line "farm-to-market" economy is emerging, but there are interesting hints of what may indeed be a startling change. One of these hints is the rapid but so far little-publicized growth of local exchange and trading systems, or LETS. An amazing array of sole traders and local businesses are discovering that it makes sense to receive payment in local barter currencies, which are given names such as "bobbins," "acorns," or "beaks."

What happens is that local people form a club to trade among themselves, using their own system of accounts. They compile a membership directory of offers and requests—goods, services, or items for hire—which are priced in local credits. Members use the directory to contact one another whenever they wish. By 1995, an estimated 30,000 people were participating in some 400 local LETS around the United Kingdom alone; similar networks have been established in sixteen other European countries. All this despite the fact that LETS is by and

Home page of the first issue of *Is Fashion Silly?*, fashion e-zine published by Pitti Immagine, 1995

(Archives Pitti Immagine)

large a completely manual system. People sit for hours in each other's kitchens filling out ledgers and sorting little bits of paper. If something so unwieldy, cumbersome, and slow can grow so quickly, its potential once on-line and accelerated up, as is now happening, could be fantastic.

Fashion is right in the middle of this phenomenon. People in developed economies spend about as much on clothes as they do on food—and the food chain is already being reconfigured by the Internet and smart logistics. It is only a matter of time before consumers start to demand closer contact with the people making their clothes—and also start to resist paying the high profit margins now taken by intermediaries.

Internet academics have coined the ghastly word "disintermediation" to describe the potential of the Internet electronic commerce to cut out the middleman. Internet connectivity among small businesses is growing fast. A report by the International Research Institute found in 1997 that six out of ten companies in the United States and Europe either use the Internet or plan to use it shortly. A big part of electronic commerce in the coming period will be business-to-business transactions. But the experience of other new technologies—for example, satellite dishes—suggests that consumers will get connected very quickly once they decide that the on-line world has something valuable to offer them. And what it offers is customization and lower costs.

Fashion and Customization

Although it is being presented in some business media as a new management fad, the concept of customization is the latest twist in a hundred-year-old struggle between standardization and customization. Back in the nineteenth century, for example, the department store Montgomery Ward boasted about the fifteen different kinds of penknives and sixty different kinds of clocks they were able to offer. Full-scale industrial alternatives to standardized production date back to 1923. Then, Alfred Sloan and Harley Earl introduced the annual model change at General Motors. When you consider that Ford's Model T began production in 1911, and that by 1924 a new model was launched every year, you could say that "pure" mass production (or Fordism) lasted precisely thirteen years. James Woudhuysen, a design-management professor, is adamant, saying that "customisation, insofar as it represents a longing for individuality, is the expression of very long-standing human desires."

Another reason for customization is that quality by itself no longer differentiates products and services. Quality is a starting point and is no longer the way to win. Consumers have become spoiled by the wide range of choices among more-or-less perfectly performing products. Customization is a logical response.

But a return to preindustrial modes of production is not imminent. An economy in which every product is made-to-order by a gnarled old craftsperson, wearing an apron and sitting at a workbench using ancient tools, makes an appealing advertising image—but it is a fantasy. Few enterprises will offer "pure" customization—a one-to-one service that offers people anything, anytime, anywhere.

What is happening is that companies are using degrees of customization in a range of responses to new market and technological conditions. Five degrees of customization have been identified by Professor Henry Mintzberg:

❶ pure standardization: epitomized by the Model T Ford

❷ segmented standardization: five varieties of cornflakes, but still just cornflakes

❸ customized standardization: customers select "extras" such as special buttons from menus

❹ tailored customization: for example, a suit based on a preexisting prototype that is nonetheless cut just for you

❺ pure customization—something made-to-order by an artisan

Mass Production in Lots of One

Customization confronts us all with new tasks of organizational design. It is not just about preindustrial ways of making things. A postmodern mood swing against mass society does not undermine the economic logic of large-scale production, even for small enterprises.

A simple question helps to clarify this issue: who is the customer, anyway? In the building industry, for example, the customer could be the architect, the contractor, the builder, or the client. In fashion, too, the customer might be a distributor, a mail-order company, a media conglomerate, or a consumer.

True customization—substantive, two-way interactions between suppliers and customers—resembles the economic relationships that prevailed before industrialization. But things today will never be the same. The scale and complexity of the infrastructure that makes customization possible in the new economy changes the nature of the process. Oliver Morton, in a special survey for *The Economist*, called it "mass production in lots of one."

In today's marketplace, the distinction between the terms "product" and "service" is becoming blurred. Consumers, who have become more discriminating, more aware, and more demanding, increasingly focus on more than the physical product and its functionality. Service and a sense of personal connection to the company become increasingly important. Service is becoming part of the product itself.

The scope of business processes is evolving in ways that we are only beginning to understand. A cloud of communication is enveloping enterprises and connecting them to each other, and to consumers, in unexpected ways. Most managers and entrepreneurs have been sensitive to their customers' needs and input for some time. They have been "customizing" without using the word. The trend is sure to continue—in thousands of different ways.

Design for Customization

In theory, customization offers people anything they want, at any time, according to any specification, anywhere they want. In practice, there are few markets in which companies can profitably offer true customization. Besides, evidence that consumers actually want all their products and services to be customized is mixed, to say the least. But given that the trend is toward customization, how can companies use design? What does it mean to design for customization?

First, customization needs connectivity—effective communication among the players. As production becomes more fluid, and design technologies interact with flexible manufacturing and prototyping technologies, a more or less direct informational connection between the enterprise and the consumer emerges, and it becomes possible to create unique objects to order.

Customization also demands that consumers become active participants in development processes, moving them closer to the core processes of the enterprise. This demands a new kind of infrastructure involving a flat organization and new work processes.

Most important of all are new distribution concepts. Logistics is one of the least glamorous but most potent support systems for continuous innovation and customization. Logistics, which is a bridge between demand creation and physical supply, makes products available. Logistics is an advanced form of customer service. The process of managing the storage and movement of materials, parts, and finished inventory from suppliers, through the firm, to the customer is a process that in the future will determine the success or failure of commercial fashion projects.

Conclusion: Only Connect

Flat organizations, new distribution channels, and close contact between customers and producers are processes, and these processes have to be designed. Manufacturing effectiveness has historically been viewed in terms of the physical flow of materials. Viewing manufacturing, including the fashion industry, in terms of information flows will be central over the next decade. Customization will be delivered, to varying degrees, by information systems that support adaptive production. The result will be evident in the product—but the means will be achieved by a continued move away from matter to service.

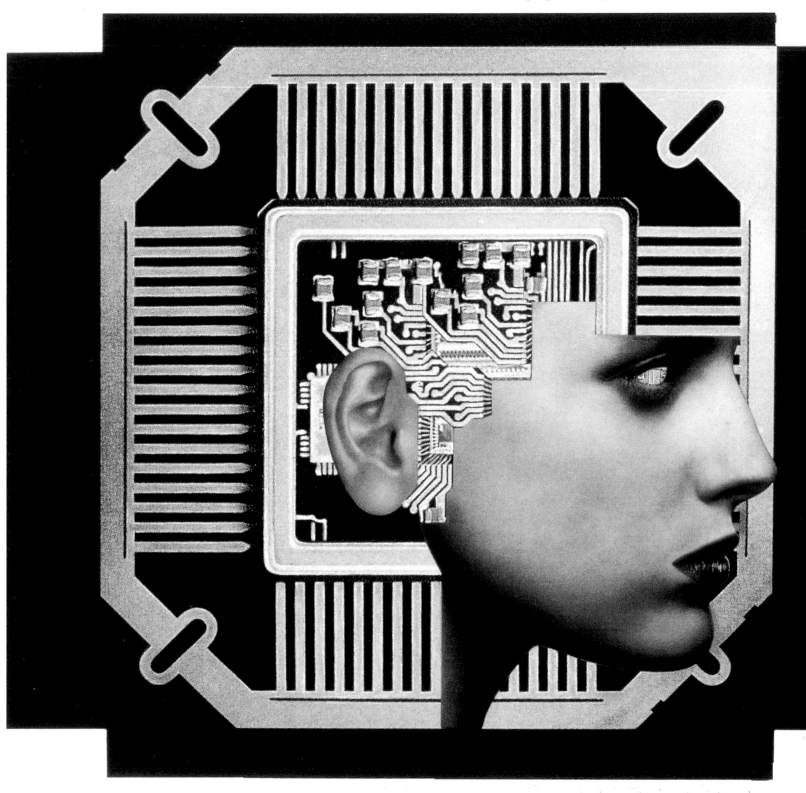

Deena des Rioux, *64 Pins*, digital graphics on polyester, 1997 (Courtesy of Silicon Gallery, Philadelphia)

BUSINESS, AND INDUSTRY

THE STYLE ENGINE

G.M.

That which is well known, because it is well known, is actually quite unfamiliar. Fashion is seen by everybody; it offers an everyday spectacle; its appearances are numerous and seductive. The discourses that fashion can generate are endless and endlessly repeated. What is difficult to see is the engine that drives fashion, the industrial organization that produces it. And yet this is one of the most interesting and original aspects of fashion, an aspect that links up with the concrete plane that lies beyond its apparent frivolity and insubstantiality.

The fashion industry generates an important economic flow, producing wealth in an exceedingly complex and original manner, and it is one of the industries that is not only surviving but prospering in a time of overall dematerialization of merchandise. Fashion is a hybrid industrial product, the result of a combination of material and immaterial elements. Fashion products are material goods with cultural content, similar in many ways to the film, pop music, or software industries.

Fashion creates wealth by combining in a single product fibers and meanings, fabrics and signs. The same product may have a different value according to the quantity of fashion that it contains: a cotton T-shirt, for instance, if it contains fashion, if it has style, will bring a higher price than one without such content. The activity of the textiles industry, which is the primary component of the fashion industry at large, is not merely the production of fabrics; it also transfers various messages "into" fabrics. The apparel industry performs a similar role in the production of outfits that are, in the final analysis, forms meant to sheathe their wearers with visual messages. For that matter, the consumption of fashion is itself a hybrid activity, somewhere between material and immaterial, functions of use and functions of meaning. The transformation of the fashion industry into a hybrid cultural industry is a recent one. It occurred in conjunction with the development of increasingly flexible and dynamic technologies within the various companies and with the devel-

156

opment of mass media in society, encouraging the circulation of information and entertainment, and enhancing their influence on everyday life.

The introduction of innovative technologies has profoundly modified the organizational models of industrial manufacturing. The old industrial capitals of Europe and America are full of abandoned industrial areas. More than 20 percent of Milan, the venue offering the greatest visibility for Italian fashion, is occupied by enormous machine-tool, steel, and chemical plants and factories, now padlocked and empty.

Many forms of classical industrialization in the oldest industrialized nations have disappeared. The fashion industry, which in Italy is the second-largest category in the trade balance and alone pays for the foreign debt created by Italy's importation of petroleum, was one of the first industries in the 1970s to abandon the old idea of the huge factory with assembly lines as too rigid and colossal to adapt to a continually changing manufacturing cycle; the industry succeeded in reorganizing into an informal structure with small, specialized production units. Fashion did not create the districts, the suburban or outlying areas where the small and midsized companies that perform a number of various interconnected activities are located. But this varied system of location of the companies, which is also a varied system of relationships among the various phases of the manufacturing process, has become its most distinctive model. The prevalence of the network-style organizational system was largely determined by the need to speed up product innovation, a typical requirement of the fast-changing market of fashion. Fashion innovation, for that matter, does not involve a technological quality in a new function, but rather in a new form, a new color, a new cultural quality of the product—in other words, a

new collection. In all of the companies that belong to the textiles and apparel industry (threads and yarns, fabrics, apparel), production is retooled at least every six months. While a product of the "classical" industries usually has a life span of at least a couple of years, and in many cases of many years, fashion products must necessarily change in order to adapt to cultural shifts in taste. This continual evolution calls for an overall organization and a process of control and oversight that are quite sophisticated, with creative skills employed to crucial effect at every step of manufacture, from yarns and threads to prototypes to the communications—advertising and publicity— that accompany the finished products. It is only in this way, which in the final analysis is a process of cultural processing, that the system of fashion manufacturing succeeds in ensuring a continual consonance with the shifts in mass culture, which is the context in which fashion products acquire meaning and value.

Seest thou not, I say, what a deformed thief this fashion is, how giddily 'a turns about all the hot-bloods between fourteen and five-and-twenty? . . . All this I see, and I see that the fashion wears out more apparel than the man. But art not thou thyself giddy with the fashion too, that thou hast shifted out of thy tale into telling me of the fashion?

W. Shakespeare, *Much Ado About Nothing*, 3.3

THE RATIONALITY OF THE FASHION MACHINE

Andrea Balestri and Marco Ricchetti

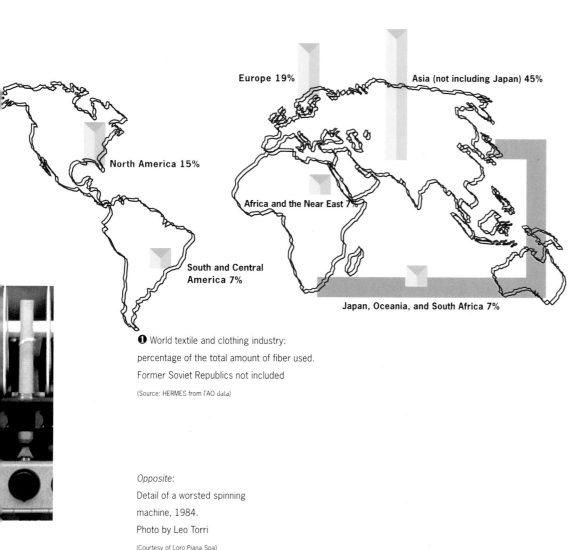

Europe 19%

Asia (not including Japan) 45%

North America 15%

Africa and the Near East 7%

South and Central America 7%

Japan, Oceania, and South Africa 7%

❶ World textile and clothing industry:

percentage of the total amount of fiber used.

Former Soviet Republics not included

(Source: HERMES from FAO data)

Opposite:
Detail of a worsted spinning
machine, 1984.
Photo by Leo Torri
(Courtesy of Loro Piana Spa)

The Textile and Apparel Industry, and the Supply of Fashion Products

The production of clothing is found virtually everywhere on earth; it is one of the oldest activities recorded by history. ❶

This activity has taken a variety of forms, differing in terms of raw materials, manufacturing processes, aesthetic codes, and final products. Every people and every nation has its own specific array of techniques, lore, and knowledge applied to the production of threads, yarns, fabrics, and finished garments. Linked to this body of professional knowledge and experience, accumulated over centuries of manufacture of textiles for clothing, we find a number of the most distinctive manifestations of the cultural identity of nations and peoples, such as the kimono or the sari. Moreover, the apparel textiles industry is a major source of jobs, as well as an important component of the many economic systems around the globe.

The manufacture of yarns, threads, fabrics, and clothing—even when, as is the case in many parts of the world, this industry attains a high degree of technical refinement or results in a vast and expressive array of costumes—is still not the same as the complex variety of manufacturing activities and services that we think of when we use the term "fashion industry." Technical knowledge and skills and exceedingly refined manufacturing traditions are certainly major components; the fashion industry, however, adds an important design dimension, which is capable of providing a continual and varied flow of products. This dimension is marked, in particular, by the ability to single out, in an international context, the spirit of the time in all its variability. Thus, the fashion industry provides consumers not only with clothing but also with an existential platform, on which they can find recognition, establish their own identity, and keep that identity up-to-date. To paraphrase a famous motto of Charles Revson, founder of the Revlon Corporation, we might say that in our factories we manufacture clothing, but in our stores we sell hope.

It is precisely the combination of the general body of technical and organizational knowledge, the ability to forecast the desires of consumers, and the ample use of the tools of communication that sets the fashion industry apart, distinguishing it from the mere production of yarns, threads, fabrics, and clothing. The fashion industry, from this point of view, is not limited to a given array of fabrics or outfits, but rather consists in the ability to create a substantial mass of new products, with a strong cultural content that is in tune with the desires of consumers in a sizable portion of international marketplaces.

Fashion products are inextricably tied to the development of the customs that they attempt to accommodate and rely on innovation and publicity. For this reason, the organizations that generate these products make use of a broad variety of competitive tools: technical skills, the aesthetic sense, intuition, rationality, risk and initiative, and operating routines. Put in those terms, the question of the economic foundations of the fashion industry can be examined through a number of immediately evident methodological problems.

One of these problems, which is particularly confusing and complex, has to do with the definition of the boundaries that mark the area occupied by the fashion system on the interior of the apparel textiles industry, and the evaluation of the portion of that industry that can be said to involve the manufacture of fashion goods. A second problem involves breaking down the value of articles of clothing (expressed by the retail price) into the components generated by immaterial and knowledge-intensive functions, which create both the surplus value of fashion and the simple manufacturing activities. Then there is a third problem of equal importance: that of supplying an economic explanation for the enormous material and immaterial investments that at least twice a year the fashion system makes in terms of sample lines, fairs, spectacular events, and advertising and publicity.

The Importance of Fashion in the Textiles and Apparel Industry

In order to respond in a systematic way to the first problem, one would need the patience and working method of an entomologist. An almost insurmountable obstacle in an undertaking of this sort is constituted by the nature of the statistical sources available and the systems whereby manufacturing processes and products are currently classified on an international level.

In the same spirit in which, in the second century A.D., Ptolemy presented the cosmological foundations of astronomy, we have attempted to estimate the relative dimensions of fashion manufacturing, borrowing a number of concepts from the work of a group of American economists and sociologists—especially Gary Gereffi, Terrence Hopkins, and J. Wallerstein. These authors have carefully analyzed the sources of supply for the distribution of apparel in the United States, making a distinction among three types of channels: boutiques, department stores, and generic clothing stores. The conclusions they have reached in their work are of particular interest, because they have to do with a major market (the United States) and because they distinguish explicitly between fashion products (fashion oriented) and simple apparel (mass market). In chart ❷, the various countries that export clothing to the United States are arranged in a series of concentric circles (which are, in fact, reminiscent of those theorized by Ptolemy). The central nucleus represents the suppliers of the boutiques (the most specific channels for fashion products). As we move toward the outermost circles, we find lines of products with less and less fashion content. The research undertaken has shown that the countries that supply the boutiques are Italy, France, Great Britain, and—to some extent—Japan. In the next two circles, which show the suppliers of department stores, we find countries

❷ **Production frontiers for global sourcing by U.S. retailers: the apparel industry**

Retailers and Main Sourcing Areas

• *Fashion-oriented companies, rings 1, 2:*
Armani, Polo/Ralph Lauren, Donna Karan, Gucci, Hugo Boss, etc.

• *Department stores & specialty chains, rings 2, 3, 4:*
Bloomingdale's, Saks Fifth Avenue, Neiman-Marcus, Macy's, Liz Claiborne, The Gap, The Limited, etc.
(generally better quality and higher priced goods than those sourced by mass merchandisers and discount stores)

• *Mass merchandisers, rings 2, 3, 4:*
Sears Roebuck, Montgomery Ward, Woolworths

• *Discount stores, rings 3, 4, 5:*
Walmart, K Mart, Target

• *Small importers, rings 4, 5*

(Source: Gereffi, 1994)

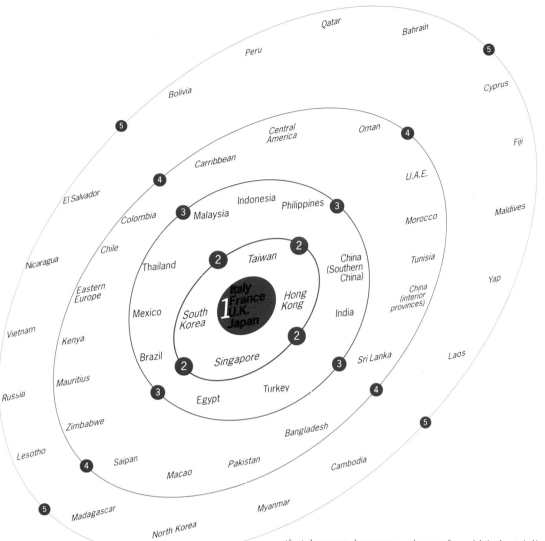

❸ The importance of fashion in global apparel export

(Source: HERMES from WTO data)

that have undergone a phase of rapid industrialization over the last quarter century (Central and South America and the Far East), where major American labels often operate their own factories or have outsourcing arrangements. And lastly, in the outermost circles, we have countries that constitute the latest generation of suppliers, with standard products, where price is the sole competitive advantage.

This set of circles constitutes a useful framework for understanding the scale of the high-surplus-value manufacturing of fashion products, which we can estimate at roughly 30 to 40 percent of the total value of world apparel exports. One important fact is that, of this share, one-third comes from just three counties: Italy, France, and Great Britain. **❸**

Risk in the Manufacturing Chain Involving Textiles, Apparel, and Distribution

The fashion industry that developed in the wake of the spread of ready-to-wear during the late 1960s laid its foundations on the difficulties intrinsically bound up with the forecasting of the direction of consumer tastes in terms of size, shape, weight, color, use, and price. In countries with high per capita income, the market has long since been transformed into a mosaic of segments comprising ever smaller numbers of consumers, whose purchasing decisions are an act of affirmation of personal identity and so

many expressions of desire. This has led to an incremental change, both in the variety of styles of dress and in their variability over time.

The personalization of consumption and consumer goods can be seen in a particularly eclectic style of dress. The growing possibility of choosing from among an extensive array of clothing multiplies the complex problems involved in attempting to align production with the shifting demands of the marketplace. In every season, in every shop that sells clothing, there takes place a confrontation and comparison of the decisions made by the customers and consumers with the decisions made by the owners of the shops and, indirectly, with those made by the manufacturers of threads, yarns, fabrics, and apparel. The costs of discrepancies between the choices made by the consumers and the decisions made by store owners and manufacturers are of substantial importance and can be even greater than many of the more usual cost components found in manufacturing, both to the system of distribution and to the industrial sector.

Prior to the advent of the ready-to-wear clothing industry, in the atcliers of the major couturiers this problem simply did not arise, or in any case the risks were quite limited. In absolute terms, only a relatively small number of items were being produced, and those items were cut and sewn only after the customers had expressed their choices with a formal contract (a deposit). The risk of problems of assortment was limited to the stock of fabrics purchased. This situation changed radically once items were being produced on an industrial scale (thousands and tens of thousands of items) without any type of contract or commitment on the part of the end consumers.

The new fashion system that has developed over the past three decades presents itself as a world of spectacle, but it is, in reality, an organic set of conventions established among manufacturers, created over time to contain the risks inherent in the unpredictability of consumers' choices. The display windows of shops, labels of the designers, and runway presentations are nothing more than the visible tip of an iceberg, an enormous piece of a greater machinery, comprising organizations and events whose role it is to channel the exceedingly varied supply of products with short life cycles, while also keeping those products in line with the decisions of

consumers. In other words, a set of forces, a field, is created in which supply and demand are structured in accordance with the material—and especially immaterial—properties and qualities that surround the basic functions (the need to clothe oneself, folk traditions, and so forth). The considerable size—in terms of resources allocated—of this component of the complex fashion machine might at first glance seem disproportionate, but it can be understood, in economic terms, by examining the specific characteristics of the products and the markets around which it is structured. ❹

The Coordination of Production and Distribution

The consumption of clothing does not follow linear, predictable lines, and above all, the forces that drive that consumption change continually; thus, marketing plans have exceedingly brief life cycles. The insatiable demand for new things, on the one hand, and the explosion of arrays of and variants on products, on the other, work together to make the problem of coordinating decisions concerning both demand and supply (models, quantities, colors, price ranges, delivery times) more complex.

The comparison between the manufacturing programs adopted by producers and distributors, and the actual choices of consumers takes place several months after the fact, well after the supply decisions of the shopkeepers (sell-in) and the manufacturing decisions of the industry have been irrevocably made. The venue in which the comparison is made are clothing stores. The operators of retail outlets order "in the dark" and thus, in the final analysis, commit to paying for the clothing that they reasonably expect to sell. Their guiding light, the polestar by which they navigate, is the information that they have accumulated over time, their sensibilities and sensitivity to style, and the financial resources of the particular group of customers that frequent their stores. If the storekeepers' predictions prove to be wrong, the unsold merchandise will crowd the shelves, becoming an increasingly awkward and burdensome presence. This inevitably leads to the collective ritual of the end-of-season sales; in the Italian market, these mark-downs now account for 18 percent of all clothing purchases by Italian families. The costs of these forecasting errors are largely borne by shopkeepers, which drives them to search constantly for new ways of reducing their risks.

The problem of coordinating industrial and distributive decision making within the fashion system, however, is not limited to the assortment of products

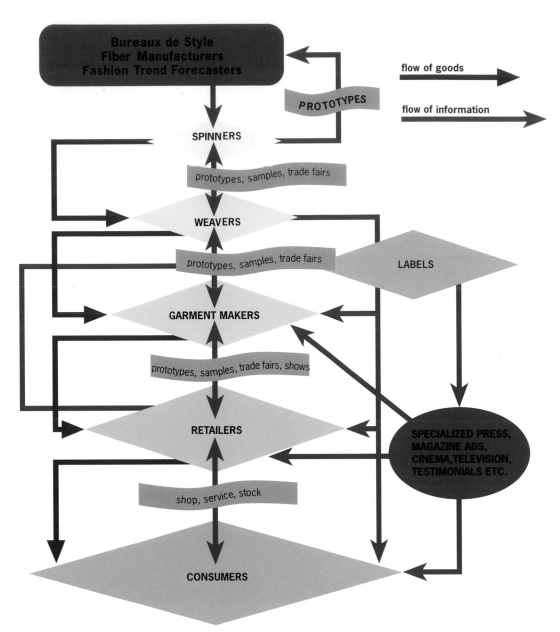

in clothing stores. Rather it is continuously present throughout the entire chain of production and demands the alignment of the decisions of a considerable array of players, from the production of fibers to the actual assembly of the clothing, including the production of yarns, threads, and fabrics. Unlike what happens between shopkeeper and consumer, however, in the relationships between manufacturer and retailer, and among the manufacturers in the various stages of the manufacturing cycle, risk is reduced through the adoption of a system of manufacturing to order. In theory, production begins only when there are signed contracts: everything that is manufactured, therefore, has already been sold, and contracts are not signed on the basis of manufactured merchandise, but only on designs. The designs are materialized with the creation of prototypes (samples, collections).

A second important form of risk reduction has to do with the process of selecting among the designs. This process is lengthy and complex, and comprises the examination and evaluation of thousands of pos-

❹ Markets, products, information: the force field of the fashion industry
(Source: HERMES)

Preceding pages:
Angelika Ullhofer, 1988, outfit by Versace.
Photo by Pino Guidolotti

NUMBER OF FABRICS DEVELOPED BY WEAVERS

(over 60,000 exhibited at Premiere Vision)

NUMBER OF FABRICS INCLUDED
IN COLLECTIONS

NUMBER OF FABRICS
BOUGHT
BY THE MARKET

5 Selection of fabric
variants
Source: HERMES

sible variants, the comparison of designs in the various stages of production, the consideration of information concerning social and cultural trends, and the filtering of the whole process through a set of sensibilities developed and refined over time. It ultimately leads to the trends of a single season: colors, cuts, materials, and new products. This result, from the point of view of the consumer, is generally perceived as the product of a flash of creative genius that, amazingly, is unleashed in a coordinated manner in the houses of the leading designers. The operation of this marketplace—in which there is a confrontation between designs, which take the form of prototypes, samples, and collections, on the one hand, and sensibilities and programs of future sales, on the other—solidifies in an intense exchange of ideas and information.

It is worth pointing out that, save for special cases, the intellectual ownership of the production of yarns, threads, fabrics, and clothing cannot be patented or protected. The investments made by various manufacturers translate, once they are made public, into information that can be easily appropriated by the competition at no cost. Something similar can also be found among consumers, where interpersonal relationships lead to the attribution of a special value to the exclusivity (personal or in terms of groups) of the outfits or the shoes that are worn.

The intensity and sheer volume of information being circulated can be shown by just a few statistics. At Première Vision (the best-attended fair of the worldwide textiles and apparel system), according to figures provided by the operators of the fair in

chart **5**, every six months the participating companies present some 60,000 fabrics, with fabric offered in an average of ten different colors. The companies in the textile district of Prato (the largest agglomeration of manufacturers of fabrics for the apparel industry) boast that every six months their sample lists—examined attentively by tens of thousands of fashion manufacturers and designers—offer an array of 60,000 new fabrics, with their set of various colors.

The long process of selection—through meetings, discussions, and exchanges of information—progresses to a reduction of the array of choices and a restricted and more consistent set of variants. Every season, well ahead of the actual appearance of the products in the stores and roughly two years before the items are displayed on shelves, the Bureaux de Style (a number of specialized institutions), along with manufacturers of chemical fibers, associations of manufacturers of natural fibers, and other public institutions, publish an array of heavily illustrated books, prepare color charts, and suggest new concepts. This is the first input of information received by the fashion machine. As soon as this information begins to circulate, however, it loses its one-dimensional nature. The spinning mills—who are part of the earliest stages of the textile chain of production—react to the initial indications and suggestions and produce the first samples, which are then taken into consideration by the Bureaux; some of these samples are entered into Bureaux reports. In all of the stages of the manufacturing cycle—from thread or yarn to finished outfit—it is the material aspects of the product—manifested in prototypes and samples of thread, yarn, or fabric—that determine its success or rejection. A long series of individual meetings, discussions, and exchanges of information and ideas, then leads to a progressive reduction in the field of offerings. At this point, the weavers establish a new and broader body of communications and circulation of information: once again, models, prototypes, and samples are presented, and the foundations are laid for the collection that will be presented at the textiles fairs, which are held just following the yarn and thread fairs.

By the time the yarn and thread fairs take place, work on the collections for the textiles fairs is already well underway; in turn, the clothing manu-

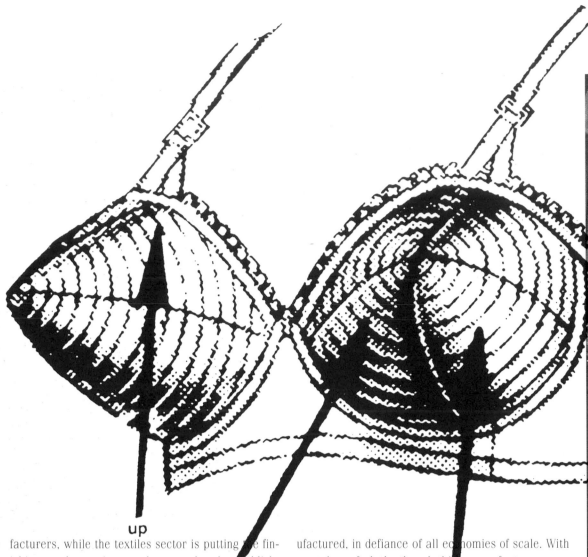

up

strong

hard

FIORUCCI

facturers, while the textiles sector is putting the finishing touches on its samples, are already establishing the overall features of the collection they are planning. Members of the various sectors meet at the fairs where—following a careful examination of feels and finishes and stitchings, and a thorough selection of samples—a certain number of threads and yarns and fabrics are chosen, each in a variety of colors. The design directors of the clothing collections, with the array of samples they have picked up at the various fairs, prepare their first sketches, and then make selections from those initial drawings. The place where this entire complicated process attains a unified whole is at the fair. By the time the fair occurs, as we have said, part of the overall task of orientation and selection has already been completed. The fair presents a series of reasonably well-defined themes. But it is at the fair that each manufacturer puts its information on the table, displaying the results that have been subjectively developed over the lengthy process of the preceding months. The fair is the culmination of this laborious process, everyone communicates everything, and there is maximum circulation of information in the system, in a confined space and over a short period of time.

Next begins the production of samples to be sent to customers. Here, too, as with the production of prototypes shown at the fairs, single items are man-

ufactured, in defiance of all economies of scale. With swatches of cloth, the clothing manufacturers can complete the clothing prototypes, which they then present in meetings with retailers, in runway shows, and at fairs. The production of prototypes constitutes a trump card of remarkable importance, as is demonstrated by the great amount of time purchasing managers of clothing manufacturers devote to feeling the finish of fabrics or materials for knitwear, or the great attention paid to runway presentations.

We have therefore worked our way around to our starting point, the point where the decision is made concerning sell-in on the part of the retailer. The retailer must select and determine not only the size of the order but also its makeup in terms of lines, styles, and colors, and its consistency in terms of prices. In theory, it is only after this crucial passage that the real process of production is activated, more or less simultaneously, in every link of the chain. We say in theory because of the lead time required in every phase of production (spinning, weaving, finishing, and assembly): fabrics need to be produced several weeks before finished garments, threads and yarns need to be ready several weeks before fabrics. The consequence of these delays is that part of the fabric orders placed by garment makers (and of threads and yarns by the spinning mills) actually take place in the dark, before cus-

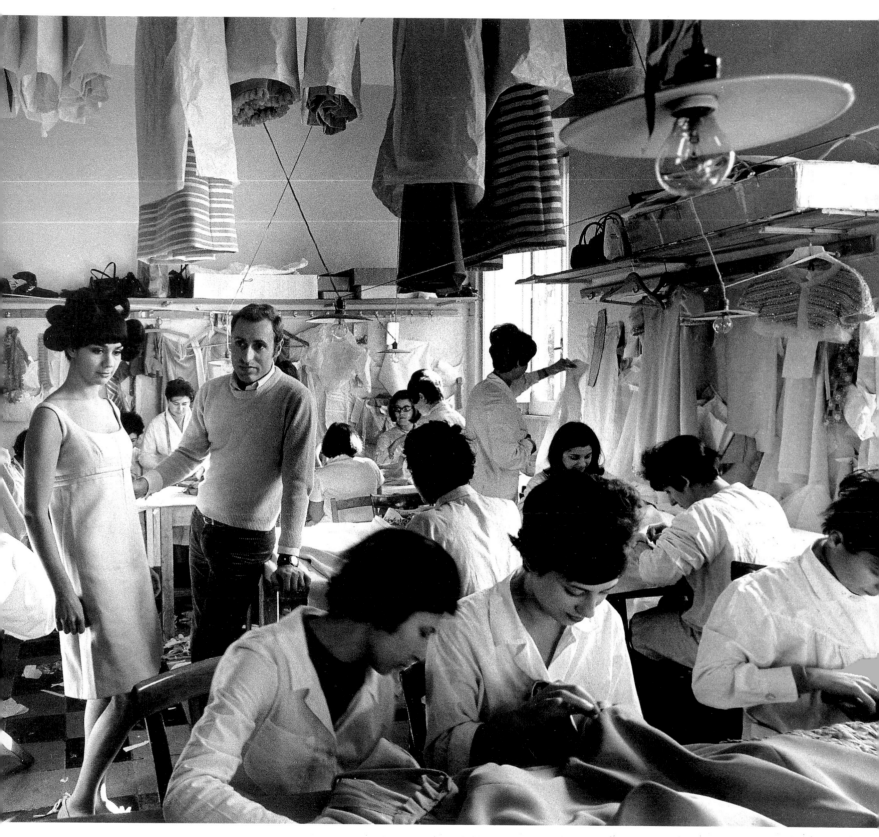

Fashion atelier.

Photo by Gianni Berengo Gardin

(Contrasto)

tomers have placed their orders. This makes the intense exchange of ideas and information that precedes orders and manufacturing even more important.

In any case, at the end of the process that culminates in the apparel fairs the system has established a general alignment with regard to the chief trends, colors, and themes that each designer and company will interpret in accordance with its own positioning on the market and its own style—thus, the risk for the system as a whole, and for the individual companies, has been considerably reduced. There remains, nonetheless, the single most important point of uncertainty. A single, decisive subject, the consumer, has apparently had no input into this circuit of communications. Only apparently, however—in fact, communications have overflowed from the sector of the professionals into that of the specialty fashion media and the more general channel of the mass media; they have intertwined with the production of culture and entertainment, and runway presentations and fashion labels have attracted the attention of the consumer and, in general, of public opinion at large. The ground has been prepared, therefore, so that the choices of the consumer, and especially the desires of the consumer, should be in line with those that the industry is ready to satisfy.

The Creation of Value

We have already referred to the difficulties involved in establishing distinctions between simple textile and apparel products and the products of the fashion industry. For these same reasons, we find another complex issue when we try to break down the value of clothing between basic product and surplus value, further complicated by the immaterial functions that are specific to fashion. In economic terms the fashion industry is a powerful engine that increases the value of the simple activities of the manufacture of yarns, threads, fabrics, and apparel. ❻

The methods for creating surplus value are many: research into manufacturing processes and new products, design, the production of prototypes (the sample ranges of the threads and yarns or the fabrics and the collections of outfits), the routine activities of marketing, runway presentations, showrooms, royalties, communications, the location of the retail outlets, and the preparation of display windows. There should be no difficulty in recognizing the contributions of all of these functions to the creation of surplus value in terms of fashion. In the case of the location of the sales outlets, however, we should emphasize a few interesting aspects. Under normal conditions, the costs of rental space are limited to

the display of products and the accommodation of potential customers; these are fundamentally technical matters. Given the same floor space, however, the differences in rental costs for a shop in a normal shopping center and for a prestigious boutique on the via Montenapoleone in Milan or on the via della Vigna Nuova in Florence come under the heading of fashion functions. Location in certain shopping areas constitutes a powerful communications tool, which enables customers to single out a number of selective reference points in the vast map of tens of thousands of options that are available to those customers when they decide to purchase new clothing. The function of communication served by the retail outlet is so critical that fashion manufacturers are beginning to seek direct control of those outlets, so as to have close contact and unfiltered communications through display windows, the layout of the store, customer service, and the ideal assortment of products. Out of this toolbox of instruments that add value to fibers and simple manufacturing activities, we might mention the resources devoted to transactions performed throughout all of the links of the production chain: gathering information, finding partners, establishing specific techniques, and planning the assortment and timing of production.

Concerning runway presentations—which in terms of function fit into the intersection between communications and marketing—there is not much left to say. Far more important in general terms of coordinating the manufacturing decisions are the trade fairs, where nearly all members of the industry

❻ Value chain in the fashion system

(Source: HERMES)

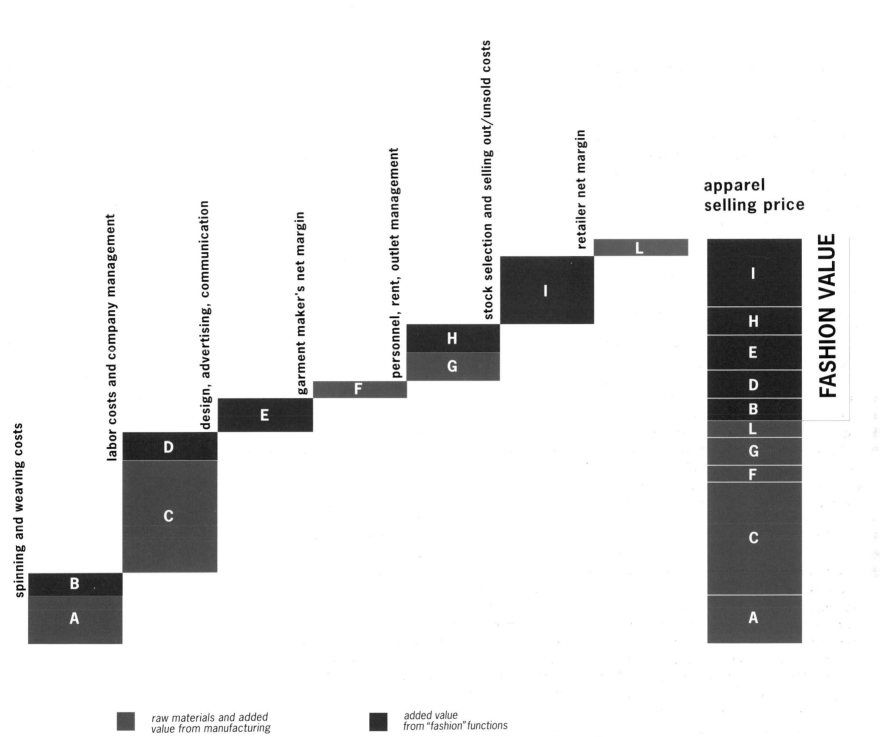

spinning and weaving costs

labor costs and company management

design, advertising, communication

garment maker's net margin

personnel, rent, outlet management

stock selection and selling out/unsold costs

retailer net margin

apparel
selling price

FASHION VALUE

raw materials and added
value from manufacturing

added value
from "fashion" functions

❼ Added value created by "fashion" functions:

style and design consultants; royalties; prototyping; new product design, research, and engineering; marketing; participation in trade fairs, shows, showrooms; stock selection costs; communications, promotion, showcases, and outlet location

(Source: HERMES)

(along with the powerful mass media) meet to exchange information. Despite this powerful organizational machine, which in a certain sense is similar in function to the role that stock exchanges play in the capital markets, a major part of the costs of coordination and synchronization of decisions among various actors in the fashion system is comprised by errors in forecasting. A number of well-known management consulting companies have estimated that, in terms of percentage of apparel retail prices, the stock that remains unsold by the end of the season amounts to 15 to 20 percent. By extending this method to other categories in the operating cost of stores and the manufacture of apparel, we can estimate, with some degree of accuracy, the portion of added value explained by fashion functions. ❼

This simple exercise in accounting casts a completely new light on the world of fashion. For example, if we call the retail price of an article of clothing 100, the costs of the component fibers are equal to no more than 3 to 4 percent. In the case of textiles, that percentage rises to 10, but roughly one-third of this same category of cost is accounted for by fashion functions: that is how much manufacturers of cottons and wools spend on research into new products, production of samples, style consulting, marketing, participation in fairs, coordination of production, and publicity and advertising. As the reader may note, the costs to shops of errors of assortment are certainly higher than the cost of fabrics, threads, and yarns used in the manufacture of a jacket or a sweater, and it is the substantial weight of those errors (which in real terms, for the Italian market alone, amounts to billions of dollars) that ultimately justifies the investment into research, design, marketing, and publicity and advertising.

If we return to our initial problem, our calculations show that the simple fact of moving within the context of the fashion system leads on average to a doubling of the base value of clothing.

The Success of Italian Fashion

The textile and apparel industry has spread around the world, and everywhere manufacturers are working to increase the quality of their product. On the whole, nonetheless, the creation of fashion is still concentrated—as we have seen—in a limited number of countries, and among these, Italy stands out, both in manufacture of fabrics and of apparel.

The failure of the Italian textile and apparel industry to comply fully with the predictions of conventional theories of international trade, which periodically call for the complete migration of that industry to countries with low labor costs, derives specifically from the connotation of the fashion system in the terms that we have just described. We must recognize that a part of the inability of those theories to properly predict the future depends—more than on any weakness of the theory—on a lack of statistical information (concerning international trade, manufacturing, employment) organized so as to distinguish within the context of the textile and apparel industry between fashion-intensive activities and products.

The findings of a research project undertaken by M. Fortis establish, better than any other commentary could, the extent of the remarkable Italian success story. In 1992, Italian per capita exports of products from the sector that includes the fashion system, furnishings, housewares, and Mediterranean food were greater than Germany's per capita exports of transportation products or Japan's per capita exports of electric and electronics products. Working on the trade categories used by the United Nations, Fortis observed that, as far as the fashion system is concerned, "out of eleven sectors examined, Italy was the leading world exporter in eight cases and was the leading nation in terms of trade surplus in seven sectors: leather (first in both cases), leather articles in leather (first and second), wool fabrics (first in both cases), travel accessories (third and fourth), men's apparel (third in both cases), women's apparel (third in both cases), knit outerwear (second and first), ties (first in both cases), footwear (first in both cases), eyewear (first in both cases), and gold articles and jewelry (first in both cases)." ❽

These structures and methods—which have made Italy so successful in a sector that history and economics have tended to relegate to nations with lower labor and manufacturing costs—raise a fascinating question for anyone attempting to analyze the characteristics of the world of fashion.

Many commentators have repeatedly emphasized the influence of specific historical traditions, especially the so-called Renaissance effect, which supposedly still persists in the culture and particularly

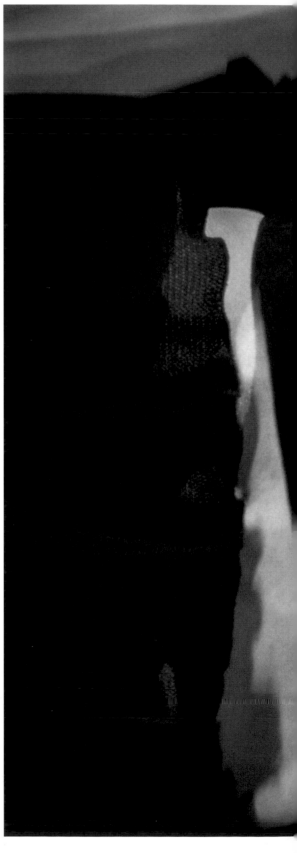

Chanel, ready-to-wear collection, spring-summer 1995. Photo by Thierry Orban (Sygma-Grazia Neri)

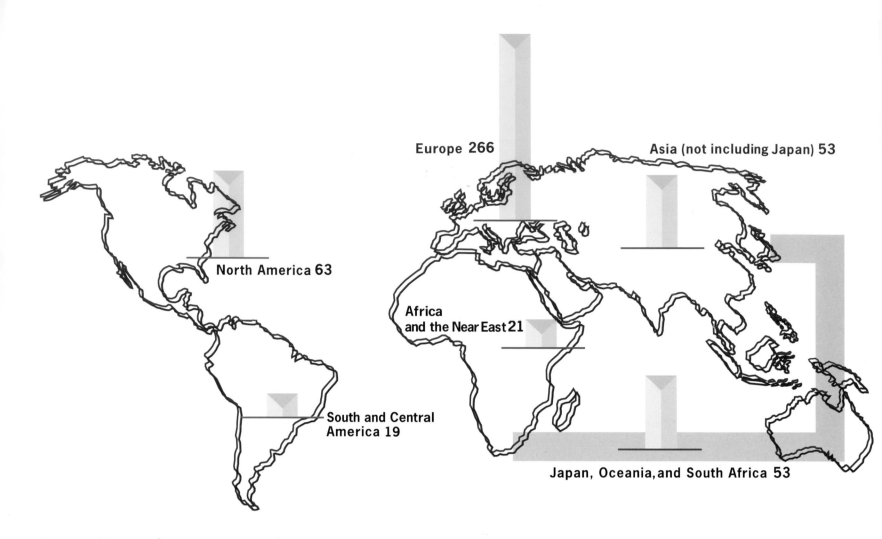

Europe 266

Asia (not including Japan) 53

North America 63

Africa and the Near East 21

South and Central America 19

Japan, Oceania, and South Africa 53

in the aesthetic sense and the crafts skills of the Italians. This interpretation is elegant, but it associates the distinctive skills of the Italian textile and apparel industry with abilities (cultural traditions and sense of beauty) that put on a secondary plane the organizational abilities, management skills, and, in general, the methods proper to modern economic science and management, without which it is unthinkable to try to work in an open global market such as that of fashion. A number of specific aspects of Italian economic development in the postwar period can help us to reconstruct the economic rationality of Italian style.

The first distinctive element is the fact that the manufacturing sector is still substantially intact. While other industrialized nations, following mere advantages of cost, have progressively transferred blocks of productions overseas, Italy continues successfully to preserve all the phases of the textile-apparel cycle, from the production of yarns and threads to the assembly of suits and outfits, including the crucial phase of finishing (which, interestingly, is often described in Italian as the nobilitazione—or ennobling—of textile fibers), and it is the only country that still has companies, facilities, and bodies of professional workers in the production of all textile fibers: silk, wool, cotton, linen, cellulose, and synthetic fibers.

The second distinct element is that in Italy there is a major machine-tool industry that produces the equipment (for spinning, weaving, dyeing, finishing, and assembling clothing) used by textiles companies. The close relationship between manufacturers of machinery and the users of that machinery has often been decisive in terms of the introduction and diffusion of innovations common to the fashion sector: the twist of the threads and yarns, the effects on the finish, or feel, of the fabrics.

This heritage of specialization and networks of relationships finds a special form of organization in the industrial districts. The Italian fashion industry, in fact, is localized into an archipelago of specialized regions: Como for silk fabrics; Biella, Prato, and Vicenza for wool yarns and fabrics; Castelgoffredo for women's stockings; Carpi and Treviso for knitwear; Empoli for leatherwear; Pesaro for jeans; and so on. The industrial districts are configured as special manufacturing structures, merging advanced technical and organizational solutions with the craft traditions whose presence serves as a remarkable platform for creativity, allowing the rapid production of prototypes, short-run series, and a great array of variants.

The third distinctive factor is administrative in nature. For many years, Italy has regulated distribution, limiting the spread of modern commercial

❽ T&A Export per capita, in US Dollars; CIS (ex-USSR) countries not included Source: HERMES from WTO data.

Preceding pages:
Hand dyeing department in Prato.
Photo by Cesare Colombo.

Chanel, haute couture collection, fall-winter 1989. Photo by Bernard Descamps (Agenzia Vu/Grazia Neri)

structures. This explains the remarkable assortment of retail outlets for independent boutiques in the historic city centers of Italy. This entirely Italian anomaly (through independent retailers, some 70 percent of apparel sales take place in Italy; as opposed to 45 percent in Germany, 40 percent in France; and 16 percent in Great Britain) has enhanced the pluralism of channels of communication between consumers and apparel manufacturers. The great number and awareness of boutique owners has encouraged manufacturers upstream to develop a more creative and original product.

In Italy, the concentration of professional skills applied to all phases of the long manufacturing and communications cycle—which extends from the conception of the product and the production of yarns and threads all the way down to the shelves in retail outlets—is exceptionally powerful and is marked by a remarkable variety of operators. Over the past thirty years of the successful system, a heritage of manufacturing and organizational experience and of testing and exploring new areas of understanding has been developed. Companies and people have created—and bestowed upon the cultures of individuals, companies, and whole local systems—a special skill for seeking out and selecting variants, and a gift for learning quickly from new practices, and finally, a talent for industrializing the results of all this.

THE VALUE OF STYLE: DISMANTLING AND ASSESSING THE STYLE ENGINE

John Durrell

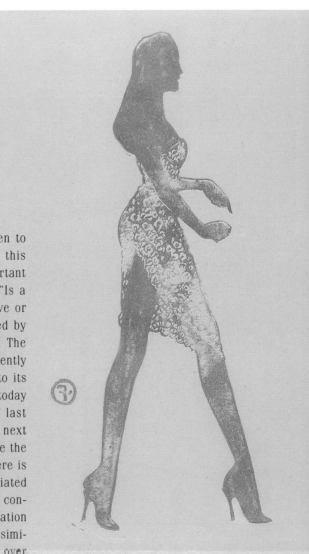

Illustration by François Berthoud.

Putting style into an economic context is not a precise process. We all know that the right style can make a business perform better, but can that improvement be measured? Even in fashion, arguably the most style-driven business in existence, there is far more to financial success than just having the right design. Style alone is not enough. Isolating style as an independent factor and measuring its effect precisely is an impossibility. That said, some of the most dynamic companies in recent decades have grown and prospered through the development and marketing of globally recognized styles. The names are familiar. Gucci, Armani, Ralph Lauren, Donna Karan, and many others have built international businesses around their particular concepts of style.

The value created by style is undeniable. Measuring it is the challenge. Financial and commercial markets are some of the most effective, objective means of measuring and realizing value. Looking at how these markets have systematically valued and rewarded companies with strongly differentiated stylistic messages is one method of approximating the value that style creates. But the first question to be answered is "What is style?" Defining style could be a career in itself.

Such a subjective factor will always be open to discussion and debate. For the purpose of this examination it is necessary to set aside important but ultimately personal questions such as "Is a given style good or bad?" or "Is it attractive or not?" The definition is necessarily simplified by permitting style to be embodied by brands. The underlying assumption is that a brand consistently communicates a specific stylistic message to its markets. For example, the Ralph Lauren of today has a continuity with the Ralph Lauren of last year, as well as with the Ralph Lauren of next year. This does not mean that the designs are the same from year to year, but, rather, that there is a consistency of quality and meaning associated with the collections that will carry over in consumers' minds from year to year. The implication is that a given brand will use design to make similar statements within its own market context over a long-term period.

Another element intrinsic to style is time. By and large, brands cannot prosper by simply recycling the same designs from season to season. Fashion is extremely time sensitive. The driving forces are clear. Designers know that markets respond powerfully to innovation. Competitors

176

Patrick Cox, advertising
campaign, 1997.
Photo by Katz Pictures
(Courtesy of Patrick Cox Inc. New York)

PATRICK ⚜ COX

aggressively appropriate new design characteristics. There is a constant appetite for the new, the fresh. Developing the vast number of designs that support a brand from collection to collection requires tremendous imagination and creativity. Maintaining the quality, relevance, and consistency of design over a period of decades is a challenge that relatively few design houses have met successfully.

All other things being equal, a fresh design is generally worth more on the market than an aging one. Last season's designs are worth less than this season's. Prices are cut to clear older goods out of retail space so that more current designs can be properly displayed. The speed with which a collection ages has business effects that ripple from the retailer back to distribution and manufacturing points with astonishing swiftness and considerable effect on profit. So the value of design newness is inexorably linked with valuing style. Again, this market value of design newness can be measured, albeit in an approximate manner.

In the simplest terms, markets value style along at least two dimensions: brand differentiation and newness of design. Examining valuations and brands demonstrates that the greater the differentiation a brand achieves, the greater the premium accorded the company by financial markets (see graph 1). This insight illustrates that the value created at the corporate level is based on clearly differentiated brand identities. Brands with relatively low differentiation—such as Reebok or Guess?—have nonetheless irrefutably built identifiable positions in the market. These brands are not commodities, but a question arises as to whether they have adequately differentiated themselves from their competitors and so created a premium value for the business. The results suggest that they have not.

Conversely, companies that represent strongly differentiated brands—for example, Nike, Tommy Hilfiger, Gucci, Oakley, or Polo/Ralph Lauren—are awarded a premium value by financial markets. This premium ranges from a multiple of two to nearly four-and-one-half times the value of companies with less-differentiated brands. These multiples readily translate into significant amounts of cash. For example, Gucci's high level

of brand differentiation translates into an additional premium market valuation of approximately $2.8 billion above the base market value of the company as measured at a price-to-sales ratio of one. There are clear financial rewards for companies with successfully differentiated brands.

Accepting that any results of this type will be approximate, the conclusions drawn from the analysis are clear. The strong brand differentiation that a coherent style has established for Gucci has in turn created additional value in the financial market in excess of $2 billion. Taking a different perspective, if Guess? were able to establish a differentiation level on a par with Tommy Hilfiger, the company could add over $600 million to their own market capitalization.

What is also apparent is that once a particular degree or critical mass of differentiation is achieved, the financial markets attach more value to the company, at progressively escalating rates. There is a point of radical departure from the undifferentiated standard, shown as falling between eighty and ninety on the scale in the graph. Once a brand achieves a critical mass of market differentiation, value rises at an increasing rate.

Objectively valuing style in financial terms required developing an original methodology based on four simplifying constraints or definitions. An important step was to examine only companies that were good proxies for the brands themselves. This meant ruling out companies that held a range of brands (e.g., Mondi) or that had fashion brands mixed with other non-fashion-branded businesses (e.g., the champagne and spirits business of LVMH). It would be possible to carry out similar evaluations for these types of companies at the brand, line, or even collection level, but doing so would require access to internal company accounts.

Focusing on companies with stock that is publicly quoted on U.S. exchanges ensured clarity and consistency of financial reporting and accounting procedures. An additional benefit of U.S.-quoted companies is the large, experienced, and liquid capital market. This is less likely to produce valuation anomalies, either too high or too low. The most practical valuation measure to

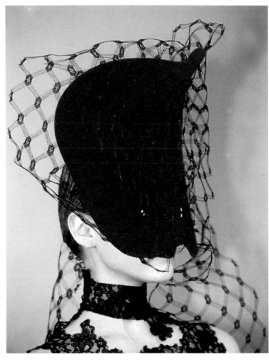

Philip Treacy, hat and veil,
1996. Photo by Ben Coster
(Camera Press/Grazia Neri)

Opposite:
Photo by Paolo Roversi

Overleaf:
Fashion in the urban
landscape in New York,
1997, billboards.
Photo by Enzo

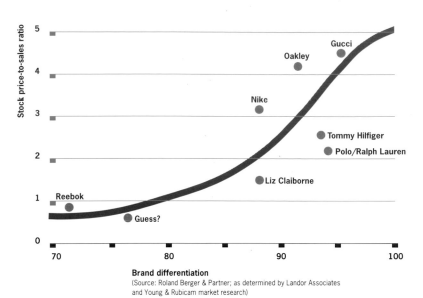

Graph 1
Market valuation of brands, 1997

Stock price-to-sales ratio / Brand differentiation

(Source: Roland Berger & Partner; as determined by Landor Associates and Young & Rubicam market research)

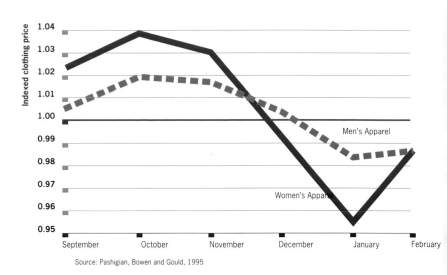

Graph 2
Seasonal clothing price variation

Indexed clothing price

Men's Apparel

Women's Apparel

Source: Pashigian, Bowen and Gould, 1995

apply is the price-to-sales ratio. This compensates for the broad size variation of the companies, so that a Nike ($6.47 billion in sales in 1996) may be meaningfully compared with an Oakley ($218 million in sales in 1996). Examining price-to-sales ratios is a clear measure of "winning" in the commercial marketplace. Admittedly, price-to-earnings or price-to-cash-flow ratios would produce more accurate measures of value creation. Unfortunately, significant differences in the operating practices of the companies themselves introduce variations that obscure the relationships derived from direct profit analysis. This profit-based approach was not found to produce reasonable approximations of relative market value.

Brand differentiation has a clearly established meaning to enable comparisons across brands: the originality and distinctiveness of the brand, relative to other familiar brands in the product category. The intent is to measure consistently the degree of difference and unique aspects of a brand, as perceived by consumers. The market research for this work involved interviewing a sample of over 40,000 adults in twenty-seven countries. The data shown is for the U.S. market, the largest group sampled, to enable the most direct link with financial market valuations.

Clearly, brands are highly valued by financial markets if they are perceived as strongly differentiated by consumers. The role of an individual design in establishing this differentiation and valuation premium is equally direct, if more short-term. Since design itself is time sensitive, the value created by style could reasonably be expected to fluctuate over time. As research into price variations of men's and women's clothing

demonstrates, this is indeed the case (see graph 2). Within a given season, price may drop by more than 7 percent for women's clothing in general. Men's clothing moved across a narrower range of approximately 2 percent. Women's clothing, with a greater emphasis on style and fashion, was found to have more than three times the variation of value with regard to time.

More expensive and implicitly more style-oriented items were also found to lose value at a greater rate than comparable but more moderately priced items. The general conclusion is that the more important the style component is to the consumer, the more rapid the decline in value as a particular design ages. It should be kept in mind that these measurements apply only to price variations in a season. As goods age and leave their season, the decline in value will become even more pronounced.

In general, a given design has a life span of one season or less in which to capture its maximum economic value. One season is not long enough to build a brand. Brands are soundly established, based on the capacity of a company, often under a talented lead designer, to produce a plethora of designs over the long term that consistently reflect and reinforce the meanings associated with that brand. The value of a single creative design is fleeting. The need for, and value of, a stream of coherent, creative designs is considerable. Financial markets recognize this, and reward the companies that consistently produce the flow of designs that will differentiate a brand. Markets, in fact, do value style. Valuing style in the fashion industry has ramifications beyond this industry alone. Other consumer businesses are

Laurie Simmons,
Walking Purse, 1989
(courtesy of Metro Pictures, New York)

Drawing by Lorenz,
The New Yorker

*"The hell of it is those punks pump over fifteen
billion dollars into the economy every year."*

using style as a progressively more powerful differentiating factor in their markets. By and large, the quality and functionality of consumer goods and services are becoming givens. Microwave ovens heat food. Watches tell time. Airlines deliver passengers to their intended destinations. Personal stereos play music. Automobiles provide mobility. The objective functions that these and other consumer products fulfill is rapidly tending toward the commodity end of the spectrum, undifferentiated from the competition and increasingly exposed to pricing pressure.

One answer for these types of industries is to differentiate through design—design that has a limited life span. In other words, style. The garment industry has known for centuries how to meet the clear functional requirements of its markets: warmth and modesty. Other consumer industries are increasingly able to meet the functional requirements of their particular markets. Now there is an opportunity for them to profit from the market influences of style in the same manner as style's most expert practitioners, the fashion houses.

For the fashion industry, style is a necessity, but it is not enough. It has never been enough. Style needs to be charged with meaning, then promoted, manufactured, and delivered to the consumers who value it and will pay for it. This requires an extensive operational infrastructure involving thousands of companies and millions of people. The companies that profit from brand differentiation and a consistent flow of creative design cannot afford to depend on style alone for competitive advantage. The financial value created by style is realized by high performance throughout the many activities that support the business, from designer to consumer. From the viewpoint of a company, a clear understanding of the interaction of style with these support functions is a manager's primary responsibility. Building an integrated view of style within the context of the company's functions and the dynamics of the market is the key to capturing and securing style's value.

Acknowledgments

Thanks to Loren Kinczel of Harvard University; original brand-differentiation research made available by Gene Bendow of Landor Associates, London, and by Young & Rubicam; research on seasonal effects on clothing prices was research published by Peter Pashigian, Brian Bowen, and Eric Gould in "Fashion, Styling and the Within-Season Decline in Automobile Prices," *Journal of Law and Economics* (University of Chicago), October 1995.

INNOVATIVE ACTIVITY IN THE FASHION INDUSTRY

Cristiano Antonelli

According to conventional analytical criteria, the fashion industry can be characterized as a mature or traditional activity that has long since ended the most innovative phase, in the narrowest sense, of the life cycle of product and technologies. It would seem that the fashion industry, then, is destined—at least in countries with high per capita income—to face significantly lower rates of growth in terms of volume and employment, as well as stagnation in terms of productivity growth. This sort of industry is, in fact, characterized by exceedingly low levels of what are considered to be the classic indicators of innovation. The volume of so-called research and development activities fails to amount to even 1 percent of the turnover. As for patents, which are traditional markers of innovation, very few are issued to companies in the fashion industry. Thus, according to these indicators, it is generally thought that there is relatively little innovative activity in the fashion industry. It is also believed that in countries exposed to international competition, and with a high pay scale, manufacturing for the fashion cycle must necessarily fall prey to competition and thus decline rapidly. According to these same prophecies, the individual companies in the fashion cycle could survive only through multinational growth, by moving their production directly to companies with low labor costs.

All we need, however, is a brief exploration of the empirical evidence—especially in the Italian case, but also in Europe at large—to see that these predictions do not correspond to the facts. In reality, the export flows of the Italian fashion industry are increasing sharply, dizzyingly, year after year. The overall productivity continues to grow, often at rates well above the average rates of the industrial manufacturing sector; labor productivity has reached exceedingly high average rates, as have the rates of capital investment in manufacturing processes.

So the predictions seem to be applicable in a sector in which, in general, no one has thought of applying them. The electronics industry, in fact—which, again according to a conventional analysis, should enjoy better health in developed countries than does the fashion industry—has repeatedly undergone terrible crises in Europe, crises that have wracked entire segments of the manufacturing sector. Manufacturing, moreover, has shifted to other areas of the global economy.

In order to understand this apparent paradox, it is probably necessary to rethink all of the fundamental categories of innovative activity. Let us take a step backward. Joseph Schumpeter, the German eco-

Still lifes for Ermenegildo Zegna.
Photos by Gianni Pezzani

nomist whose work still constitutes the foundation of the economic study of technological development, offers a very broad definition of innovation: it is a process that leads not only to the introduction of new products, but also to new manufacturing processes, new markets, new factors in production, and new organizational models. Technological change is the process of generating and spreading innovation throughout the manufacturing process of an entire economic subsystem. Innovative activity, in this sense, must then be understood as the more general process of generating new technologies—of product and process—and new models of organization, and will include the broader process of intraindustry and interindustry diffusion, which allows an innovation, once it has been generated, to be adopted by all potential users and applied to a wide array of production processes and specific situations.

In effect, this broad definition of the process of innovation appears to be applicable to the fashion industry: a complex interindustry structure that we should identify as a sector, or chain of production, and that comprises the machine-tool and chemicals industries (which supply capital goods and such fundamental intermediate input as textile fibers and dyes), textiles companies (such as spinning and weaving mills and finishing plants), as well as furniture manufacturers, leather tanners, shoe manufacturers, woodworkers, and construction firms. Economic analysis, on the other hand, has generally emphasized only the processes introducing original innovations, attributing to them a fundamental role in the explanation of growth rates of companies and of productivity. In this context, when we speak of the diffusion of innovation, we mean the concept in a narrow sense: the phenomenon whereby competitors of innovative companies imitate the original innovations that those companies developed. In the case of fashion, and other sectors as well, we should instead speak of processes of diffusion in a different sense, referring to the slipstream effects that innovation, introduced in a certain segment of the manufacturing chain, can induce even in other areas.

Of course, innovation in the narrower and more usual sense—i.e., the original generation of a new capital good—does have positive and substantial economic effects for a given economic system. It allows the development of a new industry and pro-

vides the extraordinary profits associated with a temporary monopoly. The speed, however, with which innovations that may be apparently less significant are adopted and introduced in downstream industries can have major and positive economic effects, especially when the chain of production is sufficiently long and articulated, as is certainly the case in the fashion industry. An elevated propensity for the timely adoption of innovations, supported by high levels of investment, leads to a general increase in productivity and a consequential drop in costs and prices, and—in the end—an increase in sales and a larger share of the international market.

In these cases, we may speak of a process of interindustry modernization or of the creative application of new intermediate products in areas that had not previously been considered. This process does not introduce radically new technologies. It does, however, constitute a full-fledged case of innovation. For example, if it is true that the development of new textile fibers is a product innovation of considerable importance to the chemicals industry, of no less importance are the innovative processes developed by textiles companies when they combine synthetic fibers with natural fibers, creating new mixed fabrics. Among other things, because of these innovations the companies of the apparel industry can introduce, in turn, major innovations in the production of clothing, and the textiles manufacturers can find in the home-furnishings market a major new outlet for the production of fabrics.

The difference between the spread of technological change, understood merely as a process of imitation in the narrow sense, and the spread of generalized modernization through entire sectors should, by this point, be quite clear: relations among the various agents in the case of imitation are necessarily conflicting, whereas in the case of modernization they are clearly cooperative. The interests are, in fact, complementary and convergent. Companies that are capable of making creative use of products developed by innovators are, thus, additional purchasers of the products themselves. Innovative companies, on the other hand, have a considerable interest in encouraging the development of new uses for their products, as this allows them to expand demand and, therefore, total profits. That is not all: innovative companies can in turn extract useful

information from the experience of their consumers so as to introduce further innovations and to extend the use of their products to other, heretofore overlooked, markets. These general considerations lead us to understand the basis of innovative activity in the fashion industry. The fashion industry is characterized—in many countries, and especially in Italy—by an activity with distinct systemic characteristics that consist of the accelerated interaction between processes of adoption of new intermediate products and new capital goods, and the introduction of new products in a context characterized by elevated levels of accumulation of fixed capital and intangible capital of a cognitive nature.

In particular, the innovative activity of the fashion industry is fed by elevated rates of creative adoption of product innovations developed in upstream industries, such as the machine-tool or chemicals industry. On the foundation of these manufacturing innovations, the fashion industry has been able to introduce a constant flow of product innovations based on combinations of design and style features that are compatible with available manufacturing technologies. The innovative content of the new products of the fashion industry, and specifically of the development of new articles of clothing or furniture and decoration, can only be evaluated if we truly understand the role played by new materials, from fibers to varnishes, from dyes to chemical components used in tanning leather. The success of a new line of clothing, then, is determined by the intrinsic combination of design and style and the specific techniques of employing mixtures of fibers in the fabric, making possible the use of looms without a shuttle and capable of thousands of strokes a minute, as well as the containment of the costs of the raw materials and the use of sophisticated finishing techniques.

The close link between product innovations and process innovations that are found in the fashion industry constitutes, per se, a substantial organizational innovation: it is based on innovative processes that have a substantial collective and cumulative effect and that are rooted in a continual process of redefinition of the specific context of commercial and productive activity of the individual companies, which undergo incessant processes of diversification, integration, and specialization, and therefore of entry into and departure from specific market segments. The process of innovation underway in the companies of the fashion industry has a cumulative character. The innovations in the companies

upstream encourage innovation in the companies downstream—but they do more. The continual search for product innovations in the companies downstream, and therefore experimentation in the field of new fabrics, encourages the development of innovative approaches in the companies upstream, which produce innovations in capital goods. The relationship among apparel companies that experiment with new models and new products, the textile companies that try new fabrics and new combinations of fibers, the finishing companies that work with new dyeing processes, and the machine-tool manufacturers and chemicals companies that develop new machinery and new intermediate products—all this is fundamental to the maintenance of innovative capacity for each of the subjects involved.

Relationships between users and suppliers become vehicles for exchanges of information and technological stimuli, both in the classic top-down relationship and in the less well-known bottom-up relationship. The innovative capacities of the machine-tool and chemicals industries are also

Still life for Ermenegildo Zegna.
Photo by Gianni Pezzani

turn, into major incentives for the specialization of individual companies and manufacturing units into single and specific segments of the overall manufacturing process, allowing companies to increase their general level of efficiency. The rise in specialization is often associated with an increase in productivity, as long as adequate intermediate markets grow at the same rate, offering specialized companies an opportunity to find a sufficiently substantial market. It is no accident that over the past twenty years, we have witnessed a parallel process marked by the progressive shrinking in the average size of companies and manufacturing units in the fashion industry and, at the same time, a substantial increase in the efficiency of individual companies and the sector, vertically integrated on the whole.

Thus, we see a new feature that typifies the innovation of the fashion industry: incessant organizational innovation that continually redefines the boundaries of companies and the models of cooperation and interaction among the individual phases of the manufacturing process.

The collective character of the innovative processes in question appears evident when we consider the multiplicity and variety of the manufacturing processes involved, as well as the great number of companies that take part in this effort. This also explains the importance of territorial proximity and the colocation of companies: over time this allows for the continuity of market relationships based on trust and reciprocity, and encourages the success of innovative activities with a strong collective component. This innovative vitality gives rise to the strong and—to many—surprising vigor and resiliency of the fashion industry, its deep roots in certain regions of the global marketplace, the barriers to entry by new manufacturers who are able to attract only the most standardized manufacturing segments, and ultimately the factors of a lasting economic and commercial success. This translates into elevated salaries, profits, elevated market shares, rates of investment, and prices, which in some cases are quite high.

In more general terms, the analysis of the innovative activity of the fashion industry emphasizes the intrinsically dynamic character of the process of innovation, in contrast with more traditional approaches involving comparative statistics. The individual act of innovation, linked to a single new product, is distinct from another model of the innovative process, based on a constant flow comprising the introduction of a variety of innovations. The fashion industry is an exemplary instance of this.

dependent on their relations with the textiles manufacturers that make use of their products; likewise, the innovative capacities of the apparel manufacturers depend upon the creativity of the textiles companies, and vice versa.

The success of a line of clothing translates into the success of new fabrics, increasing the demand for new fibers, which supports the sales of new machinery and intermediate inputs. Increased turnover draws greater investment, followed by a greater ability to adopt the flow of innovations incorporated in capital goods and creating a greater incentive for the innovative activity of companies upstream. In the companies downstream, the innovative process of companies upstream encourages a greater likeliness to invest in innovative activity, which in turn translates into a limitation of costs and prices and a rise in the quality of the products, with consequential increases in market share and aggregate demand for the system of the fashion industry as a whole.

The increase in overall demand translates, in

FROM THE APPAREL INDUSTRY TO THE INDUSTRIALIZATION OF FASHION

Giuseppe Berta

The clothing industry in the 1970s. Photo by Cesare Colombo

From its beginning, the history of the European apparel industry has been punctuated by its close interaction with the market. No other sector has been so dependent upon its relationship with distribution: as Stanley D. Chapman pointed out, the role of the commercial middleman was fundamental for many years in stimulating and guiding the industry of ready-to-wear apparel.

At the base of the apparel industry were department stores and distribution chains. They provided the information that there was a demand for ready-to-wear clothing that could be satisfied by coordinating the activity of a network of small-scale manufacturers who were capable of centralizing, accelerating, and rationalizing the work of seamstresses and tailors. Throughout the nineteenth century, the development of the apparel sector continued in this way in the United Kingdom, Germany, and France. For that matter, in England it was the department stores of Marks and Spencer, after 1920, that determined the explosive growth of the sector, creating the conditions whereby larger and more solid companies could be established.

Italy, despite the delay that characterized the dynamic of this sector, was no exception to the trend: here, too, the discovery of the potential of mass-produced apparel was managed by the organization of distribution and large chains of stores. The introduction of the apparel industry, however, was blocked by the fragmentation of the market and the stubborn survival of less modern styles of family consumption. The problem became evident as early as the 1920s, in view of what was happening in the rest of the Western world. The insufficient size of the market was blamed for the difficulties in taking industrial manufacturing beyond its initial foundations. The development of the modern apparel industry was accompanied by a constant effort to transcend the limits of the market, as if it were responsible for the technological and organizational backwardness of manufacturing processes. The apparel industry seemed to be weighed down at length by an insufficient industrial development. In the final analysis, the manufacturing process still relied too heavily on hand sewing, was insufficiently optimized and standardized, and employed procedures that made it seem like a giant crafts workshop.

From this point of view, the experience of a country like Italy, which industrialized its apparel sector later than other countries, is very significant. What happened, especially during the 1950s, follows a handbook strategy in terms of the establishment of mass production: as the mechanization of the manu-

facturing process progressed, there was an effort to eliminate the old crafts and tailoring qualities in the workforce, as if they constituted the chief obstacle to full operative efficiency. This was a reprise, with some significant new developments, of the North American approach: there was a strong move toward mass production of formal menswear. The revolution in marketing that accompanied the development of mass production was based on the presupposition of an emancipation of the industry from the bonds of the market. In Italy, this took the form of a radical transition: on the one hand, it involved a homogenization of selling conditions and prices, with the abolition of various, segmented local markets; on the other hand, it meant a total revision of the system of sizes, through a detailed anthropometric study aimed at increasing the adaptability of ready-to-wear clothing to fit the needs of individual consumers.

The development of the apparel industry throughout Europe in the years following World War II was based on a quest for the maximum attainable standardization and homogeneity. It was necessary to uproot both traditional styles of consumption and the widespread culture of tailoring, which had been a fixture in European family life for so long. The variety and versatility of styles of dress would have to be replaced with the uniformity typical of mass-produced menswear, branded as the appropriate style of decoration for modern living. It should not surprise us, then, that the subjective nature of the market, thus violated, should finally take its revenge. Following three glorious decades of postwar growth, the apparel industry was the first to detect the depth of the crisis that was beginning to affect the methods and structures of mass production. In the 1970s, there was a shift in this trend. The transformation toward models of consumption and lifestyles that took place in the wake of the youth revolution shook the entire operating system of the apparel industry. There emerged an authentic revolt against standardization and uniformity, while there was a growing popularity of casual wear.

The European fashion industry of today has two directions open to it. The first is to downsize and decline in importance: there are a number of companies, some with illustrious histories, that have decided to surrender in the face of the new situation. The second, which is challenging and difficult, involves a reevaluation of the forms of organization proper to

The clothing industry in the 1970s.
Photo by Cesare Colombo

Florence, 1966. Runway presentation
of women's fashion in the Pitti Palace

(Archivio Infinito)

the sector. In other words, companies must turn their backs on their recent development and return to manufacturing in small batches instead of mass production, with a renewed emphasis on quality and a general effort to personalize the product, as opposed to the homogeneity of previous manufacturing. And ultimately, they must face the challenge of keeping pace with the incessant variability and change of the market, rather than with the idea of its continuity.

From this point of view, fashion—and in a broader sense, the tailored quality that is associated with fashion products—appears as the most important resource in which the apparel industry can invest. This new approach leads, first of all, to a new complicity between the apparel industry and fashion designers and in the second place, to a new emphasis on modes of production capable of providing a closer relationship with the end consumers and their choices and preferences. One of the first entrepreneurs in the apparel industry to understand the scope of the innovations that were required for the survival of the European fashion industry was the late Marco Rivetti, who worked within the largest Italian apparel manufacturer at the time, the Gruppo Finanziario Tessile (GFT). Rivetti—who had been sharply influenced by the youth movement of the 1960s and was a passionate collector of contemporary art—was made director of the womenswear division of GFT, the division of the company that was in the worst shape and whose imminent demise was widely foreseen.

In the second half of the 1970s, Rivetti understood that the company could no longer survive with its old trademarks and marketing tools. In order to relaunch women's ready-to-wear, new strategies were needed; in particular, it would be necessary to mobilize an understanding of the market, which only the fashion industry possessed at that time. In Milan, in marginal forms, there was a growing new phenomenon of designers who were creating fashions that were substantially different from those of the traditional fashion houses. These designers were far more in tune with new trends, new ideas, and new forms of behavior. Rivetti got in touch with them and persuaded them to design product lines, which GFT would then manufacture. This was the origin of new partnerships between the Turin-based industrial group and fashion designers such as Armani, Ungaro, and Valentino, partnerships that increased the worldwide fame and

The wacky wardrobe of twenty-somethings according to the Italian family weekly *Epoca*, 1966
(Archivio Infinito)

fortune of the designers and led to the turnaround of an industrial sector that was widely thought to be on its last legs.

At the same time, the change in the structure of the product was reflected in a change in the manufacturing process. Suddenly, faced with the need to produce limited quantities, which were intended for a heavily segmented public and oriented to make the most of the exceedingly subjective nature of that public's decision making, it became necessary to abandon the techniques of mass production and return to the old methods of team manufacturing, with an emphasis on crafts—methods that had once been abolished as obsolete. Fashion forced us to rediscover the profession of the tailor and the seamstress, with the meticulous care for the quality of details that the profession implies. A term and a profession that had seemed to be lost once and for all was rescued and rehabilitated. The model of flexible production and the breakdown of large manufacturing units was thus introduced into a mature sector, reactivating a competitive potential that had been lost through the criteria of standardized manufacturing.

Today the alliance between the apparel industry and fashion—a phenomenon that we might classify as the industrialization of fashion—has at the very least cushioned the decline of the manufacturing structure of a sector that, because of its system of costs, appeared to be destined to succumb to the challenge of the manufacturing system of developing nations. In fact, developing nations were ready to take over mass production from Western nations, where it was no longer profitable.

In a certain sense, the development of the apparel industry was an archetype for—perhaps even a forerunner of—the process of industrialization. It was the first to recognize the solution of product innovation (which is also innovation of process and market) based on quality rather than standardization, and then pointed the way to the geographic separation of the strategic and design phases of the production cycle and the correct manufacturing phases.

FROM CHAOTIC NOVELTY TO STYLE PROMOTION: THE UNITED STATES FASHION INDUSTRY, 1890S-1970S

Philip Scranton

Over the last century, the American clothing trades and related elements of the fashion industry (jewelry, accessories, etc.) rose from derivative and disorganized stylings to establish a distinctive role in global fashion. Along the way, American design charted a path roughly inverse to that taken in France, where long-established Paris "names" (the lineage from Worth through Chanel to Dior) ultimately extended their couture specialties to include ready-to-wear lines for a broader, if upscale, market in recent decades. In the United States, by contrast, only after generations of mutating novelty in custom womenswear (modeled on Paris styles) and mass-market ready-mades did a cluster of visible designers emerge as trendsetters in the 1930s and after. This essay aims to outline briefly the dynamics of America's style engine in three eras: the 1890s through 1920, the 1920s through 1945, and the postwar period to the 1970s, focusing chiefly on women's fashions with an occasional nod toward menswear.

In the 1890s, the seventy-five million residents of the United States presented manufacturers with the largest protected market for clothing in the industrializing world, yet that market was dramatically segmented in terms of both supply and demand. Several hundred thousand tailors and dressmakers crafted custom garments for urban and small-town elites whose requirements varied with climate and sophistication. The most chic among them adopted "continental" names and/or stitched fake French labels into their wares. Mail-order distributors' fat catalogs (trumpeting the "latest Paris modes") circulated nationally, harvesting orders in rural districts, while other houses annually advertised thousands of new paper patterns for home sewers through periodicals like *McCalls* and *The Delineator*. By 1900, leading city department stores provided pattern catalogs in their fabric salesrooms, racks of ready-to-wear fashions (snapped up by several million young working women), and captive salons, which adapted to American tastes model garments that had been purchased in Paris (for menswear, in London). Ready-to-wear manufacturing wholesalers supplying retailers on all scales were equally eager copyists, each typically offering several hundred seasonal novelties, but increasingly they "laddered" their fashion echoes to match stores' emerging selling price lines (i.e., skirts at $5 or

Fur coat by Ben Kahan. Photo published in *Harper's Bazaar*, 1955, reinterpreted in 1994. Photo by Lillian Bassman (Courtesy of the Fashion Institute of Technology, New York)

$10). Finally, periodicals like *Vogue* and *Harper's Bazaar* anchored the fashion information system for radical European notions, whereas the *Ladies' Home Journal* fed more conservative palates (all included patterns in every issue).

Where were designers in this massive process of clothing a nation? Essentially invisible, except for a handful of Manhattan arrivistes. Although New York City was the hub for fashion production, the transmission network for style was diffuse, diverse, and dependent on European initiatives. Ready-mades, which had originated with staple jackets and pants for men, expanded dramatically in womenswear by 1900 and after, beginning the steady decay of custom dressmaking and millinery, along with a gradual stagnation in home sewing.

Perhaps the only genuine American design innovations before the 1920s could be found in peripheral novelties: cheap patriotic and seasonal jewelry, knit sweaters for outdoor leisure, or fancy straw hats. World War I brought an anti-fashion rage for simplicity and created a broader platform for "dress reformers," who had earlier urged American women to reject elaborate and constricting garments that ill fit the increasingly active lifestyles of the better classes. The implications of these shifts and of the transplantation of moviemaking from the East Coast to California would be realized during the interwar decades.

In the 1920s and 1930s, America's fashion chaos became, if anything, more decentered (and possibly democratic), though efforts at organizing and institutionalizing style leadership did gradu-

Outfit by Jane Derby. Photo published in *Harper's Bazaar*, 1955, reinterpreted in 1994. Photo by Lillian Bassman (Courtesy of the Fashion Institute of Technology, New York)

ally begin to gel. As styles churned rapidly and The *Delineator*'s monthly circulation passed two million (in 1928), the decade's hot new pattern company, linked with the Woolworth chain stores, was appropriately named Simplicity. Meanwhile, the fashion information system fairly exploded in tandem with decisive technological changes. Hollywood, in shifting from one-reelers shown by storefront nickelodeons to feature films filling seats in ornate picture palaces, created a network of stars, whose exotic or workaday clothing captured the imaginations of women. Radio broadcasts and phonograph music drew the attention of millions, and fan magazines exhaustively documented performers' glad rags and casual wear.

Both ready-made garment and pattern companies moved with dispatch to reproduce media-made styles for an expanding "youth" market, while film stylists (notably Adrian) became some of the first American designers who were widely recognized. Consequently, Los Angeles generated a fresh vector in American fashion: new modes of extravagant clothing for stars to wear at posh parties, on the beach or at leisure, or for public appearances at racetracks, the Brown Derby, or eventually, the Oscar ceremonies. This first initiative toward style leadership even affected the staid menswear trades.

In the 1920s, one Philadelphia clothier had made its fortune by specializing in quality, durable blue-serge suits—in all sizes but only one design—and another by producing staple white dress shirts. A decade later, men of all ages began taking their clothing cues from George Raft and Clark Gable (whose turtleneck sweater reportedly savaged the tie business). Clothes-makers expanded their lines accordingly. Of course, this only added to the diversity and confusion of styles, a matter that always threatened to leave producers with masses of season-end, devalued fashions, which could wreck balance sheets. Somebody had to manage this market.

With different agendas, three sets of New Yorkers stepped up to bat. During the Depression, labor organizers moved aggressively to take wages out of competition by confirming standard compensation schemes through the Amalgamated Clothing Workers and the International Ladies' Garment Workers' Union. Responsible, yet hard-bargaining, labor organizations (with government assistance) marginalized the notorious sweatshop contracting game, a struggle that had commenced before 1900 and reached success in the 1930s. Of comparable importance in menswear was the publishing initiative of Arnold Gingrich, who created *Apparel Arts*, a men's fashion quarterly, in the depths of the Depression as a means to signal upscale retailers and consumers about seasonal trends and novelties. *Apparel Arts* (and later, *Esquire*) quickly became the journal of reference in stylish clothing and accessories for men, featuring coverage of British fashion moments (the Ascot races), as well as articles on outfitting sons for college, sportswear for golf and tennis, and featuring photo clusters presenting the well-dressed "rich and famous" on both coasts. Other decisive publishing efforts at the time included

the launch of youth-oriented *Mademoiselle* and *Glamour* magazines and *Vogue*'s initiation of an annual American design issue (in 1938). Clearly, media in America became the core venue for fashion media-tion.

However, a third New York operation built the connection between mass media and design origination. The Fashion Group, which formed in 1931, linked elite representatives of style magazines (*Vogue*'s Edna Chase) with a cohort of women who had invisibly come to dominate American womenswear design. (In 1910, women constituted under 30 percent of those drafting clothing designs; by 1930, they occupied over 60 percent of all such positions.) From the Fashion Group's ranks, which reached one thousand members (including Eleanor Roosevelt!) in various urban chapters by 1939, came the first generation of individually acknowledged American stylists, whose initial organization represented a creative reaction to the "capricious authority of the male Parisian couturiers." Members like Dorothy Shaver, heading style segments of Manhattan department stores, used newspaper ads to identify individual designers with fashion lines being marketed. *Vogue*'s American design issues derived from the same set of connections. The group welcomed Adrian to its New York meetings on his semiannual trips to the East Coast, but was overwhelmingly devoted to women's career development in the fashion trades. American fashion might credit to its efforts the formation of an authentic style elite before and, more decisively, after World War II, led by Claire McCardell, Lilly Daché, Elizabeth Hawes, Hattie Carnegie, and others. A final element in New York's institutionalization of American design was the interwar advances in fashion education at the Pratt and Parsons schools and the eventual transformation of the city's Needle Trades High School into the Fashion Institute of Technology. Their graduates would fill design posts as the industry expanded following World War II.

Wartime again was hard on fashion, both because Paris, occupied by the Nazis, was effectively dormant and because textile supply regulations in the United States drastically limited the raw materials available for styling. Under tight con-

Elusive Elegance.
Photo published in
Harper's Bazaar, 1955,
reinterpreted in 1994.
Photo by Lillian Bassman
(Courtesy of the Fashion Institute
of Technology, New York)

straints, New York designers "performed brilliantly," as fashion journalist Virginia Pope remembered. Yet, curiously, it was during this global conflict that unexpected sources of design creativity arose from terrains well outside the newly conventional Hollywood-Manhattan axis and, equally astonishing, in menswear. The zoot suit—a fabric-intense creation with a knee- to ankle-length jacket and wide pants, pulled together by flashy ties and a six-foot "watch chain"—exemplified Hispanic and Black Americans' resistance to the dominion of Anglo culture and power. Zoots, as their wearers were known, were using clothing as a venue for protest, a pattern that had been evident among flappers in the 1920s and that would recur a generation after World War II, during the Vietnam era. Clothing that challenges hegemonic values and morals has a long history, but few flappers or hippies were maimed or killed, as were Zoots in California and elsewhere, often by military men and police who regarded them as defiant slackers.

Once Dior and Balenciaga showed their galvanizing late 1940s collections, Paris again dominated fashion, but a rough division of labor began to appear in the American market. Securing licenses to duplicate the leading modes, United States manufacturers remained acolytes to French high priests in suits, coats, and dresses, yet engaged prominent American designers for sportswear, youth lines, and business attire. (In 1956, the Fashion Group neared three thousand members, half of them in New York.) Market research indicated that three-quarters of American women were shorter than sixty-three inches, yielding a durable vogue for petite style, just as a flood of novel synthetic fibers, heavily promoted by chemical companies, widened fabric ranges and the first wave of Italian knits opened another venue for the design imagination. Manufacturers' seasonal collections expanded apace, the principal womenswear firms showing four or five lines annually. Norman Norell, a noted designer who had worked both in film styling and for Hattie Carnegie, generated up to five hundred preliminary sketches for each season, only a third of which reached the runways as sample garments. In midprice ready-to-wear, heavily advertised brand names began to command attention—notably Jonathan Logan and, later, Villager—as manufacturers reached out to consumers with their own retail chains. Meanwhile, the branching of department stores as mall anchors brought their licensed European labels and, in time, a new generation of American designers (Liz Claiborne) to the nation's burgeoning suburbs.

Television added yet another media mechanism for fashion transmission, not just the clothes displayed by Loretta Young or Lucy and Desi, but perhaps more powerfully, the styles city kids flaunted on teen programs like *American Bandstand*. Threads of bottom-up design appropriation had commenced in the 1950s with New York's jazz and beat scenes. By the 1960s stylists monitored the baby boomers' youth culture and boutiques for inspiration. In the mid-1960s, American fashion was a $20 billion business, employing over a million production workers and a like number in distribution. Though globalization would follow, with endless variations on American jeans and massive outsourcing of production to developing nations, the American "fashion machine" had reached a fragile maturity, drawing more on youth, celebrities, and relentless promotion than on Parisian motifs to celebrate style in what continued to be the world's largest and most unselfconscious consumer society.

TRADEMARKS AND FASHION LABELS

Antonio Pilati

Photo by Eric Robert
(Sygma/Grazia Neri)

Opposite:
Chanel, fall-winter 1996
collection.
Photo by Ben Coster
(Camera Press/Grazia Neri)

The high-end, distinctive area (in terms of quality, price, and design) of the textile and apparel sector that we call the fashion segment has always had a special relationship with communications—we might add, by way of definition, in the creation of the sector. A product becomes fashionable if it succeeds in associating with its useful value—indeed, almost inevitably above and beyond that value—the capacity to attract the attention of the collective, to cause discussion, and to establish itself as a significant theme of social life. This is not a common occurrence for material objects, which rarely succeed in extending past their practical function to become a core of feelings of debate, so as to capture the interest of public opinion and its vehicles (from the newspaper to the drawing room).

It is customarily the prerogative only of symbolic objects to serve as social themes, objects whose function is to provide a performance, not so much of practical utility but rather of a cognitive nature: from paintings to churches, from flags to books. The clothing of fashion—like jewelry and furniture, but to an even greater degree—recovers for material objects a symbolic dimension, which is capable of expanding to the status of a conversation or even a vision of personal relationships or ideological messages (in the form of social taste). This original feature of symbolism and communication extended into fashion with the advent

of industrial manufacturing. In the context of the expansion of size and scale of production—from a crafts level (limited numbers, local workshops, few machines) to that of multinational corporations (medium- to large-scale production, increase in invested capital, worldwide markets)—the communications structure also changed its form and method of operation.

In the period of crafts production, the social influence of fashion was based on technical flair, the configuration of the product, and the ability to influence the informal circles where opinion was shaped. The names of the creators were still of secondary importance, concealed behind the product itself: design was more important than the designer. In the earliest industrial phase of fashion, when the star system was already beginning to emerge, the name of the creator became important and, through a series of gradual changes, emphatic. The symbolic theme was focused and concentrated on an almost mythical figure, a sort of demiurge. The structure of communications, however, was still weak and dependent: it took advantage—in a parasitic and nonsystematic way—of the mythological circuits assembled by other subjects (magazines, radio, television) for their own purposes. The myth-making impulse of the mass media—which assemble an audience to the degree that they are successful in formulating a story (epic, tragic, or filled with pathos)

revolving around archetypal figures (king, hero, or star, distinguished by beauty or goodness, the "self-made man," an updated version of Cinderella)—made use of fashion designers as well, and thus helped them to step into a vaster dimension, above and beyond their limited sector.

Between mass media and fashion there was a difference in terms of efficacy that generated a number of consequences. The system of communications, which had a much faster overall rate of modernization, explored a variety of new options: it became organically intertwined with mass consumption (the explosion of advertising linked to commercial television), and it explored an increasingly close-linked symbiosis with computers and allied systems, overcoming traditional barriers and expanding intensively. The fashion system, which displayed a less cogent drive to innovate, followed in the wake of the media and took on its glittering reflection within its own field of operations, with the accompanying risk of a substantial split in direction: it expanded toward the mass market, diversifying its product range and discovering new functional uses. This unbalanced condition of slipstreaming, which lasted for at least a decade, began in the last few years to collapse and change character: fashion intensified its relationship with communications and attempted to recover its independence by forming a body of expression that was better suited to internal patterns, timing, and requirements, less dependent upon the objectives established by other systems and calibrated to its own manufacturing pace. In this intricate reconquest of public communications, the fashion industry became distinctively closer to the industries of the imaginary sphere, which control the broadest and most complex production of symbolic figures in our society. In particular, the communications policy of fashion resembles—in terms of layout and inspiration—the policy developed, over a larger scale, by the film business.

The communications model of the film business is distinguished by three chief features. The first is the high proportion of marketing and communications expenses in the overall cost of production: on average, in 1996 a film produced by a major studio in Hollywood involved expenditures of $40 million on production and nearly $24 million (roughly 37 percent of the total budget) on advertising and publicity. The second distinctive feature is the enormous importance attributed to the launch (press previews, ancillary events, documentation, and other material, to premiere) and the first weekends of showing. In this phase, the attention of the public is focused and the decision is made whether the film will reach the first rank in the collective agenda of interest and excitement. The launch becomes a showcase of events that are designed to generate visibility and affect society at large, with an effect that endures

Photo by Elliot Erwitt (Magnum/Contrasto)

That we should think it important to have our own monogram on the objects that we love (shirts, suitcases, napkin rings, and so on)—reasonable enough. But the monogram of a supplier? That really seems a bit much to me.

Georges Perec, *Pensare/Classificare*, 1989

over the long term: winning a significant "share of mind" has a considerable cost and involves an investment designed to prolong the yield of the film. The third feature is the progressive expansion of the time and channels of exploitation. The larger the investment in the launch, the greater the number of areas of the social sphere in which the events of the spectacle have an effect, and the longer the period in which the product has a "buzz," affecting the general attention. Television multiplies the formulas for the consumption of movies (pay television, pay-per-view, video-on-demand). There are a wider variety of opportunities to engage sponsors, and the merchandising can extend to numerous territories, even quite removed from the subject of the movie.

The model of the film business is followed right down to the smallest details in the communications cycle of the fashion industry. The expenses for marketing rise constantly, the runway presentations are increasingly spectacular and visible, the interest and production value of those presentations extends without halt, and the models increasingly resemble movie stars in style and behavior. At the same time, the array of objects linked to fashion and designer accessories has reached astonishing proportions, in much the same way that in the film business the return on investments in the launch of a title is a function of the ability to exploit in new territories the "share of mind" that has been attained. All the same, the resemblances, however profound, apply to a field of communications that reveals exceedingly diverse limitations and features. Movies are communications products with very specific modes of consumption that set them sharply apart from objects for material use. A movie is a unique prototype with relatively little in common with products previously consumed: the reasons for choice are therefore difficult to codify and include considerable proportions of emotion and impulse.

All of this makes relatively unimportant the use of that particular communications device that is a label or trademark, which—in products of mass consumption and in durable goods—is of crucial importance. Through the visible name of the manufacturer, the trademark projects a capital of communications that is established in precedence and formed out of expectations and judgments concerning the contents of the product, the uses of which still need to be verified: in a certain sense, the consumer takes for granted in advance (and on that basis makes a choice) the future operation of the product. With this idea in mind, the label or trademark provides concise promises concerning the use, the values associated with the name of the manufacturer or producer, and the images that form around the product. In this context, it serves as a device to limit the unfathomable variability of the future: it makes uses foreseeable and reassuring before the products are tried; it reduces through knowledge the risk of a price paid in advance for a concrete function. If, however, the consumption of the past does not exercise a major effect on future use, if creative variability fails to foresee the influence of engineering certainties upon future functions, then the mechanism of the trademark or label will have no venue in which to operate. And in the film business there are no trademarks, only stars who concentrate emotions and interests without creating stable expectations concerning the quality of the product. It is no accident that the only real instance of a trademark that exists in the film industry (the name of Disney) is linked to products (cartoons) that are quite close, in many ways, to the world of mass production: substantial shared traits, general predictability of the structure and characters, and assurance of a reproducible standard of emotional experience.

In fashion, of course, the conditions of consumption of the products of communications do not apply. Use is repeated over time; the practical applications are of considerable importance, and they give the product a life cycle that is far longer and more complex than that of consumption extending over just two hours. A reassuring device such as a trademark or label is useful for reducing the broad array of risks linked to the functions of clothing. There is, however, a more complex use of marketing in the showcase events that generate excitement and involvement, which is especially useful for products (such as movies) with few calculable parameters affecting purchase. In the case of products with practical uses, such as clothing, even if there is a major emotional component, the showcase event has a real value if it succeeds in prolonging its spectacular effect above and beyond a certain moment of excitement, consolidating that effect in a rational and stable promise: the show, besides creating stars, must form trademarks and labels. In this context, fashion establishes its own ambivalent nature, somewhere between a show and an industry, between the simulation of the stage and the concrete nature of material uses. The intermediate figure is the fashion designer, the creator who belongs to two worlds, who splits into two opposite dimensions: on the one hand, an artist who lives in the separate circle of inspiration, and on the other hand, an entrepreneur who operates in the quantitative, measurable context of balance sheets and manu-

Photo by Alberto Tolot

(Courtesy of The Manipulator)

Overleaf:

Andrea Splisgar, Pearls
before Swine, performance,
Florence, 1996.

Photo by Luigi Simeoli

facturing processes. The fashion designer as demiurge, whom the media put on a mythological and separate (nonindustrial) plane as a star for his or her amphibious function, succeeds in taking control of his or her own image, becoming master or mistress of the communications that concern them only by creating events of a certain type that go well beyond simple entertainment and do more than surprise or capture attention, alluding to a different dimension, which is preserved over time, heralding the future and providing operative reassurance. The double identity of the fashion designer offers a twist of significance to the notoriety of the spectacle, giving it a new purpose of credibility. The events that propagate the visibility of new models are formed on motifs of fanciful exhibition, but in the final analysis they direct attention beyond individual behavior, toward technical quality. The fashion designer is transformed from a star—visible inasmuch as he or she is an exceptional individual who generates events—into a trademark that makes use of the attention assembled to offer confirmation (expanding it over time) to a technical line, a specific conception of the product and its use. The name is transformed from a summary of a surprising and fascinating show into a warranty of style, a signature that conceptualizes a way of existence. Thus, the demiurge, through the device of style, is assimilated to the trademark that offers practical certainties with which to limit the risks linked to future use. In the movies, which have an irrelevant material form (a mere physical substratum to the abstraction of the image), it makes no sense for there to be a trademark or label: only in a few exceptional cases does the name of the star, especially a star director or photographer, come to be identified as a mass indicator of style, and with time become something similar to a trademark (Hitchcock, Spielberg). But in fashion, style often becomes an industrial promise, a harbinger of a functional character. It is in fact a way of using technology, of doing industrial design.

In short, the circuit of fashion communications, which appears to be one of the most complex and intricate of those used in the various segments of the economy, includes and intertwines at least three different levels of cognitive production: the level of design, of stylistic creation, that provides a primary foundation through specific technical factors for the perception of consumers; the level of events that, through spectacle, focus the general attention on the personalities (the star system) and, thus, on the products; and the level of the trademark or label, the development of marketing, that strives to condense into a structured image related to the product the selected elements of fame and recognizability established by the preceding levels.

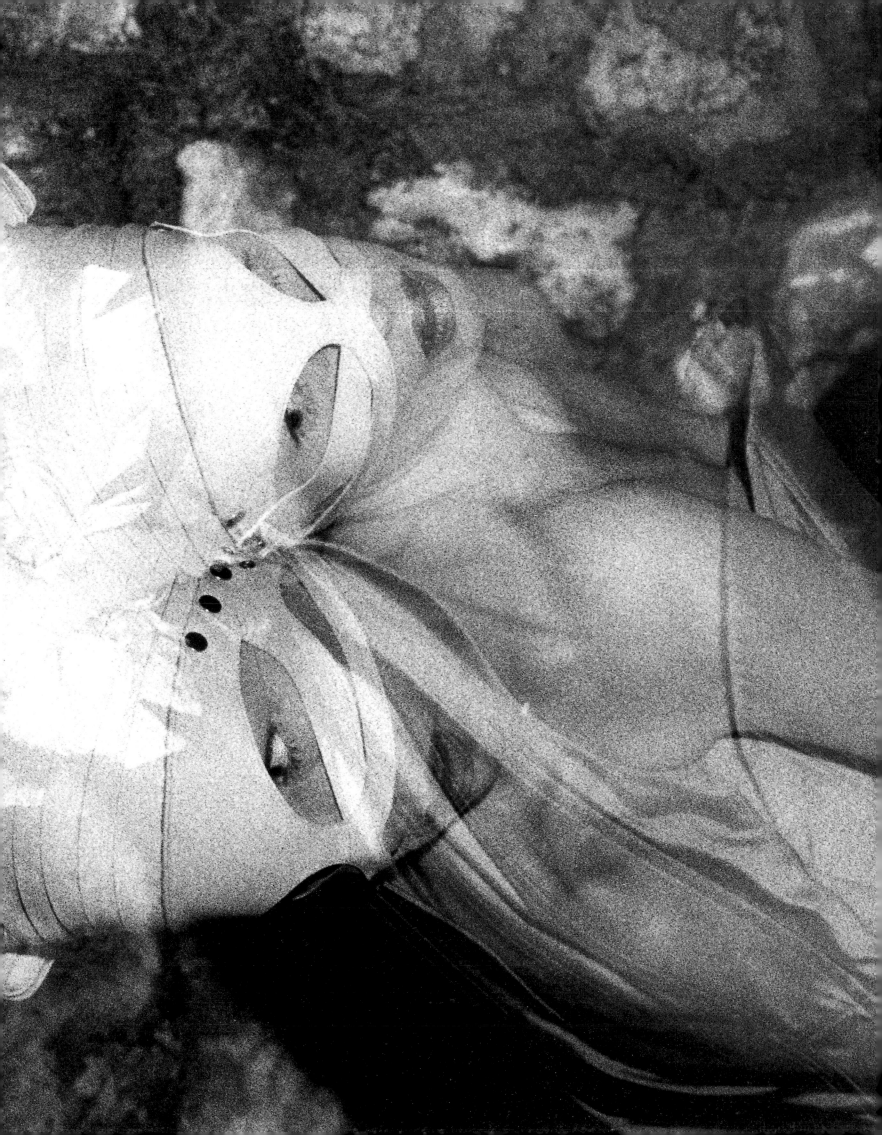

Biographies

Giannino Malossi

Giannino Malossi (born Bologna, 1954) is the author of a number of research projects concerning the mass media and culture, with a special focus on fashion and design. These projects resulted in exhibitions—"Il senso della moda" (The Meaning of Fashion; Fourteenth Milan Triennale, 1979); "Tipologie dei comportamenti di moda" (Categories of Fashion Behavior; Venice Biennale/Special Projects, 1980); "Ricerca sul decoro" (Research into Decoration; Centro Domus, 1981)—and publications, including *Liberi tutti. Vent'anni di moda spettacolo* (Everyone Free: Twenty Years of Fashion as Entertainment; Mondadori, 1987); *Apparel Arts. La moda è la notizia* (Apparel Arts: Fashion Is the News; Electa, 1989); *This was tomorrow. Pop design da stile a revival* (This Was Tomorrow: Pop Design from Style to Revival; Electa, 1990). He has been working with Pitti Immagine in the area of strategic communications since 1990 and has developed several events, publications, and exhibitions.

Peppino Ortoleva

Peppino Ortoleva (born Naples, 1948) is the author of a great number of essays and books on the history and theory of communications. Among his most recent books are *Mediastoria. Comunicazione e mutamento sociale nel mondo contemporaneo* (Mediastory: Communications and Social Transition in the Contemporary World; Parma, 1995), *Un ventennio a colori. Televisione privata e società in Italia* (Twenty Years of Color: Private Television Broadcasting and Society in Italy; Florence, 1995). He teaches the theory and techniques of new media in the undergraduate program in communication sciences at the University of Turin, and he is a partner in Cliomedia, a company that has been active for the last decade in the field of multimedia production, mass communications, and historical and social research.

Cristiano Antonelli

Cristiano Antonelli (born Florence, 1951) is professor of economic policy in the Economics Department of the University of Turin. He has also taught at the University of Sassari (Italy), the University of Manchester, the University of Paris-Dauphine, the University of Nice, and the Polytechnic of Milan. He has been a Rockefeller Fellow at the Massachusetts Institute of Technology and junior economist at the Science, Technology, and Industry Direction of the OCSE in Paris. He is managing director of "Economics of Innovation and New Technology" and coeditor of the "Economics of Science Technology and Innovation" collection for Kluwer Academic Publishers.

Andrea Balestri

Andrea Balestri (born Vernio, 1954), an economist, has directed the Centro Studi della Unione Industriale Pratese (Prato Industrial Union Study Center) since 1988; he has also run the Communications and Promotion Unit of the same organization since 1993. He regularly lectures at universities and training centers (Faculty of Engineering, Florence; Degree Course in Prato; Liuc in Castellanza; Bocconi in Milan; Hosey University in Tokyo). He is a member of the secretariat of the Club dei distretti industriali (Industrial Districts Club). He edits two periodicals (the monthly *Pratofutura* and the quarterly *Distretti Italiani*) and has published numerous articles and monographs in *Science and Experiments, La Laniera, Mondo Economico, La Nazione, Il Sole 24 Ore, L'Impresa, Sviluppo Locale, Economia e Management,* and *L'Illustrazione Italiana*.

Giuseppe Berta

Giuseppe Berta is professor of the history of industry at the Libero Istituto Universitario "C. Cattaneo" in Castellanza (Varese, Italy). He is the author of several essays on economic and social history, including *Le idee al potere. Adriano Olivetti tra la fabbrica e la comunità* (Milan: Edizioni di Comunità, 1980); *Capitali in gioco. Cultura economica e vita finanziaria nella City di fine Ottocento* (Venice: Marsilio, 1990); *Impresa, partecipazione, conflitto. Considerazioni dall'esperienza Fiat* with Cesare Annibaldi (Venice, Marsilio, 1994); *Il governo degli interessi. Industriali, rappresentanza e politica nell'Italia del nord-ovest, 1906–1924* (Venice, Marsilio, 1996). He is also the editor of *Democrazia industriale. Antologia degli scritti* by Sidney and Beatrice Webb (Rome: Ediesse, 1984). In the past, he has supervised the organization of the historic archive of the GFT Group; at present, he is in charge of the FIAT Historic Archive.

Laird O. Borrelli

Laird Borrelli received a master's degree in museum studies/costume history at the Fashion Institute of Technology and currently works in the Costume Collection at the museum at FIT. Her article "Dressing Up and Talking About It: Twenty-Five Years of Fashion Writing in *Vogue*" will be published in *Fashion Theory*.

Laura Bovone

Laura Bovone is professor of sociology in the Faculty of Political Sciences of the Università Cattolica del Sacro Cuore (Milan), where she directs the Department of Sociology and the Centro per lo studio della moda (Fashion Study Center) in collaboration with other foreign scholars interested in the subject of cultural industries. For the publisher Franco Angeli, she edits the "Produrre culture, creare comunicazione" collection. Her most important publications are *In tema di postmoderno* (Milan: Vita e Pensiero, 1990) and *La moda della metropoli. Dove si incontrano i giovani milanesi* in collaboration with E. Mora (Milan, 1997), and she is the editor of *Creare comunicazione. I nuovi intermediari di cultura a Milano* (Milan, 1994) and *Mode* (Milan, 1997).

Stefano Casciani

Stefano Casciani (born Rome, 1995) is a designer, publicist, and corporate image and communications consultant. He carries out research and planning activities on the relationship between art and design, and his objects have been presented in numerous exhibitions at art galleries and museums. In 1996, with Alessandro Mendini, he handled the layout and furnishing of the exhibition "Italy: The Art Factory" at the Louisiana Museum of Modern Art in Humlebaek, Denmark. He has been in charge of the design section of the magazine *Abitare* since 1992. He is the author of several books on the subjects of architecture and design, including *Design in Italia 1950–1990* (1991), *Architetture elettriche* (1991), *Il sogno del comando. Realtà e utopia nell'automazione domestica* (1995), and *La fabbrica dell'arte. Il design in Italia verso il terzo Millennio* (1996). He has also written many articles for magazines.

Domenico De Masi

Domenico De Masi (born 1938) is professor of the sociology of work at the Università "La Sapienza" in Rome; he began to lecture at the university in 1961. He is president of SIT, Società Italiana per il Telelavoro (Telework Italian Society) and of In/Arch, Istituto Nazionale Architettura (National Architecture Institute); founder of S3-Studium, Specialization School in Organizational Sciences; and national past president of AIF, Associazione Italiana Formatori (Italian Trainers Association). Between 1961 and 1966, he carried out organizational research and held managerial offices in companies of the Finsider Group. Between 1966 and 1979 he was teacher and manager at IFAP, the Centro Iri per lo Studio delle Funzioni Pubbliche Aziendali (Iri Center for the Study of Business Public

Functions). Since 1980 he has devoted himself exclusively to university teaching, training, and socio-organizational research. He collaborates with many important Italian companies. He has published numerous essays, by himself or with other researchers, in three main fields of interest: the sociology of urban development, the sociology of work and organization, and the sociology of macrosystems. These include *La negazione urbana* (Il Mulino, 1971); *L'industria del sottosviluppo* (Guida, 1973); *Dentro l'università* (Franco Angeli, 1977); *Sociologia dell'azienda* (Il Mulino, 1973); *I lavoratori nell'industria italiana* (Franco Angeli, 1974); *La via italiana alla democrazia industriale* (Isedi, 1977); *Giovani e lavoro* (Franco Angeli, 1982); *Trattato di sociologia del lavoro e dell'organizzazione* (Franco Angeli, 1985 87); *Il lavoratore post industriale* (Franco Angeli, 1985); *Manuale di ricerca sul lavoro e sulle organizzazioni* (Nuova Italia Scientifica, 1985); *L'emozione e la regola. I gruppi creativi in Europa dal 1850 al 1950* (Laterza, 1990); *Verso una formazione post-industriale* (Franco Angeli, 1993); *Sviluppo senza lavoro* (Edizioni Lavoro, 1994); *L'avvento post-industriale* (Franco Angeli, 1985); and *L'ozio creativo* (Ediesse, 1995). He is also the editor of the Italian edition of E. C. Banfield's *Le basi morali di una società arretrata* (Il Mulino, 1976). For the publisher Franco Angeli, he directs the "La Società" collection. He is a member of the scientific committees of the following magazines: *Sociologia del Lavoro*, *Economia e Lavoro*, *L'Impresa*, *Pluriverso*, and the Italian edition of the *Harvard Business Review*; and he collaborates with major Italian newspapers and periodicals.

John Durrell

John Durrell is a principal in the London office of Roland Berger & Partner, an international management consultancy. He specializes in the area of pricing strategy, working in a range of industries from tourism to automotive. He uses a rigorously quantitative approach to expose the systematic underlying structure of markets. He has a particular interest in the fashion industry because of the rapid product life cycle, strong brand images, and inherent product complexity.

Nadine Frey

Nadine Frey (born New York, 1956) received a bachelor of arts in classics from Princeton University and a masters of science in journalism from Columbia University. She has worked at *Time* magazine and *Women's Wear Daily* (as Milan bureau chief and associate Paris editor). She is currently a freelance

fashion writer and the Paris fashion correspondent of Tokyo's *Hanatsubaki* magazine.

Franco La Cecla

Franco La Cecla (born Palermo, 1950) is a researcher at the Arts Faculty of Bologna, teaches the sociology of interethnic relations at the Arts Faculty of Palermo, and teaches cultural anthropology at the Faculty of Cultural Property, Ravenna. He has written *Perdersi. L'uomo senza ambiente* (Bari, 1988); *Mente locale. Per un'antropologia dell'abitare* (Rome, 1993); *Il malinteso. Antropologia dell'incontro* (Bari, 1997); and various other publications, including *Bambini per strada* (Milan, 1995) and *Perfetti e invisibili. L'immagine dell'infanzia nei media* (Milan, 1996), for which he also organized an exhibition for Pitti Immagine in Florence (1995).

Richard Martin

Richard Martin, curator of the Costume Institute of the Metropolitan Museum of Art, is adjunct professor of art history and archaeology at Columbia University and adjunct professor of art at New York University. From 1974 to 1988, he was editor of *Arts Magazine*, and for twenty years he taught art history at the Fashion Institute of Technology, where he also served as executive director of the Shirley Goodman Resource Center and executive director of the Educational Foundation for the Fashion Industries. His many books include *Fashion and Surrealism*, *The New Urban Landscape*, *Contemporary Fashion*, and *St. James Fashion Encyclopaedia*. His books on Charles James and Gianni Versace were published in 1997. He has written a great number of essays for publications as diverse as *Artforum*, the *New York Times*, the *Los Angeles Times*, *L'Uomo Vogue*, the *International Herald Tribune*, the *Journal of Design History*, *Mondo Uomo*, and the *Journal of American Culture*. He is author or coauthor of several exhibition catalogs, including *Splash: A History of Swimwear*; *The Historical Mode: Fashion and Art in the 1980s*; *Jocks and Nerds: Men's Style in the Twentieth Century*; *Infra-Apparel*; *Orientalism*; *Haute Couture*; *Christian Dior*; and *The Four Seasons*. Among his recent honors are Pratt's Excellence by Design Award, the Laboratory Institute of Merchandising's Distinguished Achievement Award, an honorary doctorate from Otis College of Art & Design, election as a fellow of the Costume Society of America, and a special award for "furthering fashion as art and culture" by the Council of Fashion Designers of America in 1996. Richard Martin, curator of the Costume Institute of the Metropolitan Museum of

Art, is adjunct professor of art history and archaeology at Columbia University and adjunct professor of art at New York University. From 1974 to 1988, he was editor of *Arts Magazine*, and for twenty years he taught art history at the Fashion Institute of Technology, where he also served as executive director of the Shirley Goodman Resource Center and executive director of the Educational Foundation for the Fashion Industries. His many books include *Fashion and Surrealism*, *The New Urban Landscape*, *Contemporary Fashion*, and *St. James Fashion Encyclopaedia*. His books on Charles James and Gianni Versace were published in 1997. He has written a great number of essays for publications as diverse as *Artforum*, the *New York Times*, the *Los Angeles Times*, *L'Uomo Vogue*, the *International Herald Tribune*, the *Journal of Design History*, *Mondo Uomo*, and the *Journal of American Culture*. He is author or coauthor of several exhibition catalogs, including *Splash: A History of Swimwear*; *The Historical Mode: Fashion and Art in the 1980s*; *Jocks and Nerds: Men's Style in the Twentieth Century*; *Infra-Apparel*; *Orientalism*; *Haute Couture*; *Christian Dior*; and *The Four Seasons*. Among his recent honors are Pratt's Excellence by Design Award, the Laboratory Institute of Merchandising's Distinguished Achievement Award, an honorary doctorate from Otis College of Art & Design, election as a fellow of the Costume Society of America, and a special award for "furthering fashion as art and culture" by the Council of Fashion Designers of America in 1996.

Nancy Martin

Nancy Martin (born United States) was educated at Yale University and in Greece and has lived in Milan since 1961. She specializes in the culture of textiles. In 1987 she joined Domus Academy, teaching textile development, and in 1988 she joined the University of Urbino, teaching textile design. In 1990 she started Tessere, a virtual meeting place for people interested in textile culture. Since 1966 she has been a consultant for Solbiati Sasil SPA. She regularly contributes to fashion trade magazines and is currently working on projects for a textile grammar and a textile structure handbook.

Laura Piccinini

Laura Piccinini is a journalist who writes about fashion and popular costume. She contributes regularly to *Il Manifesto*, *D*, *Gulliver*, and other periodicals covering entertainment and youth culture.

Antonio Pilati

Antonio Pilati (born Milan, 1947) is director of the Istituto di Economia dei Media (Institute of Media Economics), Milan. He has published numerous works including *La produzione sociale della conoscenza* (Italo Bovolenta, 1984), *Il nuovo sistema dei media* (Edizioni Comunità, 1987), *L'industria dei media* (Il Sole 24 Ore Libri, 1990), *MIND. L'industria della comunicazione in Europa* (SIPI, 1993), *MIND. Media Industry in Europe* (John Libbey, 1993), *L'economia dei media: questioni teoriche* (Fondazione Rosselli, 1994), *La spesa di comunicazione in Italia. Aziende, famiglie, stato* (Fondazione Rosselli, 1995), and *Dall'alfabeto alle reti* (Edizioni Seam, 1995).

Ted Polhemus

Ted Polhemus is an anthropologist who, since the 1970s, has concentrated on the relationship between youth culture and fashion. Among his many publications are *Fashion & Anti-Fashion* (1975) and *Street Style: From Sidewalk to Catwalk* (1994), which was published in conjunction with an exhibition of the same name at the Victoria and Albert Museum in London.

Marco Ricchetti

Marco Ricchetti (born Modena, 1956) is an economist. He is the coordinator of the Economic Research Office and director of research for sales policy proposals at the national and European government level of Federtessile, where he is also adviser to the president. He is the author of several studies on economic and financial cycles in the textiles industries.

Philip Scranton

Philip Scranton is Kranzberg Professor of History at the Georgia Institute of Technology in Atlanta and director of the research center at the Hagley Museum and Library near Wilmington, Delaware. He has written five books and more than twenty articles on industrial development, most recently *Endless Novelty: Specialty Production and American Industrialization, 1865–1925* (Princeton University Press, 1997).

Valerie Steele

Valerie Steele is chief curator of the museum at the Fashion Institute of Technology. A cultural historian, she taught for a decade in the Division of Graduate Studies at FIT. Steele is the author of several books, including *Fifty Years of Fashion: New Look to Now* (Yale University Press, 1997); *Fetish: Fashion, Sex, and Power* (Oxford University Press, 1996); *Women of Fashion: Twentieth-Century Designers* (Rizzoli, 1991); *Paris Fashion: A Cultural History* (Oxford University Press, 1988); and *Fashion and Eroticism* (Oxford University Press, 1985). She is also coeditor of *Men and Women: Dressing the Part* (Smithsonian, 1989). She supervised the organization of the exhibition *Art, Design, and Barbie: The Making of a Cultural Icon*, for which she wrote the catalog (Rizzoli, 1995). Steele has lectured at such institutions as the Kimbell Art Museum, the Valentine Museum, the American Studies Association, the American Historical Association, Fordham University, the Chicago Historical Society, the Seminar on the History of Psychiatry and Behavioral Sciences at New York Hospital–Cornell Medical Center, the Association of Women in Apparel Resources, and the World Congress of Sociology, in Madrid. She is editor of the new quarterly journal *Fashion Theory: The Journal of Dress, Body, and Culture* (Berg Publishers) and has also contributed essays to many other periodicals ranging from *Aperture* and *Artforum* to *Visionnaire* and *Vogue*. She has served on the board of directors of the Costume Society of America and the advisory board of the International Costume Association (based in Tokyo) and is a member of the Fashion Group International.

John Thackara

John Thackara (born 1951), an expert on design, innovation, and new media, is director of the Netherlands Design Institute, a think-and-do tank in Amsterdam. Thackara worked in book publishing and journalism in Europe and the United States for ten years. During this period he was also director of research at the Royal College of Art in London. In 1993, Thackara was appointed as the first director of the Netherlands Design Institute; his first project there was the cofounding of "Doors of Perception," an influential conference concerned with the social and cultural consequences of the Internet. Thackara is active in the European Commission's research program I-cubed (Intelligent Information Interfaces); he was an organizer of the EU-sponsored European Design Prize in 1994 and 1997; and he is chairman of the European Design Summit (EDIS). His latest book is *WINNERS!: How Today's Successful Companies Innovate By Design* (1997). His earlier books include *Design After Modernism* (1988); *T-Zone* with R. Miyake (1991); and *Lost in Space: Travels In Aviation* (1994).

Bibliography

General Bibliography

Amendola, E. P. *Vestire italiano. Quarant'anni di moda nelle immagini dei grandi fotografi.* Rome: Oberon, 1983.

Anspach, A. *The Why of Fashion.* Ames: Iowa State University Press, 1967.

Apparel Arts. Milan: Electa, 1989.

Ash, Juliet, and Elizabeth Wilson, eds. *Chic Thrills: A Fashion Reader.* Berkeley: University of California Press, 1992.

Ashelford, Jane. *The Art of Dress: Clothes and Society, 1500–1914.* London: National Trust, 1996.

Barnard, Malcolm. *Fashion as Communication.* London: Routledge, 1996.

Barthes, Roland. *Système de la mode.* Paris: Editions du Seuil, 1967.

Batterberry, Michael. *Fashion: The Mirror of History.* New York: Greenwich House, 1982.

———. *Mirror, Mirror: A Social History of Fashion.* New York: Holt, Rinehart and Winston, 1977.

Beaulieu, Robert J. *Fashion Textiles and Laboratory Workbook.* Encino, Calif.: Glencoe, 1986.

Beauman, Sally. *Danger Zones.* New York: Fawcett Columbine, 1996.

Bell, Quentin. *On Human Finery.* London: Hogarth Press, 1976.

Bergler, Edmund. *Fashion and the Unconscious.* Madison, Conn.: International Universities Press, 1987.

Berlin en Vogue: Berliner Mode in der Photographie. Tubingen: Wasmuth, 1993.

Bianchino, Gloria. *Moda dalla fiaba al design. Italia 1951–1989.* Novara: De Agostini, 1989.

Bixler, Susan. *The New Professional Image: From Business Casual to the Ultimate Power Look.* Holbrook, Mass.: Adams Media, 1997.

Bolognese, Don. *Drawing Fashions: Figures, Faces, and Techniques.* New York: F. Watts, 1985.

Breward, Christopher. *The Culture of Fashion: A New History of Fashionable Dress.* Manchester: Manchester University Press, 1995.

Bucci, Ampelio. *L'impresa guidata dalle idee. Management dell'estetica e della moda.* Milan: Domus Academy, 1992.

Butazzi, Grazietta. *1922–1943, vent'anni di moda italiana. Proposta per un museo della moda a Milano.* Exhibition catalog, Museo Poldi Pezzoli, Milan. Florence: Centro Di, 1981.

Calasi, Betta, and Charlotte Mankey. *Essential Terms of Fashion: A Collection of Definitions.* New York: Fairchild Publications, 1986.

Calefato, Patrizia, ed. *Moda & mondanità.* Bari: Palomar, 1992.

Capucci, Roberto. *Roberto Capucci. L'arte nella moda: volume, colore, metodo.* Milan: Fabbri, 1990.

Ceriani, Giulia, and Roberto Grandi, eds. *Moda. Regole e rappresentazioni.* Milan: Franco Angeli, 1995.

Chaumette, Xavier. *Le tailleur: un vêtement-message.* Paris: Syros-Alternatives, 1992.

Chenoune, Farid. *A History of Men's Fashion.* Paris: Flammarion, 1993.

Clancy, Deirdre. *Costume since 1945: Couture, Street Style, and Anti-Fashion.* New York: Drama Publishers, 1996.

Colas, René. *Bibliographie générale du costume et de la mode.* Paris: Gaspa, 1991.

Colcridge, Nicholas. *The Fashion Conspiracy: A Remarkable Journey through the Empires of Fashion.* London: Heinemann, 1988.

Components of Dress: Design, Manufacturing, and Image-Making in the Fashion Industry. London: Routledge, 1988.

Conformismo e trasgressione: il guardaroba di Gabriele d'Annunzio. Una mostra di Pitti Uomo Italia. Firenze: La Nuova Italia, 1988.

Craik, Jennifer. *The Face of Fashion: Cultural Studies in Fashion.* London: Routledge, 1994.

Curcio, Annamaria. *La moda. Identità negata.* Milan: Franco Angeli, 1990.

The Cutting Edge: Fifty Years of British Fashion, 1947–1997. Woodstock, N.Y.: Overlook Press, 1997.

Damase, Jacques. *Sonia Delaunay: Fashion and Fabrics.* New York: Abrams, 1991.

Davis, Fred. *Fashion, Culture, and Identity.* Chicago: University of Chicago Press, 1992.

De La Haye, Amy. *Surfers, Soulies, Skinheads, and Skaters: Street Styles from the Forties to the Nineties.* Woodstock, N.Y.: Overlook Press, 1996.

Descamps, Marc-Alain. *Psychosociologie de la mode.* Paris: Presses Universitaires de France, 1979.

Diamond, Jay. *Fashion Advertising and Promotion.* Albany: Delmar, 1996.

———. *The World of Fashion.* San Diego: Harcourt Brace Jovanovich, 1990.

Dorfles, Gillo. *La moda della moda.* Genova: Costa & Nolan, 1984.

Elzingre, Martine. *Femmes habillées: la mode de luxe   Styles et images.* Paris: Editions Austral, 1996.

Ewen, Elizabeth, and Stuart Ewen. *Channels of Desire: Mass Images and the Shaping of American Consciousness.* New York: McGraw Hill, 1982.

Fashion & Cosmetics Graphics. Tokyo: P.I.E. Books, 1995.

Fashion Apparel Manufacturing: Coping with Style Variation; 1982 Report of the Technical Advisory Committee. Arlington, Va.: American Apparel Manufacturers Association, 1982.

Fashion Insignia: Patches & Emblems. Tokyo: P.I.E. Books, 1991.

Finkelstein, Joanne. *The Fashioned Self.* Philadelphia: Temple University Press, 1991.

Fischer-Mirkin, Toby. *Dress Code: Understanding the Hidden Meanings of Women's Clothes.* New York: Clarkson Potter, 1995.

Flügel, J. C. *The Psychology of Clothes.* London: Hogarth Press, 1930.

Forty, A. *Objects of Desire: Design and Society 1750–1980.* London: Thames and Hudson, 1986.

Fox, Patty. *Star Style: Hollywood Legends as Fashion Icons.* Santa Monica: Angel City Press, 1995.

Fraser, Kennedy. *The Fashionable Mind: Reflections on Fashion, 1970–1982.* New York: Knopf, 1981.

Frings, Gini Stephens. *Fashion: From Concept to Consumer.* Upper Saddle River, N.J.: Prentice Hall, 1996.

Garland, Madge. *The Changing Form of Fashion.* London: Dent, 1970.

Geringer, Susan. *Fashion: Color, Line, and Design.* Encino, Calif.: Glencoe, 1986.

Giorgetti, Cristina. *Moda maschile dal 1600 al 1990.* Firenze: Octavo, 1994.

Glamour Dos and Don'ts Hall of Fame: Fifty Years of Good Fun and Bad Taste. New York: Villard Books, 1992.

Glynn, Prudence. *In Fashion: Dress in the Twentieth Century.* London: G. Allen & Unwin, 1978.

———. *Skin to Skin: Eroticism in Dress.* New York: Oxford University Press, 1982.

Goschie, Susan. *Fashion Direction and Coordination.* Encino, Calif.: Glencoe, 1986.

Grandi, Silvia. *La moda nel secondo dopoguerra.*

Bologna: Clueb, 1992.

Gronow, Jukka. *The Sociology of Taste.* New York: Routledge, 1997.

Gross, Kim Johnson. *Work Clothes.* New York: Knopf, 1996.

Grumbach, Didier. *Histoires de la mode.* Paris: Editions du Seuil, 1993.

Habitus, abito, abitare. Progetto arte. Milan: Skira, 1996.

Halbreich, Betty. *Secrets of a Fashion Therapist.* New York: HarperCollins, 1997.

Harris, Christie. *Figleafing through History: The Dynamics of Dress.* New York: Atheneum, 1971.

Hebdige, Dick. *Subculture: The Meaning of Style.* London: Methuen, 1979.

Hewitt, Sally. *The Clothes We Wear.* Austin, Tex.: Raintree Steck-Vaughn, 1997.

Hollander, Anne. *Seeing through Clothes.* New York: Viking Press, 1978.

———. *Sex and Suits.* New York: Knopf, 1994.

Horn, Marilyn J. *The Second Skin: An Interdisciplinary Study of Clothing.* Boston: Houghton Mifflin, 1981.

Howell, Georgina. *In Vogue: 75 Years of Style.* London: Condé Nast Books, 1991.

Il tempo e la moda. Milan: Skira, 1996.

In Black and White: Dress from the 1920s to Today. Columbus: Wexner Center for the Arts, Ohio State University, 1992.

I piaceri e i giorni. La moda. Venice: Marsilio, 1983.

Jacobus, M., ed. *Body/Politics.* New York: Routledge, 1990.

Johnson, Jeane G. *Clothing, Image, and Impact.* Cincinnati: South-Western, 1990.

Kaiser, S. B. *The Social Psychology of Clothing.* New York: Macmillan, 1985.

Kaplan, Joel H. *Theatre and Fashion: Oscar Wilde to the Suffragettes.* Cambridge: Cambridge University Press, 1994.

Kazanjian, Dodie. *Icons: The Absolute of Style.* New York: St. Martin's Press, 1995.

Khornak, Lucille. *Fashion 2001.* New York: Viking Press, 1982.

Kidwell, C. B., and V. Steele, eds. *Men and Women: Dressing the Part.* Washington: Smithsonian Institution Press, 1989.

Kondo, Dorinne K. *About Face: Performing "Race" in Fashion and Theater.* New York: Routledge, 1997.

Konig, René. *Macht und Reiz der Mode.* Düsseldorf: Econ-Verlag, 1971.

Kunzle, D. *Fashion and Fetishism.* Totowa, N. J.: Rowman and Littlefield, 1980.

La moda italiana. Milan: Electa, 1987.

La mode en direct. Paris: Centre Georges Pompidou, 1985.

Landi, Paolo. *Lo snobismo di massa.* Milan: Lupetti, 1991.

La Rocca, Santa. *Le imprese basate sulla creatività artistica.* Milan: Franco Angeli, 1991.

Lauer, Jeanette C. *Fashion Power: The Meaning of Fashion in American Society.* Englewood Cliffs, N.J.: Prentice Hall, 1981.

Laver, James. *Costume and Fashion: A Concise History.* New York: Thames and Hudson, 1995.

Leuzzi, Linda. *A Matter of Style: Women in the Fashion Industry.* London: Franklin Watts, 1996.

Levi Pisetzky, Rosita. *Il costume e la moda nella società italiana.* Turin: Einaudi, 1978.

L'homme-objet: La mode masculine de 1945 à nos jours. Exhibition catalog, Musée de la Mode. Marseilles: Musées de Marseilles, 1996.

Lipovetsky, Gilles. *L'empire de l'éphémère.* Paris: Gallimard, 1987.

Lurie, Alison. *The Language of Clothes.* New York: Vintage Books, 1983.

Mackie, Erin Skye. *Market à la Mode: Fashion, Commodity, and Gender in the* Tatler *and the* Spectator. Baltimore: Johns Hopkins University Press, 1997.

Martin, Richard. *Bare Witness.* New York: Metropolitan Museum of Art, 1996.

———. *Fashion and Surrealism.* New York: Rizzoli, 1987.

———. *The Historical Mode: Fashion and Art in the 1980s.* New York: Rizzoli, 1989.

———. *Jocks and Nerds: Men's Style in the Twentieth Century.* New York: Rizzoli, 1989.

———. *Swords into Ploughshares.* New York: Metropolitan Museum of Art, 1995.

McCracken, G. "Clothing as Language: An Object Lesson in the Study of the Expressive Properties of Material Culture." In B. Reynolds and M. Scott, eds., *Material Anthropology.* New York: University Press of America, 1985.

McDowell, Colin. *The Literary Companion to Fashion.* London: Sinclair-Stevenson, 1995.

Moda Italia: Creativity and Technology in The Italian Fashion System/Moda Italia: Creatività, impresa. tecnologia nel sistema italiano della moda. Milan: Editoriale Domus, 1988.

Modes et publicité, 1885–1986: le regard de Marie Claire. Paris: Herme, Marie Claire, 1986.

Moss, Miriam. Street Fashion. New York: Crestwood House, 1991.

Muller, Claudia. The Costume Timeline: 5000 Years of Fashion History. New York: Thames and Hudson, 1993.

Naylor, Brenda. Fashion Sense. London, 1976.

O'Connor, Kaori. The Way We Wear. London: Vermilion, 1985.

Oliver, Valerie Burnham. Costume/Clothing/ Fashion Information Access: Sources and Techniques. Costume Society of America, Region 1, 1993.

Owen, Elizabeth. Fashion in Photographs. 1920–1940. London: B. T. Batsford, 1993.

Packard, Sidney. The Fashion Business: Dynamics and Careers. New York: Holt, Rinehart and Winston, 1983.

Pagès-Delon, M. Le corps et ses apparences: l'envers du look. Paris: L'Harmattan, 1989.

Pante, Robert. Dressing to Win: How to Have More Money, Romance, and Power in Your Life. Garden City, N.Y.: Doubleday, 1984.

Parente, Diane. Mastering Your Professional Image: Dressing to Enhance Your Credibility. Ross, Calif.: Image Development and Management, 1995.

Peltz, Leslie Ruth. Color, Line, and Design. New York: ITT Educational Services, 1971.

Phillips, Pamela M. Fashion Sales Promotion: The Selling Behind the Selling. Upper Saddle River, N.J.: Prentice Hall, 1996.

Polhemus, Ted. Fashion & Anti-Fashion: Anthropology of Clothing and Adornment. London: Thames and Hudson, 1975.

———. Pop Styles. London: Vermilion, 1984.

———. Street Style: From Sidewalk to Catwalk. New York: Thames and Hudson, 1994.

Pontarollo, Enzo. Le trame della maglia, le strategie della moda. Milan: Franco Angeli, 1992.

Pringle, Colombe. Telles qu'Elle: cinquante ans d'histoire des femmes à travers le journal. Paris: Elle, B. Grasset, 1995.

Quips and Quotes about Fashion: Two Hundred Years of Comments on the American Fashion Scene. New York: Pilot Books, 1978.

Ragone, D., ed. Sociologia dei fenomeni di moda. Milan: Franco Angeli, 1986.

Remaury, Bruno. Repères Mode & Textile. Paris: Institut Français de la Mode, 1997.

Riviere, Margarita. La moda, comunicación o incomunicación? Barcelona: G. Gili, 1977.

Roach, Mary Ellen. New Perspectives on the History of Western Dress: A Handbook. New York: Nutriguides, 1980.

Robinson, Julian. The Golden Age of Style. London: Orbis, 1976.

The St. James Fashion Encyclopaedia: A Survey of Style from 1945 to the Present. Detroit: Visible Ink, 1997.

Schnurnberger, Lynn Edelman. Let There Be Clothes: 40,000 Years of Fashion. New York: Workman, 1991.

Schreier, Barbara A. Mystique and Identity: Women's Fashions of the 1950s. Norfolk: Chrysler Museum, 1984.

Severa, Joan L. Dressed for the Photographer: Ordinary Americans and Fashion, 1840–1900. Kent, Ohio: Kent State University Press, 1995.

Simmel, Georg. Die Mode. 1895.

Simon, Donatella. Moda e sociologia. Milan: Franco Angeli, 1990.

Smith, Pamela. Collecting Vintage Fashion & Fabrics. New York: Alliance, 1995.

Soli, Pia. Moda. L'immagine coordinata = Corporate Identity. Bologna: Zanichelli, 1990.

Solomon, M. R. The Psychology of Fashion. Lexington, Mass.: Heath, 1985.

Sommers, Susan. Italian Chic: The Italian Approach to Affordable Elegance. New York: Villard Books, 1992.

Sproles, George B. Changing Appearances: Understanding Dress in Contemporary Society. New York: Fairchild Publications, 1994.

———. Fashion: Consumer Behavior toward Dress. Minneapolis: Burgess, 1979.

Sproles, George B., ed. Perspectives of Fashion. Minneapolis: Burgess, 1981.

Stauder, Rudy. Il femminese. Guida serissima al linguaggio della moda nelle riviste femminili. Legnano: Landoni, 1978.

Steele, Valerie. Fashion and Eroticism: Ideals of Feminine Beauty from the Victorian Era to the Jazz Age. New York: Oxford University Press, 1985.

———. Fetish: Fashion, Sex, and Power. New

York: Oxford University Press, 1996.

———. Paris Fashion: A Cultural History. New York: Oxford University Press, 1988.

———. Women of Fashion: Twentieth-Century Designers. New York: Rizzoli, 1991.

Storia delle mode, storia della moda. Milan: Longanesi, 1981.

Tabori, Paul. Dress and Undress: The Sexology of Fashion. London: New English Library, 1969.

Tapert, Annette. The Power of Style: The Women Who Defined the Art of Living Well. New York: Crown, 1994.

Tolstoi, Tatiana. De l'elegance masculine. Paris: Acropole, 1987.

Vergani, Guido. La sala bianca. Nascita della moda italiana. Milan: Electa, 1992.

Versace, Gianni. Vanitas Designs. Milan: Leonardo Arte, 1994.

Volli, Ugo. Contro la moda. Milan: Feltrinelli, 1988.

Watson, Linda. Vogue: More Dash than Cash. London: Condé Nast Books, 1992.

Wilson, Elizabeth. Adorned in Dreams: Fashion and Modernity. Berkeley: University of California Press, 1987.

Wolfe, Mary Gorgen. Fashion: A Study of Clothing Design and Selection, Textiles, the Apparel Industries, and Careers. Tinley Park, Ill.: Goodheart-Willcox Co., 1997.

Bibliography on Specific Topics

Albrecht, D. Images et marchandises in Hollywood 1927–1941. Paris: Autrement, 1991.

Antonelli, C., ed. New Information Technology and Industrial Change. Norwell, Mass.: Kluwer Academic Publishers, 1988.

Arrow, K. "Economic Welfare and the Allocation of Resources for Invention." In R. R. Nelson, ed., The Rate and Direction of Inventive Activity: Economic and Social Factors. Princeton, N.J.: Princeton University Press for NBER, 1962.

Boscarelli, L., ed. Il successo con le operations. Produzione e mercato: la via italiana all'eccellenza. Milan: Isedi, 1993.

Bovone, L., and E. Mora, eds. La moda della metropoli. Dove si incontrano i giovani milanesi. Milan: Franco Angeli, 1997.

Bowen, B., E. Gould, and P. Pashigian. "Fashion, Styling, and the Within-Season Decline in Automobile Prices." Journal of Law and

Economics (University of Chicago), Oct. 1995.

Braudel, F. *Capitalismo e vita materiale.* Turin: Einaudi, 1976.

Brusatin, M. *Storia dei colori.* Turin: Einaudi, 1983.

Bucci, A. *L'impresa guidata dalle idee. Management dell'estetica e della moda.* Milan: Domus Academy, 1992.

Davis, F. *Fashion, Culture, and Identity.* Chicago: University of Chicago Press, 1992.

Douglas, M. "On Not Being Seen Dead: Shopping as Protest." In *Thought Styles.* London: Sage, 1996.

Ejzenstejn, S. *Il colore.* Venice: Marsilio, 1984.

Fortis, M. *Crescita economica e specializzazioni produttive.* Milan: Università Cattolica, 1996.

Goethe, J. W. *Farbenlehre.* Cologne: Du Mont Buchverlag, 1978.

Goffman, E. *Frame Analysis.* New York: Harper & Row, 1974.

———. *The Presentation of Self in Everyday Life.* New York: Doubleday, 1959.

Hirschman, A. O. *Shifting Involvements: Private Interest and Public Action.* Princeton, N.J.: Princeton University Press, 1982.

IRPET. *Dove e come nasce il prodotto moda.* Milan: Franco Angeli, 1991.

Langlois, R. N., and P. Robertson. *Firms, Markets, and Economic Change.* London: Routledge, 1995.

Leonard-Barton, D. *Wellsprings of Knowledge.* Boston: Harvard Business School Press, 1995.

Lotman, Ju., B. Uspenskij, et al. *Tesi sullo studio semiotico della cultura.* Parma: Pratiche, 1980.

Machlup, F. *The Production and Distribution of Knowledge in the United States.* Princeton, N.J.: Princeton University Press, 1962.

McLuhan, M. *Understanding Media.* Harmondsworth: Penguin, 1964.

Miles, I., et al. *Knowledge-Intensive Business Services.* EIMS Publication 15. Brussels, 1995.

Noble, D. *America by Design.* New York: Knopf, 1977.

Nonaka, I., and H. Takeuchi. *The Knowledge-Creating Company.* Oxford: Oxford University Press, 1995.

Ortoleva, P. *Un ventennio a colori.* Florence: Giunti, 1995.

Porter, M. *The Competitive Advantage of Nations.* New York: Free Press, 1990.

Putnam, R. *Making Democracy Work: Civic Tradition in Modern Italy.* Princeton, N.J.: Princeton University Press, 1993.

Quintavalle, C. A. "La scena della moda." In E. P. Amendola, *Vestire italiano. Quarant'anni di moda nelle immagini dei grandi fotografi.* Rome: Oberon, 1983.

Ragone, A. *Consumi e stili di vita in Italia.* Naples: Guida, 1985.

Richardson, G. B. "The Organization of Industry." *Economic Journal* 82 (1972): 883–96.

Rosten, L. *Hollywood: The Movie Colony.* Harcourt, Brace, 1941.

Sapir, E. "Fashion." In *Encyclopaedia of Social Science.* New York: Macmillan, 1931.

Scitovsky, T. *The Joyless Economy: An Inquiry into Human Satisfaction and Consumer Dissatisfaction.* New York: Oxford University Press, 1976.

Veblen, T. *The Theory of the Leisure Class.* New York: Macmillan, 1971.

Williamson, O. E. *The Economic Institutions of Capitalism.* New York: Free Press, 1985.

Bibliographies for Individual Essays

The Circularity of Production and Consumption, or the Reflexivity of Fashion

Bovone, L., ed. *Creare comunicazione. I nuovi intermediari di cultura a Milano.* Milan: Franco Angeli, 1994.

Bovone, L., and E. Mora, eds. *La moda della metropoli. Dove si incontrano i giovani milanesi.* Milan: Franco Angeli, 1997.

Douglas, M. "On Not Being Seen Dead: Shopping as Protest." In *Thought Styles.* London: Sage, 1996.

Goffman, E. *Frame Analysis.* New York: Harper & Row, 1974.

The Rationality of the Fashion Machine

Arrow, K. *The Limits of Organization.* Norton, 1974.

Boscarelli, L., ed. *Il successo con le operations. Produzione e mercato: la via italiana all'eccel lenza.* Milan: Isedi, 1993.

Braudel, F. *Capitalismo e vita materiale.* Turin: Einaudi, 1976.

Bucci, A. *L'impresa guidata dalle idee. Management dell'estetica e della moda.* Milan: Domus Academy, 1992.

Davis, F. *Fashion, Culture and Identity.* Chicago: University of Chicago Press, 1992.

Fortis, M. *Crescita economica e specializzazioni produttive.* Milan: Università Cattolica, 1996.

Gereffi, G. "The Organization of Buyer-Driven Global Commodity Chains: How U.S. Retailers Shape Overseas Production Networks." In Gary Gereffi and Miguel Korzeniewicz, eds., *Commodity Chains and Global Capitalism.* Praeger, 1994.

Sapir, E. "Fashion." In *Encyclopaedia of Social Sciences.* New York: Macmillan, 1931.

Scitovsky, T. *The Joyless Economy: An Inquiry into Human Satisfaction and Consumer Dissatisfaction.* New York: Oxford University Press, 1976.

Stigler, G. J. "The Economics of Information." *Journal of Political Economy.* 1961.

Innovative Activity in the Fashion Industry

Antonelli, C. *The Dynamics of Localized Technological Change.* Forthcoming, 1997.

———. *The Economics of Localized Technological Change and Industrial Dynamics.* Norwell, Mass.: Kluwer Academic Publishers, 1995.

Antonelli, C., ed. *The Economics of Information Networks.* Amsterdam: Elsevier, 1992.

———. *New Information Technology and Industrial Change.* Norwell, Mass.: Kluwer Academic Publishers, 1988.

Antonelli, C., P. Petit, and G. Tahar. *The Economics of Industrial Modernization.* London: Academic Press, 1992.

Arrow, K. "Classificatory Notes on the Production and Transmission of Technical Knowledge." *American Economic Review* 59 (1969): 29–35.

———. "Economic Welfare and the Allocation of Resources for Invention." In R. R. Nelson, ed., *The Rate and Direction of Inventive Activity: Economic and Social Factors.* Princeton, N.J.: Princeton University Press for NBER, 1962.

———. "Methodological Individualism and Social Knowledge." *American Economic Review* 84 (1994): 1–9.

Carlsson, B., and G. Eliasson. "The Nature and Importance of Economic Competence." *Industrial and Corporate Change* 3 (1994): 687–712.

Dasgupta, P. "The Economic Theory of Technology Policy: An Introduction." In P. Dasgupta and P. Stonema, eds., *Economic Policy and Technological*

Performance. Cambridge: Cambridge University Press, 1987.

Dasgupta, P., and P. A. David. "Information Disclosure and the Economics of Science and Technology." In J. Feiwel, ed., *Arrow and the Ascent of Modern Economic Theory*. New York: New York University Press, 1987.

———. "Toward a New Economics of Science." *Research Policy* 23 (1994): 487–521.

David, P. A. *Knowledge Property and the System Dynamics of Technological Change*. Proceedings of the World Bank Annual Conference on Development Economics. Washington: World Bank, 1993.

———. "Positive Feed-backs and Research Productivity in Science: Reopening Another Black Box." In O. Granstrand, ed., *Economics and Technology*. Amsterdam: Elsevier, 1994.

David, P. A., and D. Foray. "Accessing and Expanding the Science and Technology Knowledge Base." *STI Review* 16 (1995): 14–68.

Den Hertog, P., et al. *Assessing the Distribution Power of National Innovation Systems*, Pilot study. Apelddoorn, Netherlands: TNO, 1995.

Foray, D. "The Economics of Intellectual Property Rights." In J. Hagedoorn, ed., *Technical Change and the World Economy*. Aldershot: Edward Elgar, 1995.

Freeman, C. "The 'National System of Innovation' in Historical Perspective." *Cambridge Journal of Economics* 19 (1995): 5–24.

Griliches, Z. "Issues in Assessing the Contribution of Research and Development to Productivity Growth." *Bell Journal of Economics* 10 (1979): 92–116.

Langlois, R. N., and P. Robertson. *Firms, Markets, and Economic Change*. London: Routledge, 1995.

Leonard-Barton, D. *Wellsprings of Knowledge*. Boston: Harvard Business School Press, 1995.

Loasby, B. J. *The Organization of Capabilities*. Department of Economics, University of Sterling, 1995.

———. *Understanding Markets*. Department of Economics, University of Sterling, 1994.

Machlup, F. *The Production and Distribution of Knowledge in the United States*. Princeton, N.J.: Princeton University Press, 1962.

Marshall, A. *Principles of Economics*. London: Macmillan, 1890–1920.

Metcalfe, J. "Technology Systems and Technology Policy in Historical Perspective." *Cambridge Journal of Economics* 19 (1995): 25–47.

Miles, I., et al. *Knowledge-Intensive Business Services*. EIMS Publication 15. Brussels, 1995.

Mowery, D. C. "The Boundaries of the U. Firm in R&D." In N. R. Lamoreaux and D. M. G. Raff, *Coordination and Information: Historical Perspectives on the Organization of Enterprise*. Chicago: University of Chicago Press for NBER, 1995.

———. "The Relationship between Contractual and Interfirm Forms of Industrial Research in American Manufacturing, 1900–1940: Explorations." *Economic History* 20 (1983): 351–74.

Nelson, R. R. "The Role of Knowledge in R&D Efficiency." *Quarterly Journal of Economics* 97 (1982): 453–70.

Nelson, R. R., ed. *National Systems of Innovation*. Oxford: Oxford University Press, 1993.

Noble, D. *America by Design*. New York: Knopf, 1977.

Nonaka, E., and H. Takeuchi. *The Knowledge-Creating Company*. Oxford: Oxford University Press, 1995.

Reich, L. *The Making of American Industrial Research*. Cambridge: Cambridge University Press, 1985.

Richardson, G. B. "The Organization of Industry." *Economic Journal* 82 (1972): 883–96.

Rosenberg, N. "Technological Change in the Machine Tool Industry, 1840–1910." *Journal of Economic History* 33 (1963).

Sah, R., and J. E. Stiglitz. "The Architecture of Economic Systems: Hierarchies and Polyarchies." *American Economic Review* 76 (1986): 716–27.

Scotchmer. "Standing on the Shoulders of Giants: Cumulative Research and the Patent Law." *Journal of Economic Perspectives* 5 (1991): 29–41.

Senker, J. "Tacit Knowledge and Models of Innovation." *Industrial and Corporate Change* 4 (1995): 425–48.

Stigler, G. J. "The Division of Labor Is Limited by the Extent of the Market." *Journal of Political Economy* 59 (1951).

Von Tunzelmann, G. N. *Technology and Industrial Progress: The Foundations of Economic Growth*. Aldershot: Edward Elgar, 1995.

Williamson, O. E. *The Economic Institutions of Capitalism*. New York: Free Press, 1985.

———. *Markets and Hierarchies*. New York: Free Press, 1975.

Winter, G. "Knowledge and Competence as Strategic Assets." In D.J. Teece, ed., *The Competitive Challenge*. Cambridge: Ballinger, 1987.

Wright, G. "The Origins of American Industrial Success, 1879–1940." *American Economic Review* 80 (1990): 651–68.

From Chaotic Novelty to Style Promotion: The United States Fashion Industry, 1890s–1970s

Chipman, Victoria. "Altered Forever: A Women's Elite and the Transformation of American Fashion Work and Culture, 1930–1955." Thesis, University of California, Los Angeles, 1990.

Dickson, Carol. "Patterns for Garments: A History of the Paper Garment Pattern Industry in America." Thesis, Ohio State University, 1979.

Hall, Lee. *Common Threads: A Parade of American Clothing*. Boston, 1992.

Jarnow, Jeannette, and Beatrice Judelle. *Inside the Fashion Business*. New York, 1965.

Kidwell, Claudia, and Margaret Christman. *Suiting Everyone: The Democratization of Clothing in America*. Washington, 1974.

Next page: Mask by Gio Ponti,
fabric by Roberto Capucci. Photo by Pino Guidolotti